Love + Peace
Barbara
&

Miracle Mission to Medjugorje

A Journey of Faith

Barbara Lorenzo

En Route Books and Media, LLC
Saint Louis, MO

Make the time

En Route Books and Media, LLC

5705 Rhodes Avenue

St. Louis, MO 63109

Cover credit: Sebastian Mahfood from author photo taken
in 2014 of a mosaic on a wall at Mother's Village

ISBN-13: 978-1-956715-32-3

Library of Congress Control Number: 2022933395

*This book is dedicated to
my Mom, my beacon of faith,
and my beloved brother Paul.*

Trust in the Lord with all your heart, on your own intelligence rely not; in all your ways be mindful of him, and he will make straight your paths.

Proverbs 3:5–6

"Dear children, in a motherly way I am calling you to return to the joy and the truth of the Gospel, to return to the love of my Son—because He is waiting for you with open arms; that everything you do in life you do with my Son, with love; that it may be blessed for you; so that your spirituality may be internal, and not just external. Only in that way will you be humble, generous, filled with love and joyful; and my motherly heart will rejoice with you. Thank you."

Medjugorje message, March 18, 2021

The four pilgrims, Ed, Mom, Me, and Paul (1991)

Acknowledgments

Give thanks to the Lord, who is good,
whose mercy endures forever.
(Psalm 106:1)

First and foremost, I want to thank God for my husband who has walked this journey, patiently waited as I put this manuscript away for months on end, read, listened, and stood by me for the duration. My children, Julia, Michael, and Matthew who made my heart open to truly comprehend the love and depth of a mother's heart. My brother Joe who coached me in the early days of getting this story unearthed. My family who are woven into this story. My gratitude to Fr. Sean, who invited me to serve in the Parish of Our Lady of the Mount and lead a pilgrimage to Medjugorje. He has been a spiritual guide, a shepherd in the truest sense. In the darkest of times, he guided with sincerity and hope. Mary Laing Robinson, my faith companion, friend, mentor, and proofreader and editor of my earliest manuscripts, reading over and over and sharing my progress. Cecille Zalamea, a fellow writer and friend who read, prayed, and gave valuable input to this project. I am grateful for the students at Saint James School in Basking Ridge, NJ, who were my first audiences as I unraveled this story of conversion and love of Our Lady. Thanks to Fr. Richard Carton, who sat through my talk before his junior high students. I am grateful for your prayers and reassurance of my witness. I am appreciative of the NJ Angels, whose prayer, support, and friendship carry and inspire. The Walking with Purpose bible study team from PVB, whose hunger for faith emboldens my faith adventure. For the Friday Rosary group, who lift up all things to Our Lady and her Son in gratitude and intercession. For the Spiritual Directors who have strolled with me always pointing to the movements of God within. For Beth Mansbridge, whose gift of editing has made this manuscript readable and helped me get to the finish line.

Contents

Prologue

I began writing this story because it needed releasing from within. During a spiritual direction session with a priest at the start of a sabbatical year, guidance was desired. His words of wisdom were "to rest, be quiet, listen and be attentive to what God wants from you."

Through our conversation, he invited me to consider my cradle Catholic faith before this happenstance and after. The foundation was there, for sure, but the zeal was not; my walk with God was on the surface. I had not absorbed the depth that was offered. The intensity I was feeling post this experience and for years after filled me with fervor and genuine love of my faith.

This mission threw me upside down. I was motivated by raw, uncorrupted love that makes your heart hurt. Love that comes unconditionally from our inner core, like a child's. I wanted to do anything to help, while struggling with the fact that the world as I knew it was about to be rocked. This story is about the journey of abrupt and gradual changes, resulting in the fueling of my soul.

It begins with an extraordinary event which began in 1981, in a small town in Eastern Europe: six children experienced a miracle. Since then, thousands of people have been touched by the events of those days, which continue to transpire through visions and miracles. My story is one of many born from these happenings.

Each chapter begins with a message—a message I believe was given by the Mother of God. The children, referred to as visionaries, have been given thousands of messages from Mary, the Blessed Mother. Throughout history, the Mother of God has appeared all over the globe, sharing prophetic messages of world events, offering protection, peace, hope, miracles, and always directing us to her Son Jesus. The history of this miracle of Mary's presence among us is told in full at the end of this book.

My story begins in 1991. Disturbing news, the kind that feels like a punch in the stomach, gripped my family. This would affect each of us. My oldest brother Paul was fearful to reveal the truth. Truth that had been buried. Submerged deep inside as he popped pills, listened to reports of new trial cures, and met with doctors. From New York, my newlywed husband and I visited my brother in Miami, Florida. We were there to strategize, to help figure out how to tell Mom and Dad that Paul was dying.

We sat in the lush tropical side yard on a breathtakingly beautiful day. The last thing I wanted to think about or talk about was the reason for our being there. I loved coming here to share stories, laugh, cook, eat, and just be together. This was changing way too rapidly for me to grasp. My heart hurt.

He was sitting next to me, reclining. I stared at him as beads of sweat collected on his forehead. For a moment, there was peace.

His desperate blue eyes met mine. "What am I going to do, Barb?"

I racked my brain for an answer, for something, anything that would bring comfort. I was silent. Nothing came to me. I sank down into the cushions to ease the hurt. I gazed up to the sky, wishing for answers. My dear brother waited patiently for me to respond. He was sick, very sick. He sat slumped, his body frail. His illness had been a secret for years. But I had known.

Paul and I were close—both lovers of art. He had pursued art education, and I had embarked into the world of fashion. He was the brother I clicked with, the one I admired most. I had four brothers: three older and one younger. Paul and I were seven years apart. He loved hearing stories about the knitwear firm, and I loved hearing about the students in the artistically gifted school where he was the assistant principal. We talked frequently. A few years prior, on an ordinary day of the week after returning home to my little studio in Manhattan, he called. As we chatted, he told me of some weird health issues he was having. This was the beginning of the HIV/AIDS crisis. I knew the symptoms and already knew people who were experiencing them. Out of concern, I asked him if he had HIV. I didn't expect the answer I got, which was "Yes."

Oh, no. I was devastated. People were dying of it.

He told me the details of how long he had known. He was going to cure himself, and he felt very confident about his doctors. He sounded relieved to tell me but asked me to keep this *secret*. Not to tell anyone in our family. They cannot know. He was going to cure himself, he repeated. I could also hear the fear in his voice. I sat stunned; this could not be happening.

As life would have it, the contrast of emotions burst wide open. One week after my devastating conversation with Paul, my boyfriend, Michael, proposed to me, and in the whirl of hugs, champagne, and extraordinary joy, I shouted, *"Yes!"*

I spoke to Paul and shared the great news. I also asked him to allow me to tell Michael the secret. Paul understood; he was excited for my future but scared for his own. The wedding was set for June 1990. Our large family gathered, and, as we immersed in the joy, the secret remained. I kept glancing at Paul and Ed, his partner of sixteen years. No one questioned. They both looked healthy and great. Oh, yeah. The other news was that Ed was HIV-positive, too. We carried on with the festivities, cheered, and toasted our blessed union.

Now, almost a year later, Michael and I were here together to support Paul.

Paul and I were two souls bound by this secret. In an odd way, the secret had strengthened our connection while it burdened my heart. Paul had entrusted me with the few words that changed everything. My lips had stayed sealed. But the moment we had hoped and prayed would never happen, was here. We had hoped he would be cured, the secret would dissolve, and it would never have to be shared. It would be erased. Unfortunately, this was not the case. We were filled with the fear of losing this battle now that he'd been told he had only months to live. Paul would have to tell our parents and he needed help on how to do it ... how to let his secret out.

After a lapse, Paul got my attention. "Barb, maybe this isn't the end. What about Fatima or another holy place of miracles?"

"You might be on to something. Miracles have happened there. Let's think about this, but you still have to tell Mom and Dad."

Thoughts raced through my mind of other places I had read about. Yes, a holy place—a healing place—that was the answer! Our fear waned. I told Paul to make that long-over-due call. Tell the secret to Mom and Dad over the phone. That would be the best way. Allow the news to be absorbed by all those miles between him and them.

Little did we know that around that same time, while we were in Miami deliberating over holy places, seven hundred miles away, in Myrtle Beach, our mom sat in a pew in St. Andrew Catholic Church, listening to a talk given by Wayne Weible, about a village called Medjugorje, a holy place where miracles were happening. The Blessed Mother was allegedly appearing daily, and people were being healed.

The conversation with my brother Paul feels like a lifetime ago. It was before a multitude of life-changing events occurred. Paul was so beaten, so ill. When I close my eyes, I can still see his desperate, weary face as I sit in this predawn light, the glare of the computer screen bright and the last sentence of the first draft completed.

The story of Paul and our journey is out of me and saved—our determined search for a miracle lies far behind us. I had felt compelled to write about it since it happened. Maybe just for me and my family. The task always seemed insurmountable. Still, I've always shared the story with anyone who would listen.

After the journey of our search for a miracle, I left my career in the fashion world and became a teacher. I had a baby, and through several coincidences or blessings, I shifted into the position as a librarian in a Catholic school—after the horrific events of 9/11/2001 and the miracle that my husband was safe in Texas, not in his office fifty-four flights up in Tower Two. I was talking to my mom; she insisted it was time to share our story of hope and faith. Not us, but me. I needed to tell all about Our Lady and what we had witnessed.

My first audiences were the students at Saint James. Twelve- and thirteen-year-olds sat transfixed in their seats as the appropriate words poured out of me about Our Blessed

Mother and the apparitions and how the miraculous journey unfolded.

One day, a girl came up to me and said, "Mrs. Lorenzo, you should write about this."

That was the push I needed. She planted a seed that would finally take root.

This was why I had sought spiritual direction as I deliberated over the writing of the story. The priest explained how events shift our understanding, fissures of light begin to alter perspective, and we become responsive to the workings of God in a deeper way. I was certain this happened to me. He suggested I sit and write; just begin.

I see, feel, and think differently. That blink of time with Paul, talking about miracles—our words hitting the air and evaporating into the universe—was the beginning of a new life.

Sometimes, thoughts voiced *do* become reality. Sitting in the church in Myrtle Beach that evening, my mom didn't even know her second born was sick. But all the events were falling into place like cards shuffled, then put in order. We were talking, thinking, and imagining solutions, completely unaware of God shifting the universe to lead us to unknown places.

I was about to learn that unexpected transformations *are* possible.

1

The Decision

"Dear children! This time also I am inviting you to prayer. Pray that you might be able to comprehend what God desires to tell you through my presence and through the messages I am giving you. I desire to draw you ever closer to Jesus and to His wounded heart that you might be able to comprehend the immeasurable love which gave itself for each one of you. Therefore, dear children, pray that from your heart would flow a fountain of love to every person, both to the one who hates you and to the one who despises you. That way you will be able through Jesus' love to overcome all the misery in this world of sorrows, which is without hope for those who do not know Jesus. I am with you and I love you with the immeasurable love of Jesus. Thank you for all your sacrifices and prayers. Pray so I might be able to help you still more. Your prayers are necessary to me. Thank you for having responded to my call." November 25, 1991

Michael and I returned to New York. We had just gotten in when the phone rang. I heard Paul's tearful voice in the receiver.

His voice quivered and he struggled, saying, "Mom and Dad are wonderful. We are so lucky, Barb. They are incredible. They told me how much they loved me and would help me through all of this and do whatever I needed."

He had just finished the call. I could only imagine my poor parents sitting quietly, with miles between them and their son. I knew Paul needed them, and he was able to let it out: all the hardships, fears, hopes, the physical and mental roller coaster he had ridden. Paul poured out the words that had gushed from his lips. He had finally unburdened himself and told them the whole truth. He sobbed, he told them of how long he had carried this secret, the uncertainties, his deteriorating health, his failing blood tests and all the horrific facts.

He told Mom and Dad how he had tried to cure himself and had hoped to never have to tell. He shared about his phenomenal doctor, who scoured, read, and presented new treatments as the race to live stretched. This man wanted Paul to be a success story and live a long, healthy life on the other side of this disease. Paul spoke of the trials, grueling side effects and all the gory details. He sobbed, telling them that it didn't work. He had to say the words, "I am dying, Mom and Dad. I am sorry."

Mom and Dad listened, and loved. Paul was telling me the replay and kept repeating "how lucky we are, Barb." He was their child, their second born. He told me how nervous he was. I could picture Mom in the bedroom, sitting on the bed, her head resting in her hand, and Dad in the kitchen at the table, his brow and face contorted as he listened on the other extension, his fingers gently thumping the table.

The three were tethered in a triangle of shock. It all boiled down to love and the basic force within us to care.

This conversation was so loaded—but how awesome! They heard him; they listened as the gravity of his truth stung their hearts; they loved and did not condemn.

I thought about what may have really been going on in their minds. Did they want to shout at him while they remained silent? Did his anguish trump any anger? They had gushed compassion. I agreed we were blessed!

The perspiration was dripping down my arm as I sat on my little navy blue couch in my tiny New York City studio. I was grasping the phone tightly. Paul continued talking for over an hour, filling me in on the banter of unconditional love and then his sentiments about our family and his future. We cried together and ended the call, saying "I love you." If only I could have reached through the phone and held and hugged my brother tightly. I didn't want to hang up. Miami and Manhattan were too far apart.

***

As I look back, I realize that conversation marked the second difficult truth my brother Paul had to admit to our parents. The first hard truth had been revealed years before, when he expressed his love for Ed, who would be his partner for the next sixteen years. Exposing that truth was a giant step for him. Years of suppressed confusion and inner struggles were finally an open discussion. The secret left my parents shaken and filled with questions and regrets.

We were a big Catholic family living in a perfect little bubble. Learning that their second born was living a life so far from the foundation of their teachings, my parents were rocked to their core, while the thought that he had struggled without their help saddened them. Mom and Dad had raised us with firm morals, discipline, and adherence to Gospel values. All of us attended Catholic schools, and every night, without fail, eight voices joined in prayer around the dinner table.

Our family was a product of the 1950s: Dad, a hardworking veteran with common sense; Mom, wise, organized and diligently faith-filled. Every Sunday we sat in the pew in this order: Kathy, the oldest, followed by Paul, then Rick, Greg, I was next, then the youngest, Joe. During our childhood we made several relocations of residences as Dad moved up the corporate ladder with General Motors. Those moves drew us tighter and more cohesive as a family.

Therefore, the reality of Paul's news made the challenge to understand him immense. For a while the desire to change him became the focus of my mother's prayers. The desire to deny his reality tested my parents' hearts. The search for knowledge about his truth took Mom into the library stacks, and the struggle to comprehend it challenged each one of my siblings in varying degrees.

My parents made one thing clear to us all: "Paul is our son, your brother, and you will not reject him. You may not agree with him, but above all else we will love him."

Paul had come out with this truth as an adult living independently, twenty something years old and residing in Miami, Florida. The oldest in the family, Kathy, was married; the third child, Rick, was married; and the three youngest were still living at home.

Time progressed and we moved forward. Life went on, years transpired, we remained a tight family. Paul created his niche in Florida in art education. Ed worked as a teacher. We gained insight, we adjusted, we gathered for weddings, baptisms, anniversaries and holidays, and the family grew and grew. Ed embraced us, and we, him. Mom and Dad showed love by their example, and we followed. Life, for a time, was smooth.

***

Then the awful news that the latest secret revealed: Paul was declining rapidly. It pierced our hearts. And to pile it on further, Ed was coping with his early stage diagnosis the natural way—with immunity boosters and homeopathic regimens. Paul was signing on to the earliest drug therapies and test medicines to combat the virus, but they left him with miserable residual effects. Ed's health was strong—no symptoms yet—but he was scared. The conversations in Miami of miracle cures and holy places of healing helped fuel us, for a moment, with hope. Those thoughts made us step out of the coldness and fear to stoke optimism.

Mom was upset with me. Why had I not told her?

"Why, Barb," she boldly cried, "*why?* We could have been with him longer at your wedding a year ago. We could have all stayed and been together and helped him more. Why didn't you tell me?"

I responded with the truth that Paul had entrusted me and asked me not to, so I kept quiet. I felt horrible for Mom, felt guilty I hadn't leaked it and was confounded by what I had done. Maybe things would be different now, if Mom had known.

Mom absorbed the shocking news with great distress. She and my father loved us profoundly, and this new truth was unfathomable to grasp. Mom did not judge, but looked to her faith, dropped to her knees and began to pray with her whole being for her son. Through copious tears, my parents clung to each other and God.

Then, *wait a minute*! Mom recalled the talk, the miracle place, the place of the apparitions of the Blessed Mother in Yugoslavia. The talk Mom had gone to when two people at their parish shared a story of Medjugorje.

Who was it? Yes, Wayne Weible, an author of a book about Medjugorje. He was the one who spoke, relating the happenings in the small rural village. Mom had gone with her friend. They listened, learned, and believed that miracles were occurring; people were returning cured. Yes, that had happened weeks before Paul's cry for help. It all came back in a flashing moment. Mom relayed it all to Dad, then proposed it to Paul, to go to this place.

He said yes! There was hope!

Mom told me, and I said, "I am in. Let's go!"

Mom wanted a miracle. She wanted a miracle with every cell in her body. She wanted her son cured. She wanted him healthy. She wanted Paul to grow old and continue working with the children as a teacher and assistant principal. She did not want to contemplate the idea of burying her son. She wanted him here, on this planet, with the rest of us. She wanted him to bury *her*.

So, with his "yes," her prayers flowed constantly.

2

Preparation

"Dear children! Today also I want to call you all to prayer. Let prayer be your life. Dear children, dedicate your time only to Jesus and He will give you everything that you are seeking. He will reveal Himself to you in fullness. Dear children, Satan is strong and is waiting to test each one of you. Pray, and that way he will neither be able to injure you nor block you on the way of holiness. Dear children, through prayer, grow all the more toward God from day to day. Thank you for having responded to my call." September 25, 1987

The trip was now indisputably in motion! My role, to orchestrate the plans. I was the sibling who didn't have little ones at home and could easily make the trip. I was traveling overseas often with my work, so investigating what was necessary for a journey to Yugoslavia was not overwhelming.

I made calls, Mom gathered brochures. I traveled to Myrtle Beach. Mom and I strategized on the living room floor, with plans and pamphlets from various tour companies spread out before us. It came together quickly. We called Paul and Ed in Florida to fill them in on the details. The four of us would make the "pilgrimage," the term the tour companies used in reference to this excursion. Even the word *pilgrimage* was empowering. It sounded like a prayer.

We decided on Marion Tours as our sponsor and proposed the dates. Once confirmed, we booked the tour. We'd leave from New York on August 8, 1991, and return on August 17.

With all my being, I wanted to be on board with Mom's rock-solid faith, but a part of me was skeptical. I was unsure, wavering and had many questions. I was a secular cradle Catholic, resembling a visitor at an elite buffet. I chose those ideologies that fit my lifestyle. Religion was not a top priority. In my early twenties I attended Mass almost every Sunday—when I felt prompted to go—but that was it. My belief was there; it was my grounding, my foundation. I said thanks to the Almighty when things were good and prayed when things went awry. My faith was in my head, not my heart.

Because Michael had previously been married, we had gone through the steps of an annulment prior to our wedding. I knew I wanted to be married in the Church. That process pulled me close for introspection and caused me to re-address my faith but did not leave a lasting impression. I was also going to be a stepparent, which I took seriously. When these adolescent boys, Michael and Matthew, were with us, I knew they'd be watching my choices, so Sunday Mass would be a priority.

As for the Rosary, I had not prayed one in years. I also did not pick up the Bible to search for answers. My grade in Catholicism was a C, at best. I was spiritual, that was for sure, and searched for answers to my existence, but the church was not always where I sought those answers. I was a participant of the Forum, a secular self-actualization program, and read many self-help books to guide me through my questioning. New Age ideologies caught my attention. My search was for transformation and understanding.

Why? I asked God, why did this happen to my brother? Did God know, before Paul's birth, about his sexual orientation? Did He know the decisions Paul would make? Did God know he would experience grave illness? Was the eternal plan so clear and defined? Then the questions of our free will and the impact of our choices rolled around in my brain.

From the divine perspective, what was the reason Paul and my family had to go through all this? My questions led to an endless stream of more questions without answers. Mom handed me the book, *The Message*, by Wayne Weible, and firmly instructed me to read it. I was sensing Mom's frustration in my lackluster faith. I hoped to find meaning in the pages of this book.

I read and absorbed all of it in wonder and awe. The revelation that the apparition of the Blessed Mother was currently happening and had been going on since 1981 left me stunned. From my elementary religion classes, I was aware of other apparitions, but the duration was not as long. This was profound. The thought was unbelievable, mystifying, even. I grappled with the fact that we were headed to the place where six children allegedly saw the Blessed Mother and conversed with her, just steps in front of them, like I talk to my own mother. A place where, solely based on belief, thousands of people had gone to see, hear and experience conversion or healing.

Did I have the faith required to make this journey? Who knew for sure, but I wanted the miracle for Paul and maybe that was enough. Mom had a close and powerful relationship with Our Lady. I guess being the mother of six gives one a good reason to talk to the Mother of Jesus on a frequent basis.

Mom shared stories with me about her grandmother, who had lived with Mom's family when she was young. The wise elderly woman inspired Mom and fueled her faith. Her grandmother, Briede, went to daily Mass, and Mom tagged along during the summer months of her elementary school years. Through this union of young and old, my mother's concrete faith formed.

I was definitely a work in progress. I pored through the book. Wayne Weible had experienced a conversion and actually heard the Blessed Mother speak to him. He was a reporter and a journalist, so writing was his gift. Our Lady actually asked him, by speaking to his heart, to write of the events that occurred in the remote little village. I couldn't put the book down—it was profound and enlightening. As I mentioned, through my Catholic education I had learned about the apparitions of Our Lady of Guadalupe in Mexico, Our Lady of Lourdes in France and Our Lady of Fatima in Portugal. The stories had stayed with me. I needed to believe and trust with all my heart, but it was challenging and contrary to my current state of faith.

To rely on belief—instead of the fear that coursed through my heart when I listened to my siblings' reports of Paul's deteriorating health—was a struggle. They were visiting him the summer before we planned to leave. They told me Paul was worse. He was declining rapidly. The various medications to extend his life had wreaked havoc on his system. He was transfusion dependent now.

I was scared. "What if?" questions plagued my mind. What if Paul needed medical attention and we had an emergency? Where would we go? What if we had a problem with his medicine? What if the Communist government confiscated his medicine? What if we could not keep the medicine cold, as it needed to be? There were more and more questions. I fretted with every waking hour and tossed and turned at night as the worries raged in my mind.

I spoke to his home health nurse, who was a godsend; she cared so much and gave me advice. I planned to pack some foods that would help if he had certain ailments. She gave other recommendations that would assist in a pinch. Knowledge and preparedness seemed to help calm the fear.

An external factor bursting across the news was the civil war blossoming in Yugoslavia, between the Croatian and Serbian people. It also kept me tossing at night. There was volatile unrest in that region of the world, with skirmishes erupting daily. Then the huge question came: Should we even make the trip, considering the health decline and civil unrest variables?

Mom thought we should consider calling off the trip due to the political clash brewing. My father was nervous and distressed. Amidst a myriad of emotions, he spoke his mind. He wanted a miracle for Paul just as much as we did. Nevertheless, he had reservations about his daughter, his bride of over forty years and his dying son traveling to a country in conflict.

We had a three-way conversation. Dad and Mom, on the two extensions in Myrtle Beach, and I joined from Manhattan. We played the "should we, shouldn't we volley" back and forth until Dad expressed that we had given Paul hope and this trip was his son's last wish. I believe, as the words left his mouth, he was convincing himself that we had to proceed. Therefore, knowing all the concerns, we unanimously decided to move forward and not cancel. The journey was going to happen. We were committed to going.

My new husband, on the other hand, traveled extensively and was extremely unsettled about the budding war. His concerns about my welfare and that of my brother, Mom and Ed were unwavering. That scared me most. Civil unrest and a potential war more than disturbed him and he wanted me to understand the possible dangers. He was trying to be realistic and supportive, but was anxious, as any new spouse would be. I tried so hard to be open and dismiss any skeptical ideas from my mind. I wanted to believe as I thought my mom did, that this was possible—that anything was possible with God. I sincerely was not there yet, and my husband's doubts unnerved my hopes.

After reading Wayne Weible's book, I knew I had to start praying the Rosary, which Our Lady was asking of us. I had never said the Rosary in a consistent way before, and I felt rusty. I had trouble staying focused. I'd held a rosary many times during my twelve years of Catholic school but had forgotten the mysteries and all the prayers. I just said ten Hail Marys and then an Our Father until I completed the circle. My Rosary praying was pathetic, but I had to start somewhere. Paul had given me a rosary from Rome; he had gotten it on one of his trips prior to being sick. I tried my best to get into the spirit of Medjugorje. I prayed while getting myself organized and prepared.

The day before everyone arrived, I departed for work in Manhattan. Mike and I had moved into his condo in Freeport, Long Island, and given up the studio apartment to be close to the boys. My commute into the city was by the Long Island Railroad. I was getting a very early start, so I parked our jeep at the Baldwin train station, near the stairs to the platform, and then trained into Penn Station and walked to the office from there. I was stressed and finalizing all my projects at work, passing them on to various co-workers so that all bases would be covered, and my clients would get the attention needed in my absence. My bosses were compassionate about the journey and wonderful in giving me the time off. They were trying to make it as smooth as possible, and I was grateful.

Frazzled was how I felt, but I tried to remain focused and move one step at a time. On my way home that evening I exited the train and started to walk to my car. I'd gone in very early that day. I felt fortunate that I'd parked so close to the platform steps; I was exhausted.

I couldn't find the car. It was not there. I retraced my steps and still no car. I then spiraled, thinking the stress had been too much. Maybe I'd parked farther away than I thought, so I walked and walked. Still no vehicle. No black jeep. My heart was in my throat. The realization that the car was stolen stung my gut. This can't be happening now! Is this a sign?

I am an organizer. A planner. I like to have order and know what's happening. I like control. That's my personality. I tried my best to be prepared, to refer to my list and check things off as the departure time neared.

No car? Who took it? What had I left in the car that identified where we lived? My mind raced with all those thoughts. Would the thieves come to our home? If it was some kind of sign, what did it mean? I felt a scream brewing deep inside. Oh, please help me each step of the way, I prayed.

I called the police, called my husband, and told them the particulars. At that time, Michael and I shared one car since we both worked in Manhattan and commuted back and forth. When I calmed down, I thought about what was going on and pulled myself together.

The stolen car was just another hurdle. We had bigger issues. With Paul's failing health and the civil war looming, the stolen car was an inconvenience and I wondered what else we were to face.

I had no option but to propel forward and repeat, over and over, that anything was possible with God.

3

The Departure

"Dear children, By God's will I am here with you in this place. I desire for you to open your hearts to me and to accept me as a mother. With my love I will teach you simplicity of life and richness of mercy and I will lead you to my Son. The way to Him can be difficult and painful but do not be afraid, I will be with you. My hands will hold you to the very end, to the eternal joy; therefore do not be afraid to open yourselves to me. Thank you." May 2, 2008

"Dear children! Today I invite you to pray for peace. At this time peace is being threatened in a special way, and I am seeking from you to renew fasting and prayer in your families. Dear children, I desire you to grasp the seriousness of the situation and that much of what will happen depends on your prayers and you are praying a little bit. Dear children, I am with you and I am inviting you to begin to pray and fast seriously, as in the first days of my coming. Thank you for having responded to my call." July 25, 1991

I hoped the Blessed Mother was leading Mom, Paul, Ed and me as we pushed on in faith. Michael, on the other hand, was having a tough time. The anxiety-provoking stuff was piling up and now we were missing a car. My husband was invested in this trip, but not like me. I shared a lifetime with my brother, and Michael's relationship with Paul was only a few years old. The doubts and questions were mounting as we got closer to saying goodbye. The stolen car drew Michael back and forth on the phone with the police. He stayed home from work that day, to help by renting a car so we could pick up everyone from the airport. We would have one night in our home before our departure. Mom arrived from Myrtle Beach, Paul, and Ed on schedule from Miami.

We loaded the car and headed home to our humble abode for our first physical contact since this trip took shape. All the planning had been happening long distance. I put a cool drink in everyone's hands as we sat in the living room and began to chat about our expectations and concerns. Michael started asking questions and conversing with everyone, which gave me the opportunity to take a good look at my traveling companions.

My eyes rested on Mom, who had never taken a trip without my father. She had aged. This terminal illness polluting her firstborn son was obviously taking a toll on her physically. Lines etched with worry and concern showed on her face. At age sixty-seven, she had been through a lot in the last few years. Cancer first, now this.

Mom's battle with breast cancer had happened two years before. She underwent a mastectomy. My mom was a trouper, though when she got the diagnosis, the dreaded word *cancer* played havoc on her steady temperament. Decisions had to be made about the treatment options. She always impressed me as being the optimist, never the complainer, but this illness upended her for a remarkably short time. Then she rallied. She prayed through her ordeal, with the support of Dad. When the initial healing and rest were over, she dutifully attended her physical therapy and, in a relatively short time, returned to her active lifestyle and playing her beloved golf. They had gotten the cancer and with her prognosis favorable, she was on a maintenance chemo drug and doing OK. Now that she was sitting here in our condo, I envisioned her prosthesis tucked away and the long scar near her heart hidden under the golf shirt she wore.

Mom sat on the navy paisley couch facing her very ill son. Love and sorrow reflected from her blue eyes as she surveyed Paul. I could tell she was nervous and apprehensive, yet calm all the same. This petite determined woman, with her dyed blond, beautician-set hair, was my awesome role model of strength leading us to this holy place.

My eyes moved to Paul. His arms were so skinny, his face gaunt; he had changed dramatically. He was sporting a Florida tan, but his eyes were drawn and his hands frail. I thought about the years of trial medications, the effects of which now showed. His eyes, still so blue, lacked spirit. He smiled weakly and was clearly relieved to be sitting securely near Mom, the person whose faith, love and enthusiasm showered him in life and cheered him on.

I thought back to a spectacular Christmas in Miami. It was when he had gotten the report, just weeks before. He had tested positive for HIV. He remained numbed and quiet about this news. It worked; we had no idea this bomb had been dropped. He carried on making it a magical Christmas. I can only imagine that he was petrified. The AIDS epidemic was just making headlines and taking lives with it. We were oblivious; it was Christmas, the time of peace, joy, giving, family, and love. Part of our large family gathered, and we all stayed in Paul and Ed's home: Mom, Dad, my brother Joe, sister Kathy and her husband and two children and Grandpa. After the spectacular renovations, this residence was fittingly named "The Palace." The Mediterranean Revival treasure had been condemned before they purchased it. Paul and Ed's blood and sweat were in every nook and cranny of this home. Their hands had transformed the neglected, dilapidated home and breathed new life into it.

They purchased the 1925 estate for a mere $103,000, put in over $40,000 for its restoration, and the historic preservation society issued a grant of $10,000 for their efforts. It was their pride and joy. When the home was completed, they made the cover story of *Historic Preservation* magazine.

"The Palace," decorated to the hilt, was a virtual winter wonderland. The bay of pink stained glass was a perfect spot for a towering nine-foot tree. The balsam fir was decorated with wallpaper fans and miniature white lights. It was gorgeous. Thick pine garland outlined the wood-beamed ceilings and framed the doorways. There were layers of presents under the tree. After flying in from New York's seasonal mayhem at LaGuardia Airport, I crossed the threshold of their home and my mouth dropped open! The beauty of the scene was overwhelming.

The entire week we feasted on Paul's gourmet delights, telling stories until the wee hours, and laughing until our stomachs hurt. The wine flowed and the love was flourishing and abundant. I remember being so thankful for family and so proud of Paul and Ed. I kept thinking Paul was so happy.

The juxtaposition of this week, later in time contrasted so extremely between the celebration of the birth of Christ and the hidden HIV diagnosis.

Paul had faith, he was generous, humble and he delighted in serving us all. He was an altar boy in elementary school. In high school he was awarded for his Christian leadership. I sat looking at him now, realizing that he had hidden his HIV secret from me for years. He was running a race of time. In a way, he was as determined as Mom to defeat her cancer, but the discoveries and treatments were not there. It was beyond his control. He was tired and out of breath. My gaze wandered to the cane positioned in the corner of the room, to aid him in Medjugorje. He was only thirty-nine years old. Was he as frightened as I was?

My focus shifted to Ed. He sat in the striped wingback chair. He looked scared and unsure about this whole adventure. Ed was Protestant. He never talked much about religion or faith; he did not practice and occasionally accompanied Paul to church. Ed was along for this ride. He told me he didn't know what to think about traveling to Medjugorje, but it was worth trying and maybe this would work. I caught a moment as Ed's soft brown eyes watched Paul. Ed was relieved that Paul was with his mom. I think Paul was as equally relieved; Ed had lost both his parents, so being with Mom was good for him too. She had plenty of love to go around.

In the fifteen plus years of getting to know Ed, I loved his warm smile. It lit up a room. He was affectionately sarcastic and often knocked on his own head, saying, "Knock on Wood." Wood was his last name. He had a boyish way about him. Now he looked serious and anxious. Not only was he concerned for Paul, but also carried the weight of being HIV-positive himself. I can only imagine the fear coursing through his system. He looked healthy on the outside, but beneath the skin, disease was present.

Mom brought me back from my internal drifting to review our plans. After we talked about the schedule, Mom suggested we say the Rosary. Paul and I exchanged nervous glances; it had been years since we had said Rosaries, even though I had been practicing since reading the book about Medjugorje. We held a long gaze as we retrieved our rosaries and positioned them in our hands. We both lacked confidence of leading the mysteries and some of the prayers were unfamiliar. We were grateful when Mom began.

Mom led us with her heartfelt prayers and meditations. Ed followed along. At each mystery, I listened intently to each word and began to refresh my memory and store the words Mom was reciting. Saying the Rosary felt awkward but good, like we were preparing, and it felt reassuring for what would unfold.

Michael was preoccupied with the stolen car scenario, so he moved to another room. I think this was part of God's plan. All this was too much, and the car gave Michael something concrete to focus on while the rest of us were clinging to our wavering faith.

Michael and I had been married only a year, and this was a huge test of our love—our first crisis. With so much at stake, I was trying to be calm, controlled and in charge, while I wanted time to go backwards. I did not want to go to a war-torn country with my sick brother and my mom. There was no turning back. Michael and I clung to each other that night and did not say a whole lot, silently wishing and praying it would all go well.

The next day we tearfully said goodbye at home, then again at the airport. I moved into airport mode. We stood in the lines, checked in and got set for the flights. Ed was carrying Paul's medicines in a small cooler. I viewed myself as the facilitator in this quartet; Mom was in charge of prayer; Ed took care of Paul; and Paul's job was to hang in there and think miracles are possible.

The first leg of the itinerary was New York to Rome; we departed JFK at 6:00 p.m. and arrived at 8:00 a.m. The flight went smoothly. Our next scheduled departure would be at 5:30 p.m., our layover long enough for Paul to sleep or rest at a hotel. We got to the hotel and hovered over Paul as he rested. We arrived at the airport for our next flight; we boarded with ease and took off on time. The flight, scheduled to land in Dubrovnik at six forty in the evening, made a puzzling switch midair. This was when our faith and Mary's guidance were so necessary. More tests began to unfold.

4

The Switch

"Dear children! At this time, do not only think of rest for your body but, little children, seek time also for the soul. In silence, may the Holy Spirit speak to you and permit Him to convert and change you. I am with you and before God I intercede for each of you. Thank you for having responded to my call." July 25, 2006

Buckled, settled, we were on our way! I had an invisible checklist in my head. As we moved towards our goal, I checked off the list. Each mark represented a movement that would get us closer to the anticipated encounter with Our Blessed Lady and a miracle. Mom and I inhaled deeply, relieved that we'd made it to this second flight without a hassle. I found comfort in her nearness. The Jat Airways jet departed Rome for Dubrovnik.

Once the plane was airborne, some people from South Dakota introduced themselves. They had noticed our red duffle bags with the white "Marion Tours" lettering inscribed on the side. They sported the same type of bags. The five travelers consisted of two sisters in their thirties, their parents (whom I guessed were a little younger than my

mom) and a family friend. The friend was extremely enthusiastic, chatty, and knowledgeable about the apparitions. We
exchanged basic information and learned this was their first
excursion to Medjugorje. We determined, based on the comparison of our itineraries, that we would be together for the
duration of this sojourn.

I closed my eyes to rest.

The next thing I heard was: "Seat backs upright, prepare
for landing."

I woke alert, and mentally prepared the checklist. The
tour company was scheduled to meet us at the airport, and
they would take over. This was a reassuring thought. I looked
over at Paul. He was awake and appeared rested. Ed had an
expression of, "Oh boy, here we go!" I lifted the window
shade and peeked out the window … confusion set in. I saw
a scattering of small terra-cotta roofed structures in a rural
setting. This was definitely not the historic walled city of Dubrovnik. Where were we? I did not see the grand city on the
Adriatic, the city I had looked at in the books. I fumbled for
my ticket and examined it. Clearly, it stated "Dubrovnik" as
the arrival airport. I looked out again, hoping my eyes had
played a trick and I'd see the beautiful image of Dubrovnik,
but—oh, no—it was not there! My stomach flipped. As we
landed, I saw a cinderblock warehouse-like airport building
painted a shade of bright royal blue. Where were we?

One of the daughters and I exchanged alarmed glances.

The plane landed, and we proceeded to disembark. At the bottom of the steps, our feet made contact with a broken concrete tarmac. I was nervous. We all walked in shocked silence. We entered the building, went through a simple passport area and then on to retrieve our luggage. No one spoke English. We followed the other passengers' movements. We continued through customs, with the exception of one of the daughters, whose luggage was lost. She went to locate her bag. I saw her trying to communicate with one of the attendants and, frustrated, she turned and came back to us, defeated. No one from Marion Tours had greeted us. We looked around hoping for them to appear, hoping to see red duffle bags or a sign with the words, "Welcome – Marion Tours," but nothing. I felt helpless.

As I sit here writing, I cannot recall the specifics, except that we spied a nun in a full black habit and watched where she was going. The woman from our group abandoned the hope of finding her suitcase. We told her we would loan her things. Then with a burst of confidence, she and I encouraged our group to head towards a parked bus. We both felt the nun was a sign and we followed her. We tried to engage the nun in conversation and ask for help, but she didn't speak English.

The majority of the people from our flight were getting on this singular waiting bus. Only a few did not get on, so we followed the somewhat confused crowd and boarded this aged dingy transport. The bus driver who was waiting outside the door was potbellied, shirtless, with greasy gray hair. His burly countenance, scowl and unshaven face was intimidating and downright scary.

Paul, his face pale, looked at me with disgust, questioning my ability in travel planning. He kept shaking his head in disbelief, wondering where in the world we were.

"Wish I knew," I repeated for him and for me. "It will all work out. Just get on the bus," I pleaded.

Mary, oh, Blessed Mother, help! She is leading us. I repeated this thought over and over as the worry overwhelmed, and, for one of the first times in my life, I told myself to just *trust*. We had no other choice.

The bus rumbled along a narrow road with deep canyons, vast valleys, and winding rivers. The scenery was dotted with white stone and red roof dwellings hinting of a bygone era. The rolling mountains on the horizon were spectacular. We slowed to a stop in a line of traffic, waiting to board a transport ferry. A large, weathered map glued to a billboard at the landing showed Dubrovnik. It was plainly marked. We were heading in the right direction. What a relief!

The problem, I later found out, had been that Jat Airways was Serbian, and Dubrovnik was in Croatia, and this was the beginning of the dreadful civil war. Croatia and Serbia were in a fight for independence. The place where we had landed was Tivat, in Montenegro—the country south of where we wanted to be.

For us, this crazy airport switch was unnerving—and not on my checklist. We needed to reach Medjugorje without any more delays, to ask for a miracle regarding life and death. From the dusty bus windows, I watched the sun begin to set. The roads narrowed and curved. The bus grumbled along at a decent speed. Sitting next to Ed, Paul, with the cane between his legs and fingers clasping the handle, rested his bent head on his hands. At times he shook his head and glared at me. His frustration and weariness at the disorder of this trip was getting to him. Mom prayed constantly, her eyes sometimes closed, her lips moving, but without a sound.

At a border crossing, armed soldiers stomped into the bus. This was daunting, the opposite of peace. I could hear my husband's voice in my head: "What are you doing, Barbara? This is not a good time to be going there."

My meek inner voice was shouting, You're right. What are we doing?

The soldiers wanted money, and we could not understand. Some German-speaking people on the bus told us to give the soldiers American currency. I cannot recall what we came up with, but they were satisfied and got off the bus.

We continued to a hectic bus depot. We had to transfer buses. I remember squinting at a schedule for Dubrovnik that was posted on a board. The nun helped, by pointing, to clarify the next bus we should board.

Later that evening we arrived in Dubrovnik. I saw a van with MARION TOURS on the side, waiting in a parking lot. I could now check this off my list. What a relief! As this vision appeared out the bus windows, the nine of us voiced a collective elation. I knew we now had an additional two-and-a-half-hour ride to our final destination. We were weary. Paul was hanging in, quiet and pensive, and not thrilled with his younger sister.

With welcome arms, we greeted Mario, our tour guide and driver. We were so excited; it was as if he were a long-lost relative. We were so ready to be led. We loaded our bags into the van and began our drive to the village. Ed was sitting in the front seat. I was next to Paul and Mom in the second seat, with our fellow travelers behind us. There appeared to be no speed restrictions, or at least it didn't seem that way. Mario was speeding on the narrow, winding, and steep roads. With all we had experienced, the anxiety level heightened. Ed had a petrified look on his face when he reached for the seat belt—which did not exist—and his eyes cried "Help!"

We began to chatter and tell our troubles to Mario. We learned from him about the airline's refusal to land in Dubrovnik, as originally planned. He apologized for not being there to meet us.

Finally, we rolled up to our guesthouse in the village of Medjugorje at 1:00 a.m. As we got out of the van, there, before our eyes was the towering church of St. James. Our house was across the street. Mari, our host, welcomed the nine of us into her home and showed us to our simple yet adequate rooms. She told us that breakfast would be at nine. This would give us time to rest, settle in and be able to attend the morning Mass in St. James Church. So gentle and caring, she agreed to refrigerate Paul's medicine and offered help in any way she could.

We had arrived!

5

The Trip: Day One

"Dear children! I am with you in the name of the greatest Love, in the name of dear God, who has come close to you through my Son and has shown you real love. I desire to lead you on the way of God. I desire to teach you real love so that others may see it in you, that you may see it in others, that you may be a brother to them and that others may see a merciful brother in you. My children, do not be afraid to open your hearts to me. With Motherly love, I will show you what I expect of each of you, what I expect of my apostles. Set out with me. Thank you!" March 18, 2011

My mind and body slowly churned as I awoke. The reality of what was to happen next sent quivers through me. The first light poked into the simple, unadorned room. I opened my eyes. The night before, I was beyond exhausted, but now I felt rested. Mom was still sleeping peacefully. I rolled over towards her; she lay only feet from me on the other small bed. I loved this woman. The sun was now streaming in, blanketing the room with warmth—no air conditioning in our tiny space. I rose quietly and moved towards a back door, which opened to a narrow private balcony walkway, joining our room with Paul and Ed's.

The view was serene: a countryside of red dirt paths, lined green fields, simple homes capped with terra-cotta clay roofs, all hemmed in by mountains and blue sky. We had made it! Thank you!

I listened at Paul's door and heard voices. I knocked and entered. Paul, my dear brother, looked weary, but was already up and dressed. We exchanged good mornings, smiles and hugs. Ed had given him his medicine and they were about to head down for breakfast.

When I returned to our room, Mom was up and getting herself organized. We assessed our space and decided to take out what we needed for the day and store our suitcases under the beds. We needed to clear space to walk. One small table between our beds was the only furniture. We had our own tiny bathroom, which was good. Some places were dormitory style. I didn't see any formal hotels in this village in 1991. The local residents had created simple quarters for the many pilgrims flocking here, building additions onto their homes to accommodate the faithful arriving daily.

Our host met us in the dining room when we got downstairs. She prepared a simple breakfast for us, and then pointed the way to St. James Church. Being so close to the church was a gift. This was ideal, with Paul so weak. The August sun was hot; when we moved outside the temperature was already a steamy ninety degrees and rising each hour. As we stood on the concrete walkway of our modest home for the next six days, I examined our surroundings.

The street offered a few cafés with outdoor seating and numerous storefront shops selling religious articles. The rosaries hung like necklaces on metal stands to the sides of the thresholds. People strolled by with eyes focused towards the open doors of the church.

St. James was clearly the heart of this town. A beautiful statue of Our Lady, Queen of Peace, graced the courtyard which was bordered by a circular manicured garden and wrought iron fencing. We paused to admire the serene life-sized statue. A few benches outlined the square, rightly positioned under the shade of trees. A prime spot, I remember thinking, to escape the heat. The plaza was filling with other pilgrims like us, on some mission.

We moved inside. The hugeness of this church, in contrast to the small village, was surprising. The interior was simple neutral stone floors, beige walls, and wooden pews. The people created the color and décor.

Mass in English began at ten. Luckily, we found seats and knelt down. The music began, preparing us for the liturgy and, wow, it was angelic. I looked around at the faces and wondered what brought each one here. Were they praying for miracles of various sorts?

We stood, and the entrance hymn echoed. Paul sang, I mean he really sang! His voice was clear, loud and sound bellowed from his soul! Ed and I exchanged amazed glances behind him. The disease had left him short of breath, his lungs compromised. So, to hear this strong tone was unexpected.

Mom smiled, watching Paul completely engaged in song, while Ed and I looked on in awe. The overpowering faith of the devout congregation profoundly lifted the energy in the church. The Franciscan priest said the Mass with such reverence. When Mass ended, I did not want to leave; it was so moving I wanted to stay rooted.

It was a relief to be here, but on the other hand, this holy atmosphere was definitely out of my comfort zone. I was a New Yorker working in the fashion industry. I was not accustomed to people openly exposing their Catholicism. This faith-filled place was so foreign to me, I felt awkward; still, I was determined to rise out of my own obstacles and follow Mom in determined hope.

We stuck around until the church emptied.

Then we left and strolled down the path behind the church. We marveled at the simple tranquil beauty. Beyond the added outdoor bench seating which was recently added to accommodate the massive number of pilgrims, there were grape arbors. Fields interspersed with an occasional grazing cow dotted the landscape. An older Croatian woman, with a dark scarf tied under her chin, sat, crocheting fine lace, under the shade of a tree. Her completed handiwork lay spread out on a blanket next to her, for sale. This was such a contrast to our lives in Manhattan, Miami, and Myrtle Beach.

By word of mouth, our guide learned that the visionary, Ivan, was meeting with pilgrims, so he gathered all who were ready to go. We boarded his van and rode the short distance to Ivan's house. A crowd was already gathered and more people on foot arrived from all directions.

Ivan stood on the front walkway of his family home, telling us of his experience. His humble nature impressed me as he spoke through an interpreter. He expressed his feelings at seeing the Blessed Mother, in June of 1981, for the first time. She stood before him as we were, in three-dimensional form. He was frightened at first.

Then he described her. "She is beautiful, a beauty like nothing else I have ever seen. It is hard to use the right words to explain. She has black hair, blue eyes, rose-colored cheeks, and she is young. She wears a gray dress." He went on to tell us what she wants the people to know. Ivan said, "Her most important messages for all of us were to pray, to fast, to experience a conversion of the heart and to do penance." He went on, telling us that he got over the fear and shock of the initial meeting of Mary, the Mother of Jesus, standing before him. He remarked that "after ten years, his encounters with Our Lady are quite comfortable." He shared that Our Lady stressed to all the visionaries, the importance of family prayer and making the time. Through Ivan, as per the instruction from the Blessed Mother, we also heard that we must guide and discipline our children to show, share and give love. We need to spread peace and love from our hearts and pray from our hearts to her. This was so simple and clear.

My mind was trying to grasp the reality that Ivan converses freely with the Blessed Mother, the Queen of Heaven and Earth, as she hovers before him. This was inconceivable for me. I had read about it. Hearing about it from others somehow made it easier to accept. Now, hearing it directly from the visionary, I was in awe. He spoke regularly to someone who walked on this earth over 2,000 years ago.

I was moving in a stupor as we headed back to St. James Church. Paul was quiet and feeling sick. His coloring had turned ashen, he was coughing, and he clearly felt uncomfortable. We paused and rested. The heat was getting to him. Our next stop was to hear Father Slavko speak. This would be a relief; Paul could sit in the cool air-conditioned church. Mom had asked if he wanted to continue or go rest. He wanted to stay. We entered the church, moved to a row, sat down in the pew, and waited.

Father Slavko arrived, approached the altar, and prayed. He was young, in his forties, with dark hair. He moved to the pulpit and addressed us. He had been the parish priest since 1983.

He looked out and said slowly, "Our Lady is calling you here and you must be patient yet open to receive her message."

What! Calling me here?

He instructed us not to feel frustrated, but peaceful. "She will let you know what she wants."

This was huge! All of a sudden, it was as if he was talking to me. I don't know how to explain it except that bells and alarms went off in my mind. Our Lady was calling us here!

Mentally I knew what we were doing, coming here out of faith, to Medjugorje, to pray and ask for a miracle. Hearing Father Slavko say she had called us here was penetrating in a different, uncomfortable, surprising way, especially after hearing Ivan speak. I knew my presence here was about Paul. I was the facilitator to help get us here—my role in this mission. Now I was abruptly thinking something different. This had not even entered my consciousness before. My focus was about Paul's healing. Our concern was about him. The notion that Our Lady called us all here—Mom, Paul, Ed and me, Barbara—to this place was incredible. I was hanging on this phrase. I wondered if they had heard it with the same fervor. I knew, at that moment, how critical it was to be open.

I recalled one of the messages from Our Lady: *"Dear children! I am with you. As a mother, I am gathering you, because I desire to erase from your hearts what I see now. Accept the love of my Son and erase fear, pain, suffering and disappointment from your heart. I have chosen you in a special way to be a light of the love of my Son. Thank you."*

She called us here. Mom was invited by a friend in Myrtle Beach to hear about Medjugorje before ever knowing about Paul's illness. Now we sat in the church, the heart of this holy place, contemplating the thought that the Queen of Peace was gathering us. These words tumbled in the hemispheres of my heart and brain.

After the talk, we went back to the guesthouse. It was so hot a cold shower was the perfect remedy. I let the water wash over me as all the thoughts swam in my head.

Later we joined the others for dinner. Our host served delicious meals. Our first dinner included soup with delicate noodles, homegrown tomatoes and peppers, a bean salad, breaded veal, and delicious refreshing watermelon. This journey carried so much weight—so much was at stake— that this meal fed the body and soul. Sharing our first day's happenings with fellow pilgrims made the extraordinariness of this place begin to sink in.

After dinner, we walked out into the warm twilight and headed across the street to St. James for the evening liturgy and program. Every evening they followed a schedule, which began with the recitation of the Rosary. We decided to sit outside on the benches. The seating was added to accommo- date the crowds of pilgrims from around the world coming to experience the apparitions. Loudspeakers were strategi- cally placed so we could clearly hear the readings and music from inside. With the ominous hostile situation brewing be- tween the Croatians and Serbs, we heard that the number of pilgrims was lower than normal. This was a scary thought, but also beneficial. Mass was fully attended by both local vil- lagers and visitors. I could only imagine how the numbers would have multiplied if this political situation was not brewing. For us, it was appreciated; we could get seats and move around the village without paralyzing crowds.

We took out our rosaries and joined in the rhythm and repetition of the prayers. Hearing the Croatian language was quite musical, so hearing the Hail Mary repeatedly while watching the gathering faithful, soothed my spirit. I was sitting next to Paul. He looked better after some rest and nourishment. I watched Ed and Mom reciting the prayers, their rosaries threaded through their fingers. The love between us was so thick, our eyes would meet momentarily, and we'd exchange grins. With Paul by my side, I closed my eyes and felt the breeze. The hot temperatures of the day surrendered to the sweet gentle breeze of the evening. It was refreshing.

The chorus of pilgrims and locals joined in the Rosary. In a small room inside St. James, the visionaries also prepared for their miraculous encounter. They were praying with the rest of us, and, at a precise time, Our Lady would appear to them.

I had heard that select people were invited to be present in the room when she appeared, which would be incredible to witness. I could not imagine what it would be like to see what the visionaries saw: her beauty, her three-dimensional form.

It was strange—the physical sensations as you prayed the Rosary outside of the church, with the visionaries inside the church—you felt an invisible awareness of peace blanket you. You could sense her presence. It was an unseen embrace of profound love. At that exact moment I could imagine the frequency of energy in the air emblazoned with sparks. It was unbelievable, supernatural and, at the same time, very real.

When the Rosary concluded, the Croatian Mass began. We stayed in our seats. The devoutness of the entire community was different from Masses in the US. The people here had clearly been touched in some way and Our Lady was guiding them. We followed along, not understanding the language, yet understanding every ritual in the celebration of the Mass, which is universal.

After Mass, we strolled behind the church. Paul began to cough and could not stop. My mom was stroking his back, worried about him. I moved away, off by myself. The more he coughed, the more frightened I became. It hit me in the gut. I was overwhelmed. The fear that he might die gripped my heart. All of it was more than I could handle. The emotions snowballed.

I started to move, to run, to escape. I sprinted behind the church into the vineyard. No one was on the path; I was by myself. Thoughts besieged me, so I upped my pace. I was running hard and fast, then abruptly the neon sign in my brain alerted: Danger, imminent war! I was flooded with a different kind of fear, the trepidation tremendous.

Strangely, immediately, large hands came down and lifted me into the palms. My frightened, shaking body was cradled in huge hands; I could see the lines in the fingers. I heard a voice in my head that said, ***"My Mother has brought*** *you here,"* and something more, like, *"It will be all right."* I was most clear on this male voice telling me His Mother had brought me here. In that instant I felt loved beyond reality, the feeling completely engulfing me. It was as if a syringe removed the sense of fear and replaced it with peace. Words do not exist in our vernacular to describe what I felt. It was not of this world. I lay on the ground, knees tucked under my body, my face in my hands. I was crying. I was sobbing. I was humbled.

What had just happened in those few seconds? Could it be that time stood still and I was in the hands of Christ? It all took place instantly as my guard was down. I had been scared out of my mind, and then I was stunned and calm. I struggled to get up and began to slowly move back to Mom, Paul, and Ed. I was dazed.

I crossed from the vineyard into the seating area behind the church, when a man passed in front of me. I recognized this man as Wayne Weible, the author of the only book I had ever read about Medjugorje.

I joined my family and wanted to tell them what had happened in the field, but the look on Paul's weary, sick face and the exhaustion in my mom's eyes stopped me.

What I did say was, "Mom, you are never going to believe who is here. Wayne Weible."

My mom didn't hesitate before saying, "Did you tell him about your brother?"

"No."

She said, "Go to him, he has the power!"

Mom, I thought, this is too much. Then I recalled our purpose, a miracle. Go do it, Barb! I told myself. Slowly I turned and saw him sitting alone, his head resting in his hands. I approached him.

I whispered, my voice shaking, "Excuse me," and started to cry. Through the tears, I was able to say, "I want to ask you to pray for my brother. He is sick. He has AIDS."

Wayne looked into my eyes with concern, and responded, "Is that your brother over there?" He pointed towards Paul, Mom and Ed.

"Yes," I replied.

Wayne held my hands and prayed with me. He whispered words as tears streamed down my face. His voice was calming.

He said, "There have been cures of AIDS here."

What! My heart flipped. My tears stopped, my mind trying to grasp what he had said. This was huge. It could happen here! We could witness a miracle. Paul could walk out of here healthy. I was shocked, hopeful, humbled, and speechless.

Wayne looked at me and made a request. He asked me to pray for a young Croatian girl who was ill and dying. My thoughts promptly shifted to the image of a young girl of about twelve. He had not mentioned an age, but my imagination did. He said she was dying.

"Of course," I said, "I will pray for her."

As I was about to walk away, he asked me to bring Paul back the next evening, at the same time, and he would pray with him and Ed.

I thanked him, told him I would pray for the girl and would see him tomorrow. We parted; I turned and walked back to Paul, Ed, and Mom, who waited to hear what had happened.

I told them, "There have been cures of AIDS here, Paul. It is possible!" I was ready to scream, collapse, cry, jump—such a complex jumble of emotions reeled through me.

I rested my hands on Paul's shoulders and said again, "There have been cures here!"

He looked back at me through tired, hopeful eyes. I think he was trying to grasp that reality.

We saw people moving towards the church doors; a healing service was about to begin. The door we entered opened near the altar. It was crowded and everyone was kneeling. We followed and lowered to our knees on the hard stone floor. The faces of the crowd looked up towards the priest, their expressions serious, pious. We were transfixed in that position for over an hour, and my knees were not screaming in pain as they otherwise would have been. I was transported and changed in this holy place.

Back in our modest room, my beautiful, weary mom looked at me across the space between our beds, our knees almost touching.

She said, "I am so glad we are here, Barb, I am so glad we are here." Her eyes reflected relief and peace.

Together we thanked Mary for guiding us on this passage, and we prayed for the young Croatian girl. As I stared at Mom, I thought nothing was impossible with God.

6

The Trip: Day Two

The Gospa explains the cross, the heart, and the sun to the visionaries. "These are the signs of salvation: The cross is a sign of mercy, just like the heart. The sun is the source of light, which enlightens us."

Again a shining silhouette takes the place of the cross on Krizevac. The visionaries asked the Blessed Virgin if it was She. "Why do you ask me, my angels? Have you not seen me? The world must find salvation while there is time. Let it pray with fervor. May it have the spirit of faith." November 22, 1981

The second day, I woke, slowly opening my eyes as my mind replayed the day before. I looked over at Mom, who was still sleeping. She had made this all come to be with her ardent faith. What a woman, what a mother! All the things I heard, saw, and felt, unreal. The triumphant thought of cures in this holy village had filled me with hope. This ordinary day of the week was anything but, and the anticipation of what would happen when Wayne prayed with Paul was beyond my belief.

I had told Wayne the truth the night before. I said, "My brother is dying of AIDS."

There was no hesitation in my mind. Mom could not say Paul's illness, and she did not want others to judge. Mom directed us, her obedient children, not to say what was wrong with Paul. She thought "cancer" sounded better. I was so sorry for all those with cancer. We borrowed their diagnosis, their frightening, invasive word in exchange for ours. She believed, with a diagnosis of cancer, others would have empathy, but AIDS would bring condemnation. Nevertheless, the truth spewed out of my mouth when I had approached Wayne. I could not avoid saying the truth. I asked him to intercede on our behalf. When I told Mom, she did not say a word; she was just grateful for his response, his confidence about cures.

What I did not share was the supernatural happening on the path, in my moment of panic and fear. I was not certain I really grasped it myself. Had it been my imagination? No, it was so clear. Jesus literally held me in His hands, spoke and touched my soul. Could it have been? Pure love had filled my being in that instant. Planning this journey had surfaced so many concerns, apprehensions, and sheer desperation. Now those chaotic feelings were reduced, a part of them vacuumed out and replaced by hope and love.

It was Sunday, the Lord's day of rest. *Since on the seventh day God was finished with the work he had been doing, he rested on the seventh day from all the work he had under-*

taken. So God blessed the seventh day and made it holy, because on it he rested from all the work he had done in creation. (Genesis 2:2–3)

Paul looked distinctly better. I was not convinced he really was improved, or was it my wishful eyes playing tricks. He could not get over what Wayne had said, "cures of AIDS here."

After breakfast we walked to Apparition Hill, also known as Podbrdo Hill. It was here, in June of 1981, that the children first saw Our Lady. We had wanted to be there early to avoid the scorching temperatures and crowds. This was a good move on our part. The four of us arrived at the base. A row of small touristy shops lined the street. Rosaries, displayed outside like jewelry, flanked the doorways. The actual path, beyond the shops, weaved up the hill. It was incredibly rocky and gradually steep. Mom surveyed the trail and looked down at Paul's shoes.

"Paul, why did you wear those shoes? You should have on shoes with more support. How are you going to do this in those shoes?"

Paul listened and responded, "This is what I brought, Mom. It will be OK."

Moccasin loafers were the subject of debate. Mom kept at it as Paul climbed, his cane supporting him. Her concern apparent, she was relentless, warning him to be careful and watchful of slippery or jagged rocks in his path.

He remarked that the cane would help him, and repeatedly replied, "It will be OK."

My attention shifted, while this banter continued, to the people on the hill with us.

To my surprise, I saw a crippled girl with braces on her legs, walking with two others. On her shoulder rested a large cross as she struggled up the hill. This was astounding. I saw another group climbing, without shoes, on the rough rocks. My witnessing them made the exchanges between Mom and Paul seem ridiculous and contrary to the mood here. I was in humble awe. I then noticed many abandoned crosses left upright on the trailside as I gazed towards the summit.

Mom's shoe distress was clearly aggravating Paul. Sadly, he was getting annoyed. Suddenly, Mom felt faint and dizzy. Ed and I took either arm and found a rock perch for her to sit on.

She said, "I am not going up. I will pray for you as you go."

"What? Are you crazy, Mom! You are not going up? Mom, this was where it happened." Then I stopped.

Mom repeated, "Go on, I will be fine."

"OK, Mom," I said, bewildered.

Paul, Ed, and I left her on her perch and started up the mountain. We moved silently as we stared at all the crosses left by pilgrims. The mountain overlooked the village. The view was magnificent: a patchwork quilt of earth and green, the grand spires of St. James Church in the center.

About halfway up, a large cross marked the place of the first apparition. I could not fathom Mary, the Mother of Jesus, appearing at this precise spot repeatedly; it was hard to grasp this reality.

Paul made it to the summit with Ed's assistance. This was a sacred place. We breathed it all in, found a place on the ground and sat in quiet. I prayed for Paul and Mom. I uttered in my mind, I hope I am saying this right. Please hear my prayers. Give us this miracle and make my brother well.

It was here that the conversation between Paul and me began. He looked at me, then cast down his eyes. "Barbie, I cannot pray for myself. I made some very wrong choices. I am having trouble."

I shot back, "Paul, you have to pray. It has to come from you and from all of us." I felt desperate. He wanted to live—I knew that—but his inner struggle was evident. "Paul, we are here for you! You have to ask, please."

He was not saying anything. We locked hands, and I looked to Ed for help. He had not known how to reply to this. We sat with closed mouths, eyes absorbing the beauty, each lost in our thoughts.

I dove into my inner dialogue. Our Lady, this was where it began, on this mountain. You spoke to the children. Oh, Mary, if he does not ask, will it still work? If we all pray, can he still be healed?

I waited for an answer. Nothing came. The confusion of how to ask, how to pray, what were the correct words, all plagued my mind in this dire situation. I was so naïve.

"I want to see Mom," I said, so we rose and started down the trail.

As we approached her, I said, "Hi, Mom, are you feeling OK?"

"Just fine," she said with a smile. "I said my Rosary. How was it at the top?"

"Beautiful," Paul replied, and down we walked.

I truly believe Our Lady had wanted Paul to experience the quiet, the meditative quality of the hike. Apparently, there was a purpose for Mom's dizziness. Mom prayed. After that scene, I did not recall her mentioning his shoes or any other insignificant thing for the duration of the trip. Her focus had shifted.

At the base, we asked about a phone so we could call home and let Dad and Michael know we were safe and it was going OK. Imagine: This was 1991, before cell phones. In this remote pocket of the world, the guest homes didn't even have phones for us to use. Therefore, we did what other pilgrims were doing and stood in line at a pay phone to make our call. We were able to reach Michael and Dad to report the news and asked them to call the rest of the family.

The Sunday Mass was packed; the combination of locals and pilgrims filled the pews of St. James. I watched heads bowed in prayer and hands clasped, pointing upward. This reverent kind of devotion was moving. Everyone sang, everyone's responses seemed so heartfelt, everyone appeared engrossed, focused, and attentive. The reverence increased as the Mass continued. This was something unusual. Paul sang deeply and loudly. I completely agreed with Mom's comment from the night before. It was good that we were here.

After Mass, we went to an outdoor café and dined on sandwiches. It was great to observe the happenings on the street. The hustle and bustle of locals and pilgrims from all over the world filled our ears with chatter in multiple languages. Paul was tired and wanted to rest, so Ed and Paul headed back to the guesthouse, and Mom and I explored. We walked and talked, discussing what Wayne had said. Our anticipation for the meeting that evening was growing.

Later, we agreed to sit outside again for the Rosary and evening liturgy. The sunset breeze felt so good. We were praying the Rosary, when all of a sudden, people around us started standing, pointing to the sky and looking towards the sun.

We stood, turned around and saw a round disc covering the sun so that its brightness did not make us squint. My eyes fixated. The disc covering the sun rotated from right to left, exposing rainbow-colored flares beyond the outer edge. Then the sun began to fall from the sky, so much so that I grabbed Paul's arm and we lunged backwards together, and, at some point, Ed hooked my other arm. Like a yoyo, the sun moved away from us, into the sky, and pulsated. In a moment it stopped.

The sun then appeared as it normally would. We squinted. People in the crowd exclaimed, "Did you see rosaries in the sky!"

Everyone talked about what appeared before his or her eyes. Paul, Ed, Mom, and I did not see images, but seeing the sun as we did was implausible and incredible. Our mouths hung in disbelief as we looked at each other. The fact that others saw images amazed and intrigued me. Each view was personal for everyone as they journeyed in their faith. Some were clearly seeing more than others.

What I believe we witnessed was the Miracle of the Sun. I had heard about this, and now I had seen it with my own eyes. It had happened in Fatima, Portugal, in front of 100,000 people, on October 13, 1917.

Was this really happening? During the Rosary, Our Lady appeared to the visionaries and again the blanket of love wrapped around us. The evening was not over. My heart pounded in anticipation of our meeting with Wayne Weible. His comment from the night before played over and over in my head: "People with AIDS have been healed here."

When the Mass concluded, we walked to the back of the church, our purpose clear, the feelings of trepidation, excitement and hope mingled.

As promised, Wayne was there. I introduced Paul and Ed. Mom briefly mentioned hearing him speak in Myrtle

Beach and told him that she lived there. Then we all joined hands and prayed together. His words were spontaneous and heartfelt. He then asked to pray with Paul and Ed alone. Mom and I moved to the side quietly, pleading for healing. I prayed for Mom's prayers to be answered. When they finished, we thanked him, and he left to join his group of travelers.

Ed shared what Wayne had said. "He told us to clean our insides with holy water from the fountain in the front of the church and begin to drink the water daily. Wayne said this would cleanse both the body and the soul. He also remarked, as he prayed, that he saw faces of many in purgatory praying for Paul. He said souls could pray for others but not for themselves, and Wayne reminded us to pray for souls in purgatory."

More may have been said, but that was what was told.

Now we had to continue asking Our Lady, through her Son Jesus, to hear Wayne's request, and we would continue praying and listening.

Wayne was a powerful man, as Mom had said, and Mary had called upon him to spread her message. His story of conversion was amazing. As a journalist, he had heard about Medjugorje in a discussion of modern miracles. He came, saw, converted and his life changed.

Fast forward and years later, Wayne published a book in 1999, titled *The Final Harvest*. It was his fifth book about Medjugorje. Mom came across this book at a resale bazaar in her retirement community, many years after we had returned from this trip. She had not read this book and was eager to begin. What she found while reading created a wave of astonishment. In this book, Wayne mentions meeting me and recalls my request for him to pray for my brother. Here are his exact words:

> Suddenly there was a tap on my shoulder. I glanced up: It was one of the women who were accompanying the sick man. She asked timidly, "I know people are always asking things of you, but I have a very special request. Could you please come and pray over that man up there in the front? Could you come and say a prayer over him ...? The young woman's voice trailed off and she began to cry. "He is my brother, and he is very sick. He has AIDS and he is dying. My mother and I brought him and his friend here, hoping for a healing." I felt horrible, knowing I had hesitated to do what the Blessed Virgin was asking. I had failed in this particular instance to answer the call.

You see, the Blessed Mother had urged Wayne to pray over Paul when he had heard him coughing. Let me continue with the excerpt.

The following day, they came. Both men had AIDS; the man who was so sick was Catholic, while his partner, who had been living with him for 17 years, was Protestant. The sick man was very repentant and open to what was happening in Medjugorje. He wanted a healing. The confused, frightened Protestant did not really understand what was going on. He knew nothing about Medjugorje or about apparitions, but was hoping this was all real, because they had no hope left. We prayed together, all of us, and then I put my arms around both of them and prayed to Jesus that they both might be healed spiritually and physically. I wouldn't have done that for anything in the world five years before. I wouldn't have gone near anyone with AIDS, let alone pray for the person's healing. I would have judged him in my heart, and I would have condemned him. But the thought struck me: This was also war. It was the war of good against evil, the war that raged in all of us. And it was in these situations that Our Lady was urging us to answer her call. Her messages centered on the very words of Jesus when He said, "Whatever you do to the least of Mine, you do to Me." When we can see others as Jesus sees us and respond to them without judgment, then we can say we are answering the call.

After our meeting with Wayne, Paul and Ed went into St. James Church for the healing service. Mom and I sat outside, silently absorbing all that had occurred. Was Mary going to intercede on behalf of Mom's request ... Wayne's request? Would Paul be able to continue his life, working and giving to children? If he did survive this, would his life change? What would happen in our family if we had this miracle? How would Mom endure if the miracle did not happen? These were some of the questions which spun in my mind.

I glanced over at my mom, her face so riddled with contrary thoughts. I felt so utterly sorry for her in the enormity of this. Did she have the ability to let go completely and fully entrust her son to her holy Mother?

Some parallels form in my heart between Mother Mary and my mother, in the thread of their suffering sons. As we say in the prayer given to us by our Father, *thy will be done on earth as it is in heaven.* How hard it is for parents to watch a child suffer.

When Paul and Ed came out of the church, we kissed good-night. Mom, Paul and Ed returned to the guesthouse. I wanted to walk, so I ventured off. Feeling safe, I could have strolled for hours. I didn't sense the fear that had gripped me just twenty-four hours ago, and the coolness of the night appealed. I needed to unwind and savor this place.

7

The Trip: Day Three

"Dear children! Today also I invite you to prayer, a prayer of joy so that in these sad days no one amongst you may feel sadness in prayer, but a joyful meeting with God, His Creator. Pray, little children, to be able to come closer to me and to feel through prayer what it is I desire from you. I am with you and each day I bless you with my maternal blessing so that Our Lord may fill you abundantly with His grace for your daily life. Give thanks to God for the grace of my being able to be with you because I assure you it is a great grace. Thank you for having responded to my call." July 25, 1992

"Dear children, also today I desire to call you, through this time of grace, pray. Renew my messages, dear children. Live my messages. Dear children, this time is a time of responsibility, live my messages responsibly. Dear children, I desire for you to do works, and not words. The Mother prays for you and intercedes before Her Son for all of you. Thank you, dear children, also today, for having accepted me and accepted my messages, and for living my messages." June 18, 2009 – Ivan's message from an evening encounter on Apparition Hill

After the two previous intense, miraculous days, from a sound sleep I awoke filled with promise. Mom was still resting. I decided to quietly cross the balcony to Paul and Ed's room. I wanted to check on Paul. Yes, he looked stronger; it seemed as if a daily cup of prayer, rest and water replenished his compromised body. He was filling bottles with holy water and drinking it; maybe this was really working.

On this day, we met early to travel by bus to the parish of Fr. Jozo Zovko. I was looking forward to the thirty-mile ride and venturing outside the village. Since we had arrived in the dark, this would be our first scenic excursion. As we drove out, the sky was blue, a perfect day, and the air conditioning on this coach bus felt so good. The temperatures were soaring again, and Paul looked happy to be cool. We chatted about the lush tobacco fields, precise vineyards, the rural farmland and the beauty of the majestic mountains in the distance. This was one of the moments when we were conversing normally about scenery, without all the big issues.

Father Jozo's story was woven into the tapestry of Medjugorje. Eight months before Our Lady appeared to the children in 1981, Father Jozo was named pastor of St. James Church. On the day Mary appeared, he was not in town, but a few days later learned of what had happened. He did not believe; he was skeptical. He questioned the children, but remained doubtful. One day, he was in prayer and Our Lady instructed him to protect the children. Moments later the children knocked on the door, running from the authorities.

He then believed and aided the visionaries and played an integral role in leading the faithful of Medjugorje.

Under the Communist regime, talk of the apparitions was dangerous. Father Jozo balanced between protecting the visionaries, shepherding his parishioners and avoiding collisions with the military police and government. Aware that something miraculous and wonderful was happening, he attempted to do what he could to advise the people and listen to the messages the children were receiving.

Father created a safe harbor for the children from the authorities; he gave the visionaries refuge in the sanctuary of the rectory. His willingness to help the children and share the messages from Our Lady endangered his own welfare. In August 1981, he was arrested for rebellion against the wishes of the Communist state. He was sentenced to prison. He was released after a year and a half but was not allowed to return as pastor of St. James in Medjugorje. He was assigned a parish some distance from Medjugorje. Our Lady spoke to his heart over the years. He had much to share with the pilgrims drawn to this holy village. We were going to hear his testimony.

The beauty of the church, the scenery and grounds were impressive. Lush, well-manicured gardens surrounded the church. We moved towards the open doors ... the pews inside were filling quickly. Thankfully, we got a seat about three quarters of the way back from the altar. From the stream of people still to enter, it looked like many would stand.

Someone began to lead us in a Rosary. After this, a celebration of the Mass, and the Gospel for this day was from Luke 12:32–48. Jesus said to his disciples: *Do not be afraid any longer, little flock, for your Father is pleased to give you the kingdom.* It then goes on to say, *Where your treasure is, there also will your heart be.* The Gospel reading concluded with: *Much will be required of the person entrusted with much, and still more will be demanded of the person entrusted with more."*

The parts mentioned above were what jumped out at me. "Do not be afraid." That was a tough one. I was afraid for my brother and the heart of my mom. My encounter in the vineyard had given me a sense of protection and I was trying not to be fearful, but it kept sneaking up on me. Hearing the words brought comfort. I heard with refreshed ears. I questioned "my treasure" as I listened. What was my treasure? Faith, family—for sure—and the people I love. The ending of the Gospel stating "much will be required" hit a chord. We were getting so much on this trip, and if Paul was cured, what would be demanded of him, of us? There was so much to contemplate.

Mass in this holy place mesmerized me and I found myself concentrating on every word and its significance in my life. After the liturgy, Father Jozo filled us in with a detailed account of his experiences: the story of his extraordinary dedication to the visionaries and his personal spiritual growth during the first months of her visitations.

Father Jozo spoke through an interpreter. The first message he emphasized was to offer penance or sacrifice so that we can love freely, without blocks or constraints that hold us back. When we demand sacrifice of ourselves, we show Our Lady how compassionate we are for our intentions. He remarked that when we cannot express our love, punishments are doled out, which is why we must look humbly at ourselves. We need to be free to allow ourselves to love. The Blessed Mother, through all her messages, was helping us to be free of our egos so that we could be at peace and in the freedom to love. If we have bread, we can fast. The poor and hungry cannot fast. The Blessed Mother calls us to pray, fast and pray for peace.

He remarked again, like Father Slavko, that our presence in this place was important; he added that it would have impact globally. Father told us to be open to private messages or conversions of the heart and, most emphatically, that prayer was miraculous. He reassured us that we were safe here and blessed to come, and that what we give to Jesus we give to all. He spoke of the Body of Christ and the unity in Jesus and the Holy Spirit we receive in Communion. Each of us, he said, has the opportunity for enlightenment and transformation by the bread and wine. He informed us that Mass is life. The unity of the family church should be our concentration.

Our Lady gave him a message for priests, which Father Jozo shared with us. He told us that we must pray for priests. Our Lady showed Father Jozo a wheel image. In the center was a circle representing God's love. Emanating from the center of God's love were spokes, or branches, to an outer circle. We represent the outer circle. The priests are the spokes connecting us, the believers to God's ever present love. We must allow ourselves to transform in the Mass. The frequency of energy between the priests and us is charged and necessary for our growth.

He emphasized the significance of the Bible. "Do not forget it!" he exclaimed. "Place it in a distinctive spot and read it every day." The Blessed Mother cried, when speaking to him, "Tell them that you cannot believe without revelation from God's word."

Father Jozo proposed that we locate a unique place in our homes and create a family altar. In this place should be the following basics: a picture of Mary and her Son, the Bible and holy water. A family place to worship. Read the Bible; it is the Living Word of God. Kiss the Bible. Fill your heart with the peace of the Bible. Permit this altar to be a gift of prayers, blessing and protection to your children after you die. Put your life in the care of God. Father Jozo poured these wisdoms out to us; it was up to us to listen. They came from the pleas of Our Lady.

Following Father Jozo's talk, Wayne Weible spoke. Ed's personal miracle began when the two men stood together at the altar.

Ed nudged me with his elbow and asked, "Do you see the aura of light above their heads?"

I whispered, "No."

He said, "Are you sure? I see halos."

Time lapsed, and he asked again, "Do you see the halos?" and again I replied no. This continued throughout the duration of the talk. He sat dumbfounded, staring at this special vision.

Ed received a miracle.

When Wayne began, he told us of his own conversion, his introduction to Medjugorje and the insistent plea he received from Our Lady in his heart, in her exact words: "*You are my son, and you are to do my Son's work. Write about the events in Medjugorje. Afterwards you will no longer be in this work [newspapers], for your life will be devoted to the spreading of the message.*"

In the years following, he did as Mary had asked. Currently he is the author of six plus books about Medjugorje. He continues to lead countless people on pilgrimages to this holy place. His story, which he details in his book *The Message*, was one of suffering, loneliness, desperation and, eventually, salvation and peace. The voice he heard deep inside was open to her message. I was riveted in my seat as I heard his humble, articulate story spill out. His love for Our Lady so obvious, his words touched my spirit.

Our day with Father Jozo was not yet complete. This charismatic priest laid his healing hands on all of us present, with the help of visiting priests from all over the world. We moved out of the pews and stood in the aisles, waiting for a blessing. All around me, people were falling gently to the ground after the blessing by this holy man. Only now do I understand what was happening.

The *laying on of hands* is the method used to bestow a special divine blessing. It works as a priest lays his hand on the recipient. I watched Father Jozo put his left hand on the shoulder of one of the pilgrims and the other hand on the head, or sometimes both hands cupped on the recipient's head. Next, he whispered a prayer over the person, and this was when the impartation of the Holy Spirit happened. Some fell to the ground as the Spirit entered their body. They then lay on the ground and rested in the Spirit. After moments, I watched people get up off the floor. They looked peaceful. Some simply stood firm and received the blessing. Around me, I saw many wide eyes, tears of joy falling on some cheeks and expressions of nervousness and exaltation. The energy was buzzing in this holy church.

Mom wanted Father Jozo to lay his hands on Paul and Ed. She pushed them forward and attempted to stand next to Paul. Mom was then gently nudged away, shifted by the crowd. Engulfed in the people, she moved farther and farther away. Paul, Ed, and I stood shoulder to shoulder in the aisle as Father Jozo approached. My heart was beating rapidly and the prayer in my heart was screaming, *Heal my brother, please!*

When Father Jozo's hand touched my head, my knees began to buckle. I felt energy coursing through my body, but I did not fall. This experience was so unfamiliar to me. I was scared and awed at the same time.

I turned to watch, and it was a miracle. He placed one hand on Ed and one hand on Paul. This was the moment; I knew they would be healed. … But they did not go down. *Why?* was the cry in my heart. *What happened?*

We moved back into the pew and knelt. My tears streamed. I wanted Paul and Ed to fall simultaneously and allow the Spirit to heal them, but they had not gone down.

My eyes searched for Mom. Where was she? I spied her on the other side of the church and saw a priest whisper to her as his head lowered near her ear, his hand on her shoulder. Mom turned to come back to us, her face strangely surprised.

She returned, moved into the pew and knelt next to me and said, "Barb, the priest whispered in my ear, 'It is good that you have brought your son here.'"

Once she'd said it, she bowed her head and cried into her hands. I knelt there next to her, stunned beyond belief. In this crowded Croatian church, a priest who spoke English directly affirmed the words of my mother's heart. I prayed,

Dear Mary, Queen of Peace, heal my brother for my earthly mother, if this is the will of your Son.

With the service over, Paul, Ed, Mom, and I sat on the steps outside the church. It was warm, but a slight breeze touched our faces. We hugged, shed some more tears and talked briefly about our feelings of what had occurred. Paul felt frustrated and in a state of confusion. I think he wanted to feel a bolt of lightning and know that he was better. He did not know and wanted so badly to have confirmation. He wanted to know something. Ed sat in awe; he had seen halos and looked dazed. Mom hung on each word the boys uttered, waiting for them to reveal that her prayers had been answered.

Our bus was about to depart, so we boarded and quietly returned to the village of Medjugorje. The rest of this day was meditative and silent. Our hearts were full. We attended the Rosary and evening Mass with longing, and again allowed the love of Gospa—the Croatian word for Lady, the Virgin Mary—to envelop us. It was our time to pray privately and be in communion with the Medjugorje community.

After the Mass, we heard of an extraordinary thing that was to occur. Ivan would be meeting with his prayer group on Mount Podbrdo at ten thirty that evening. Gospa would be appearing to the group and all pilgrims present could attend. The news spread by word of mouth; it was passed excitedly from one group to the next.

How exciting and astonishing! Paul felt drained from our day, so he sadly made the decision to stay back and rest. Mom, Ed and I could not wait to experience this, and we told Paul we would give him all the details. We grabbed our flashlights and headed towards the mountain. This would mark Mom's first time to go all the way up Podbrdo Hill. The first time, she had become dizzy and sat to pray. Now she felt a little apprehensive about doing this in the dark, with the terrain so rocky. The climb was challenging enough during the day.

Upon arrival at the base, we encountered the multitudes who had also gathered to ascend the mountain to be with Our Lady. What a gift this was, to be present for the apparition. I wondered if we would see anything. Profoundly faithful people surrounded us, all inspired by Our Lady, longing to be pulled into Her fold. We felt the inconceivable power of the Holy Spirit growing and igniting inside us, drawing us to the mountaintop.

We began the ascent, moving in the groove of the people as we swarmed upward. We hung on to each other, looking over our shoulders to make sure we were connected. A boy with blond tousled hair, about ten years old, walked in bare feet ahead of us.

I remarked to him, "Don't your feet hurt? It is so rocky."

He replied, with a British accent, "Lady, we are on holy ground. My feet don't hurt, and I even have a deep cut."

He motioned to me to look at his foot as he balanced on a large rock. I shone my flashlight and saw a cut the size of a quarter on the bottom of his foot. I could see it was not bleeding and he said it did not even hurt. I was stunned for several reasons: first, the pure injury—no blood, no pain, and secondly, the faith of this ten-year-old child to take off his shoes and walk barefooted in the dark.

We moved on. As we got closer to the top of the mountain, we searched for a place to settle as the multitudes milled around the top of the mountain near the small cross made of steel. Guitar music emanated from the center of the hill, from Ivan and his friends; the melody and gentle voices soothed the air. Approximately two hundred plus people gathered to witness this event. I heard dogs barking, babies crying, rocks disturbed by the stirring shoes ... and then the Rosary began. The harmony of prayer recited in the mixture of native languages sounded angelic.

In an instant, in the midst of prayer, a hush washed over the crowd. It was whispered, "She is present." A miracle occurred. It was as if a bubble descended over us and not a sound could be heard. It was complete and utter stillness, so quiet I do not ever recall experiencing absolute silence in the midst of a large crowd. The dogs, the babies, the whispers, the pebbles, the wind, nothing—all sound vacuumed out and love poured into our beings.

Then it was over, and the noise and movement ensued.

Mom said to me, "Did you see anything?"

I said, "No. Did you hear nothing?"

Her face lit up in agreement. "You are right. It was as if I was holding my breath."

Ed agreed, and we all smiled in understanding. The universe was conspiring. As if this was not enough, there were three shooting stars: one before the actual apparition to Ivan, one during and one after Our Lady was gone. This was beyond my understanding; it was extraordinary, miraculous, and awesome. The words are not available to express the feelings and observances. I can only express it like an eruption of joy so deep in my core and an insight into what was beyond our earthly existence.

Upon our reentry to the village from Podbrdo Hill, the multitudes flowed like honey, sweet and thick. Smiles adorned the faces. The participants of this pilgrimage in August of 1991, as well as the community of Medjugorje, descended from atop the mountain, down into the evening lights of the village. The love of Our Lady touched each of our hearts on this amazing evening and filled us with grace.

8

The Trip: Day Four

"Dear children, today also I am inviting you to prayer. I am always inviting you, but you are still far away. Therefore, from today, decide seriously to dedicate time to God. I am with you and I wish to teach you to pray with the heart. In prayer with the heart, you shall encounter God. Therefore, dear children, pray, pray, pray. Thank you for having responded to my call." October 25, 1989

Tuesday August 13, Ed's fortieth birthday. A wild faith journey was probably not the plan for celebrating this momentous anniversary of his birth. Yet, again, this day did prove to be miraculous!

The morning began at five thirty, with a simple breakfast, and then off to Cross Mountain, otherwise known as Krizevac Mountain. We left so early because of the heat index. There was an air of excitement as we rode in the van to the base. We listened as our guide told us of the history of the concrete cross, erected on the pinnacle of this prominent mountain. The family from South Dakota, our fellow pilgrims, joined us, so there were nine of us together for this experience.

The cross was built in 1933. An inscription on the base reads: *To Jesus Christ, the Redeemer of the Human Race, as a sign of our Faith, Love and Hope, in Memory of the 1900th Anniversary of the Passion of Jesus.* In its center was a relic from the actual cross Jesus had carried and which held Him at the crucifixion. This relic was a gift from Rome.

Ever since the apparitions began, pilgrims had gathered at the base and followed the Way of the Cross to the top. Bronze relief sculptures of the stations, created by an artist, Carmelo Puzzolo, were added in 1988. We knew from our guide and what we had heard from other pilgrims that we were to stop at each station, pray, meditate, and move on towards the summit.

We got out of the van. We each held the navy blue covered paperback book, titled *Pray with the Heart!* by Fr. Slavko Barbarić. In my ignorance of desiring a miracle, I wanted to do everything right, whatever that meant in my mind, so reading and pausing at each marker was important for this request. I made it clear to our group that this was how we were going to proceed and if they disagreed, I requested that they not stay with us. To my grateful heart, they agreed. Our prayer book would guide us for each station as we made our way. We decided to take turns reading the meditations and leading the prayers for each station. The nine of us had not only arrived at this holy place together, but shared breakfasts, dinners, and excursions, all melding us as companions on this journey and all pulling for each other.

Paul and Mom surveyed the steep trail. Paul was uncertain about doing this, not sure how high he could go, and stressed this to the rest of us. Mom agreed to stay back with him if necessary. We would take it slow. The morning was cool and fresh. However, as the sun rose higher, the tinge of heat began to piggyback the air. It looked much steeper than I had thought. The perspective from the distance skewed the reality. The trail traversed the side of the mountain. It was very rocky; the path was not smooth and worn. I would have thought after all the years of erosion from people navigating this trail, the rocks would have worn down, but no, jagged surfaces were everywhere. Paul would have to calculate his steps. The AIDS had left his feet with peripheral neuropathy, which made his feet tingle and his gait sometimes unsteady. We were definitely going to move slowly.

The reddish dirt and shades of gray from the rocks filled the landscape. There was green, but it was brush, like foliage growing wild and free. The sun was making its way out; it looked like we had another beautiful day. I could not imagine doing this in rain or inclement weather—the climb would be treacherous. I worried about Paul and Mom, with the heat, the height, his health, and her hopeful heart. We gathered at the first marker.

I read the first reflection; everything here was a first for me. This active faith was constantly surprising me. I opened my book and read.

"Jesus prays in the Garden of Gethsemane." I was thinking, Please, answer our prayers and help my brother. We want to do this right. I want to obey the rules and follow the instructions of prayer on this mountain.

This was so big, I did not want to make a mistake. I took everything seriously, as I had never before. This miracle meant trusting and believing with all my heart. I was trying. It did not come naturally to me. At times my thoughts would tell me all this was crazy, and then something would happen. I would see something, and my conviction would return. I wanted it to work, and for others, it had. There were documented miracles in this place, so this was not crazy. Paul was open to it all, and Mom was the most convinced.

I continued reading about His apostles sleeping when He had asked them to stay awake and pray. I thought as I read, *They* cannot stay awake for this, for *Him*! They saw the healings, the miracles, some saw the transfiguration; they had felt the changes within; they had been witnesses to it all. Why did they struggle to stay awake for Him? As Christ spent this night in the garden, He sweated blood, He was anxious, He prayed for His Father to take away this cup. His friends, His companions slept. How frightened and alone He must have been.

I read the reflection. The words directed us to ask for forgiveness for being halfhearted. This was so true. How many times had I prayed or asked for something without sincerity or with some level of skepticism?

I read, "Grant me that I may follow this Way of the Cross, as Mary did." This was huge. I would try. I wanted my brain to get it; I wanted my heart to get it.

When I finished reading, we said the Our Father, the Hail Mary and the Glory Be together. I felt heavy and weighted inside.

As we moved to the second marker, I looked at Paul. Please have mercy on him. Can he get beyond the burden he carries? He had endured the diagnosis and treatments of HIV/AIDS with the support of Ed and friends, but without his mom or family. He worried; he had struggled about telling us of his predicament. He could not share his fears openly. He hid this truth from us. Was it to spare us? Was it to keep from disappointing his parents? From our conversations, I think it was a mixture of many reasons.

The mood was intense among the group. We were riding on the spiritual and physical experiences we'd had thus far. Each expression was serious, concentrating on every word uttered. We gazed at each other. Paul was determined; I could see it in his gestures. We moved to the bronze marker.

The First Station

Jesus, You are condemned to death.

Someone else was reading now. I heard the words *injustice*, *violence*, and *quest for power*. What was Paul thinking?

Was he relating to Jesus' condemnation by society? I think of the thousands who suffered from HIV/AIDS. They suffered in silence, so many fearful and without hope, so many rejected sons and daughters. They struggled from injustices; they endured great maladies without compassion and some in panic.

Paul said, many times, to me, "I cannot ask to be healed, Barb. I made mistakes."

I said, "We all do."

Please, God, clean out the guilt so he feels that he can ask to be healed from the depth of his soul. Teach me to love and stand up for others, under all circumstances. Do not allow my judgments to be crowded with prejudices.

The Second Station

Jesus, You receive Your cross upon Your shoulders.

The cross Paul carried was heavy. He carried it for a long time. He asked me quietly, as we walked between the markers, "Tell the others the truth, Barb, tell them I have AIDS."

I looked at him long and hard and said, "Really, Paul? What about Mom?"

He responded, "They have to know. We can still protect Mom." He was looking at me, pleading for me to do this.

"OK, Paul." I squeezed his arm.

Mom, as I said before, was not comfortable with saying the word AIDS, so we continued our charade and said cancer. In reality, it had not come up much; people had not asked. When we were first introduced, we told the group it was cancer. She could not say the reality, and we honored our mother. One by one, I quietly told them. Paul and I wanted to protect Mom, so I asked each person to respect that. I was in awe; as each person listened, they met my eyes with sympathy and compassion. It was surprising to me that as I shared, they began to open up and unveil the burdens they carried in their hearts, the reasons why they were here. They poured out their confidences in the safety of this holy mountain. Now, acceptance and truth strengthened the bond between us.

The Third Station

Jesus, You fall for the first time beneath the cross.

Paul was transfusion dependent on this journey; he was weak, after years of trial drugs, to beat the disease. Since we had been here, I had seen him weaken, and bend over, coughing vigorously, sometimes resulting in getting sick to his stomach. He looked gaunt and so much older than thirty-nine. He leaned on the cane, which had been my grandfather's. He had died in his nineties. Paul was sick—a shadow of his former energetic self.

As the next person read the meditations, Paul seemed to gain a little strength. The group wanted him with us now, more than ever. The truth and sharing our burdens had made us closer in some way. The passage "truth will set you free" has enormity. I could see the weight leave him. The support mounted, and the eight of us lifted him up in spirit. Paul was listening to each word, allowing it to permeate his being. His empathy for Christ was showing in his expressions. Paul was continuing to move up the mountain.

The Fourth Station

Jesus, You meet Your holy Mother.

My awesome mother brought Paul here for a miracle. Mary was her model. Mom wanted to take away the cross Paul carried, but she could not. I looked at Mom. Her tearful eyes gazed upon my brother with love overflowing. I felt so glad in that instant that God had placed us here, at this exact moment in time. Mom was standing by Paul through all of this, his suffering and times of desperation. He could finally fall into the arms that bore him, as the beloved hurting child. The glances between us united us in an inseparable embrace.

The Fifth Station

Jesus, Simon of Cyrene helps You carry Your cross.

Ed was a Simon; he helped Paul with the burdens of illness. Ed was HIV-positive. He himself carried a heavy cross. He was well now. He showed no signs of illness, yet. He carried the vision of Paul deteriorating, knowing that he would inevitably be sick unless a cure was found soon. Our fellow journeymen did not know this truth of faith. Mom and I did and we prayed for Ed. He needs to be healed too. This day was Ed's birthday. Please, God, give him a long life and conversion of heart. He walked and prayed along with us, watching, hearing and being there for Paul. I admired Ed and loved him. He was standing unselfishly with Paul and lifting him when he stumbled.

As I surveyed the others, they all wanted to help Paul with his cross. Now that they knew of his AIDS infirmity, they wanted a miracle for him more profoundly. I began praying for them, for the hurts they carried, and listened with a tender, raw heart.

The Sixth Station

Jesus, Veronica offers You her veil and wipes Your face.

"Paul, stay with us," we all resounded when he looked like he might give up.

"We can move slowly."

"We want you with us."

"Do not stop yet."

He wanted to continue, but I could see his body was weary.

He smiled weakly and said, "I want to." He was pulling out all the strength he could muster.

I thought of his doctor in Florida, who was cheering him on. This dedicated doctor had listened to Paul's cries for a cure. The doctor researched the studies of trial medications and enrolled Paul, and supported his desperation for treatment. The doctor had been the one to wipe Paul's tears when another blood test came back with negative results, when the medicines did not work. I thought of all the friends and family who were praying unceasingly for Paul while we were here. They pray to wipe away the sickness.

The Seventh Station

Jesus, You fall the second time beneath the cross.

We arrived at the seventh station—the number seven, the divine number seven, the number significant in the first book of Genesis as the day of rest after creation, and the number repeatedly identified in the last book, of Revelation. It was Paul's turn to read. Everyone now knew his truth. He followed the words on the page: "You have redeemed the world by your cross," and he continued to the end.

I looked up—something was happening! I stared at him, and, in slow motion, he looked up after reading the last word. His face was changing; the lines of stress were disappearing. The lines marking the months, the years of agony, illness, pain, struggle … evaporated as if it had melted away. His face was smooth, like a child's. My heart began to beat rapidly, my eyes frozen, focused on his.

His look penetrated through my skin and to my soul, and then he said, "Barb, I am not doing this by myself, I am being helped. I am not afraid to die."

With this utterance, everything changed. His energy was restored. His voice changed from weariness to lightness and airiness. He looked like he could take off running. Exuberance poured out of him.

A shift. Oh God, is he healed at this moment, at this Station of the Cross, on this mountain so far from home? In this holy place. What happened? Thank you, thank you! I cried and laughed and smiled from ear to ear. I grabbed Mom. She saw the change. Her expression of relief, concern and profound love mingled together. She reached for Paul and held him in an embrace. Ed and I hugged. We all saw the change. We were all beaming with smiles, with tears of joy streaming down our faces.

"We must continue," Paul said.

He was the one drawing us back to the stations, asking who was reading next. He wanted us to go on. Wow!

The Eighth Station

Jesus, You console the women of Jerusalem.

Our voices heavy, we all said the words together from our books, through joyful tears. Oh, Jesus, You endured so much.

You truly are here to console and answer the prayers of a wounded mother, my mother. Our Blessed Mother, you have heard Mom beg for the life of her son. You heard her. You and your Son are with us now!

Whatever happened, the change of heart, the conversion, the healing was for all of us. We were changed. Forever changed as we feasted our eyes on the new and refreshed Paul.

The Ninth Station

Jesus, You fall the third time beneath the cross.

Paul's reverence was inspiring. He was off the ground. He was praying with his heart, his body, his soul. I saw his lips move and strangely heard his thoughts. Oh, my God, I am heartily sorry for all the wrongs, sins and choices I made. … Then he began to pray for others. I felt the pains of our fellow pilgrims. The prayer we recited from our book exited our mouths and entered the atmosphere. Strangely, I could sense the wounds of our fellow pilgrims; they were raw and open, but healing was happening, and it was replacing the injury.

The Tenth Station

Jesus, You are stripped of Your garments.

In the greatest humiliation and suffering, Jesus showed dignity. God was teaching us. I knew that greater awareness would surface eventually, but in this sculptural image in front of me, the head of Christ was up. He was looking out at us.

Forgive us for all we take for granted, and we thank You most profoundly for the new garments Paul is wearing.

The Eleventh Station

Jesus, You are being nailed to the cross.

What was happening? We were reading the painful words of torture on the cross, and Paul looked healed. The contrast was extreme. Please help us to understand Your suffering and let us thank You for what You did for us. I could not imagine Mary seeing her Son, His body ravaged, full of wounds and His torture. Since 1981, She was here helping us, healing us, teaching us. My mom just moments ago saw a transformation in her sick son: so thin, out of breath and diseased, without a cure. Now there was noticeable wellness. There was hope.

The Twelfth Station

Jesus, You are dying on the cross.

At this extreme station of the cross, supernatural love was embracing us. It was profound. In the midst of great strife, there was peace, light. It was radical, and I was in awe. We grasped the stillness; it fell like a blanket over us. I cherished the glimmer for the time that it was present. Christ was dying, and Paul may live. Have mercy on us all and thank You for the power of this most holy place.

The Thirteenth Station

Jesus, You are taken down from the cross and placed in the embrace of Your mother.

The two daughters and I read the next meditation. We looked at our mothers, and tears welled in their eyes. Our Lady was holding her battered and mutilated Son in her arms, the child she brought into this world to be the light of hope, the one who would be King. How devastated Our Lady must have felt holding her bleeding child. How lost and abandoned. How close this was to my mother's heart. Mary, thank you for my brother. Embrace him. I pray my mother be spared of this scene. I pray for this to last, for Mom's prayers and ours to be answered. Will Mom die before Paul, as it should be? Was what happened to Paul on this Way of the Cross his healing? I pray so with all my heart.

The Fourteenth Station

Jesus, You are placed into the tomb.

Paul read this one. I was about to burst, so much emotion pumped through me. The feelings besieged the extreme opposite poles of emotion. The brutal death of Our Lord and how it was; I am transported to the scene: feeling the dust in my face and throat. Jesus died so cruelly. However, the people of His time did not know what would transpire ... the triumph that would occur in several days. His rising and eternal life—do we clearly understand or grasp the meaning?

I did not want to bury my brother. I wanted to grow old with him. I was grateful for his transfiguration, his renewed strength, his loud voice as he read, his physical ability to be at the top of this holy mountain. He looked at me with renewed eyes and he gave hope to Ed.

We were at the top! Paul looked at Mom and said to her, "I am not afraid to die."

Mom responded with confidence, "You will not die."

Mom then looked up and said to Mary, "Please do not take him!"

The prayers sewed us together. They had poured forth from our cracking voices as we made our way through the stations. We had witnessed a miracle. Paul was stronger at the top of this mountain than at the bottom. Time passed, but something supernatural happened; we all saw the change in Paul at the seventh station. The transformation evident, the illness vacuumed out or pushed deep within so only health was visible. Together, we prayed a prayer of thanksgiving and a healing prayer. We lit a candle in the center of our circle at the top, directly in front of the enormous concrete cross. We joined hands and prayed. We rejoiced in what we received and asked for cures, for the hurts still inside.

We separated. We went our own ways to meditate, reflect, thank and be in our own place. I was a kaleidoscope inside. Exhausted and jubilant, I could have cried and shouted for joy. I was a jumble and in shock. I could not believe what I had seen in the last hour. I was so hopeful and wanted to share it with someone, but at the same time was drenched in feelings. I was unsteady, yet a firm believer. The stillness and beauty of nature before my eyes brought calm. The valley below: the patchwork of earth, the fields in varied shades of green, the natural clay roofs and meandering roads. In the center, bold and strong, were the spires of St. James Church. The cross before me was so unyielding and solid I was in awe and humbled. I sat for a while in stillness and relief. Oh, wonderful Mother of Our Lord, thank you for this time of unending love. Fill me with peace as this continues to unfold.

After some time, we began our descent. Paul and I were holding hands and feeling giddy, like little children free of the burdens which had plagued us a short time ago. We sang, "Let there be peace on earth …." We were laughing. It was mind-boggling that he could move and sing like this—it was incredible. Mom caught my eye, and her joy was exploding.

We continued to traverse down. Mom looked back at me at one point, with surprise and shock in her face. She asked, "Do you see what I see?"

I said, "The rocks," and she nodded.

In that moment all the rocks, pebbles and boulders transformed to the image of Our Lady with the infant Jesus in her arms. From the smallest stone to the largest bolder, everywhere my eyes could see, all revealed the same image of Mother and Child. No one else could see it, only Mom and I. Like crazy people, we started collecting the rocks in our T-shirts, stretching them out as hammocks and filling the pouches we had made. One by one, then by the handful, it was another miracle, our miracle. A miracle for my brother's mom and the sister. It was a confirmation, a kiss from heaven. Suddenly we came to our senses and dropped the rocks. We each kept one. We smiled and whispered, "Thank You," and continued. Mom still has her rock and I mine.

All this had happened before twelve noon—amazing! When we got to the base, we boarded our van and headed to the home of Ivan. He met a large group of us in front of his house. Physically, I stood there, but my mind felt challenged and overloaded. I recalled that as people asked questions, he gently moved over the inane comments and continued to take valid inquiries. He stood before us so gentle, serene, and loving. The emphasis of his talk was family, prayer, and how the Rosary could unite the family in strength and bind them in love. I was witnessing the truth of what he was uttering about prayer, conviction, and dedication to our intention. As we had just witnessed, they built strength, especially in our group.

When Ivan finished, we headed back to the house. Our morning and afternoon were extraordinary. We had played a part in several miracles and, remarkably, unknown to me, some of which were yet to be revealed.

For Ed's birthday, his gift was a day of miracles, and all this before he blew out his candles. The courage and dedication of Ed astounded me—to go halfway around the world with his sick, sick partner, a determined yet worried mother and a sister, in search of a miracle. Let alone in a country about to explode in war. He received the gift of a beloved friend who was jubilant and seemingly well and still going strong at six that evening.

We decorated the dining room with banners and crepe paper I had brought from home. The owner of the guesthouse served a delicious dinner and finished with a beautiful birthday cake. We sang to celebrate this man.

Then, Ed looked at his watch and said, "Let's hurry, or we will be late for Mass."

I smiled. This Protestant man was excited about the liturgy and the apparition of Our Lady. He was amazing and had memorized the Rosary in Croatian. Ed was affected, maybe even changed, by Medjugorje. His euphoria was evident to all of us. His new year began here, in this holy place—a new decade for Ed.

Our day concluded after the Rosary and inspiring liturgy. We sat at an open-air restaurant for a cool drink, surrounded by other crowded round tables, chatting of the events of this

day and savoring the moments. We toasted Ed and acknowledged that we did not completely grasp all that had happened. We were in a sort of euphoria as life meandered and
people strolled on the sidewalk in front of us, separated by
the simple wrought iron railing of the café. We retired for
the evening in anticipation of another day in this blessed
pocket of the world. Paul was still going strong.

9

The Trip: Day Five

"Dear children! Today I invite you to pray for peace. At this time peace is being threatened in a special way, and I am seeking from you to renew fasting and prayer in your families. Dear children, I desire you to grasp the seriousness of the situation and that much of what will happen depends on your prayers and you are praying a little bit. Dear children, I am with you and I am inviting you to begin to pray and fast seriously as in the first days of my coming. Thank you for having responded to my call." July 25, 1991

This summer of 1991, my second of married life, was such a profound turning point in my spiritual journey. I was turned inside out on this trip. I heard the Scripture, the Living Word, in a new light and it was incredibly applicable to my life. The scenes played over and over in my head ... the understanding of the apostles' presence at the miracles. I had now witnessed a physical change in my brother. His blue eyes glistened, his stress faded, his ability to climb, run, skip replaced the weary breathless boy, all on Ed's birthday. I refer to that day as Paul's transfiguration. Paul looked amazingly healthy. I also desired an immediate confirmation that he was cured, which was not going to be possible. I was in a bubble, and it was fragile. I needed to trust. What was going to happen next? What was going to happen today?

People of Medjugorje fast on Wednesdays and Fridays; this was a day to fast. Growing up, we gave up something during Lent and ate fish on Fridays. I do not remember times when I was urged to fast and give up something for another. Now, here in this holy place, almost everyone fasts on bread and water. Our Lady said to the visionaries, *"With prayer and fasting, one can stop wars; one can alter the laws of nature."* She said this to them in July of 1982. Evidence of this commitment was apparent in our guesthouse; everyone fasted, the children and adults. Frankly, they did this with admirable devotion and did not seem to complain outwardly. I was learning by observation.

The people here followed the request of their holy Mother. They had learned through Our Lady's words that fasting and sacrifice united them to Jesus. The villagers comprehended, making it their outward sacrifice on Wednesdays and Fridays. It opened their eyes in a renewal of what He had done for us. It was that simple.

I made a vow to fast the entire day. As we crossed the street for daily Mass, I surprised myself at how I looked forward to this hour in church. I found it soothing, comforting and it gave me the time to reflect. My attentiveness was, somehow, on a higher frequency. I was bursting with thanksgiving on this day. The words of Scripture spoke to me; the reflection zeroed in on judgment and condemning others.

The priest's message encouraged unconditional love. We are all God's children … if only I and the rest of humanity could embrace this and be kinder to each other.

As I sat in the wooden pew, my thoughts focused on Paul. I considered the trials Paul had experienced, the times he felt unaccepted, isolated, and had no other choice but to harbor secrets. I saw how clearly I judged others through my expectations, how I criticized and condemned mentally and sometimes verbally when they differed. I was humbled, I was sorry. The priest suggested that we look into a mirror and focus deep into our eyes and say "I love and accept you for who you are." This was a simple exercise, an attempt for truly getting to know ourselves. Taking this on and applying it might help to begin to understand and accept others. I looked over at Paul. He looked revived. It was overwhelming. What was going through his mind, his body?

After Mass, we stood outside. I felt rejuvenated and seemed to be the only one asking what was on the agenda for the day. What was next? What else did we need to do? Someone mentioned a Rosary on Podbrdo Hill; I knew instantly that I must participate. No one else wanted to join me, so I went off in solitude. Actually, it felt good to be by myself. I wanted to think and thank God for all that had happened so far; this had exceeded my expectations and conceptions. The thought of Paul healed and growing old with me, repeatedly appeared in my mind. I relished this thought.

By the time I got to the base of the mountain, the air was scorching and sticky. I glanced at the faces of the people waiting. My eyes rested on an elderly woman, her weathered face lined and tan, her hair hidden under a black kerchief tied under her chin. Her rosary was clenched in her arthritic-looking hands. Her dark shirt and skirt were simple, shoes worn and black, her ankles thick. Her eyes focused on a cross; left by a pilgrim, it was wedged on the hillside. She was a villager. I wondered: What personal witness does she carry in her heart? How many Hail Marys has she voiced? How many times has she climbed these hills? What has she seen? My curiosity tugged, but my contentment at observing her visible faith held me rooted.

People gathered, the crowd thickened, waiting and excited to pray. What a rarity; such a gathering was not often open like this at home. I heard a rumbling that Marija, the visionary, was going to talk with pilgrims before the Rosary. I quickly navigated to her home, close to Podbrdo Hill. The thoughts started to stack in my brain. I wanted to remember, so I could record all that I had seen and heard, later in my journal.

Marija's brown eyes looked tenderly on all of us as we huddled on the walkway and street in front of her family home. At twenty-six years old, she was the visionary whom Our Lady had commissioned to pray for souls in purgatory. Marija's brown hair was moist with sweat; she had been repeating this story for just over ten years and was still having daily apparitions. She looked tired. She gently asked, through the interpreter, that no one take pictures. As the crowd swelled, I would guess the celebrity status was so contrary to the humble messages of Our Lady. It was clear that Marija did not want to answer questions. She briefly wanted to share the messages, her witness of what she had seen and heard from Gospa, Our Lady. The thought astounds: Marija converses with the woman whose image is painted, sculpted, and printed more than any other female in the world. The main points she wanted to share of her conversations were: to say the Rosary devoutly, with the heart, and to read the Holy Bible with our families. She could not emphasize this enough. The unity of the family was critical. Pray for peace. She thanked us and said a prayer.

What a blessing it was to hear these modern-day disciples—each guided in simplistic language as to how the Blessed Mother wanted us to live. I wondered if I could really listen and apply this to my life. Could I do this at home, with Michael? I was not so optimistic. It was so easy here because prayer was everywhere you moved in Medjugorje. I remember having a sense of what it must have been like in the days of Jesus and his apostles. People following them, crowding them, listening intently to the words of wisdom. Countless were converted on the spot as they witnessed.

When Marija finished, I moved with the pulse of the people, back to the mountain, waiting for the Rosary to begin. I noticed others from my group arrive, but no Paul, Ed, or

Mom. About two hundred people had gathered when Father Slavko arrived, wearing his long Franciscan robes. He must have been so hot; the temperature was in the high nineties. He carried a microphone; someone with him held a speaker so the crowd could hear the meditations. He began to lead us in prayer. The rhythm of the recited prayers sounded so beautiful, the air profoundly reverent as so many languages melded in harmony with Father Slavko. He acted as the conductor, through the Holy Spirit.

The hot sun baked as we progressed up the mountain. At some point, it moved behind a cloud. A gentle breeze began to blow—so refreshing, I longed for it to continue. I studied the crowd as we prayed: the multitude, the diversity of ethnicities, ages, and faith. Some devoted pilgrims even managed to walk barefoot, maneuvering the rocky terrain. What a sacrifice! The elderly woman I had seen earlier now cradled the hand of a small child. As we prayed the Rosary, beginning with the Joyful Mysteries and followed by the Sorrowful, and lastly, the Glorious Mysteries, something was happening in the atmosphere. The weather was changing as the story of Jesus' life unfolded. It was miraculous. During the Sorrowful Mysteries I noticed black clouds rolling in. The wind picked up, the temperature dropped; the sky seemed about to explode in a violent storm. During the fifth Sorrowful Mystery, Jesus' death, the wind stilled. In the midst of this blanket of dark, heavy clouds, there was complete silence.

Everything quieted and for a moment it felt as if we were all there at Calvary, on the spot where Jesus took His last breath.

Father continued to lead us in the Glorious Mysteries. We prayed our Hail Marys through Jesus' Resurrection, his Ascension, and the Pentecost. I watched as if on the set of a film. The storm clouds faded. The great director, on cue, called the invisible hands to bring out the sun, in all its glory. The sun burst through the clouds. How did this happen? During the last two Glorious Mysteries, the Assumption of Mary into heaven and her crowning as Queen of Heaven and Earth, the sun shone brilliantly, all colors magnified. My mouth was reciting the prayers, but I was in a state of wonder. Sensations were rushing through me—the complete surprise of this environmental occurrence astonishing.

The people were quiet; the locals did not show any expression of this miracle that had taken place. The visitors looked around for other faces, other eyes, to assure them that they saw it too. We nodded to each other for confirmation. I was humbled and, more than anything, grateful for this witness. It was greater evidence of this holy place and the apparitions. In the forefront of my mind was the question, Is Paul cured?

That evening, everyone from our group shared stories from their day. Paul was quiet, contemplative. He confirmed he was feeling better. I asked him this a lot, actually to the point of annoying him. With everything that had transpired,

I felt so small in this universe, but at the same time, confident that our prayers had been heard and seen by God.

The sacrament of confession was available that evening for all who wanted to participate. The visionaries had expressed the importance of this sacrament for our spiritual growth and personal empowerment over sin. Our Lady wanted us to be clean, yet aware of our choices and behaviors. Outside and inside St. James, hundreds of people lined up, waiting. What a vision to see the multitudes of souls waiting to talk to a priest and confess all their sins, waiting for absolution, waiting for a cleansing. This in itself was miraculous.

There were signs over small tents lined up outside the church, which directed and informed us of the language of the priest inside. Ed had never encountered this; we explained that we had made our first confession before making our First Communions when we were in the second grade. He listened, grabbed a pamphlet, and moved away. We went on and he did not. We stood in two lines, waiting for the English-speaking priests. We scanned the pamphlet to be prepared before entering, Paul and I had not gone to confession in years.

We were hesitant. I was glancing at the words on the page, but thinking that the focus was on Paul, not me. I did not really want to go. It had been a very long time, and I even said, "This is for you, Paul, not me." I knew I should go through with it. Mom, frustrated at our banter, walked away.

After more time waiting, I watched Paul enter the small tent. I stood in line and said a quick prayer for Paul. My heart was racing. I was focusing on my sins and rehearsed the Act of Contrition. Trying to be clear on what I wanted to say and, looking at all these people, I needed to be brief.

The person before me came out. I proceeded with caution. I knelt down. It was dim inside. I could see the serious gray-bearded priest and hear his gruff voice. Instantly I felt like I was seven years old. My palms sweating, I began.

"Forgive me, Father, for I have sinned. It has been years since my last confession."

I continued rambling out my sins and then thought that for so many years of not going to confession, what I had said was lame. My honesty, nerves and fear collided. I felt upset. In retrospect, there was definitely an opening, a shift in my heart to get this better and for greater spiritual self-improvement. A work in progress.

Paul came out, a strange look on his face. He did not want to talk. He moved towards the church doors, clearly wanting to be alone with God. We went inside St. James, knelt, prayed, and addressed our penance. Later he told me he had expected something different, a different reaction from the priest, somehow, a different message from the one he received. He was disappointed, which made my heart hurt. I wanted him to feel peace, to feel clean and whole.

Soon there would be a healing and blessing service in the church, so we stayed. Then, a Holy Hour beginning at 10:30

p.m. The church was packed. The faithful knelt, sat, stood, prayed, thanked, and adored Jesus on the altar, in the monstrance. When I had left New York, my prayers skimmed the surface; here, I began to understand what it meant to pray with the heart. It goes so much deeper: questioning, requesting, and then transference from a mental place to an emotional place. Clearer perspective emerged in the depths. The deeper the submersion, the less aware of the surroundings and the greater the awareness of the inner sanctum, where there was peace to be found.

At some point in the later part of the day, I broke the vow I had made at the start. I blew it! I ate—my hunger pangs won. I could not even make it through this one fasting day. One day, to honor the request of the Blessed Mother, and I could not do it—after all the miracles I had witnessed. This night I was going to sleep cluttered up. All this faith contrasted with my human weakness. Actually, human weakness was what caused us to be here in this holy place. Mother Mary, help us. God help us.

10
The Trip: Day Six

"Dear children, Today I call you to a humble, my children, humble devotion. Your hearts need to be just. May your crosses be your means in the battle against the sins of the present time. May your weapon be patience and boundless love – a love that knows to wait and which will make you capable of recognizing God's signs – that your life, by humble love, may show the truth to all those who seek it in the darkness of lies. My children, my apostles, help me to open the paths to my Son. Once again I call you to pray for your shepherds. Alongside them, I will triumph. Thank you." October 2, 2010

"Dear children, today I am blessing you and I wish to tell you that I love you and that I urge you to live my messages. Today I am blessing you with the solemn blessing that the Almighty grants me. Thank you for having responded to my call." August 15, 1985

Thank God it was morning. I had tossed and turned over what was being asked of us here. Humility, the attitude I wanted to adopt for this day, be patient and watch. It was a grand holy day today, August 15, the feast day of the Assumption of the Blessed Mother. How lucky to be in this holy place on this day. We had planned this trip so quickly, I never considered a feast day of Our Lady in the plan; it just happened that way.

The Spiritual Fruit of the fourth Glorious Mystery of the Rosary, the Assumption, is *To Jesus through Mary.* We are told that Mary, at her death, left this world, her body as well as her soul, and was taken up into heaven. When the apostles went to the tomb of Mary, they did not find a body, but found fragrant lilies. We believe Mary was born without original sin, her human body pure, not corrupted nor tarnished. How magnificent! She, this blessed woman—who carried Jesus in her womb, lived, died, and then went to paradise—was appearing here, in this village!

Our last day in Medjugorje coincided with Mary's final day on earth, the day she reunited with her Son in heaven. My mom prayed so completely, from the core of her being, for her son. The profound love of a mother is like no other.

Paul's health continued to improve. We sat in front of St. James after our breakfast this day, agreeing how truly blown away we were by it all. I journaled my last notes, trying to capture as much as I could. My words, though, were not as profound as this place. It was similar to taking a photograph that does not do justice to what the viewer truly sees. I found that my words could not express the extraordinary things we had witnessed. I tried to preserve all the details.

The crowds descended for the feast day. We searched for an uninhabited peaceful spot and found one, a small old graveyard behind the church. For a brief time, we were alone.

Ed, Mom, Paul, and I lit the candle I had purchased the previous day in one of the many shops. We decided to say a Rosary, the Glorious Mysteries. Our hearts were so full there
was a cord of love pulled tight around us.

I recalled each of them sitting in our condominium only
eight days prior. Paul, so weary, gaunt, afraid. On this day in
Medjugorje, I trusted that he had surrendered his will to
God. A physical and spiritual conversion had occurred. Ed
changed from the reticent, skeptical man to looking calm,
with a childlike trust. I knew he was digesting all that he had
witnessed. Mom, amazing! She was scared, back in New
York; now she was radiant. She had given everything to Our
Lady, with her open vulnerable heart. Mom was now confident in the answered prayers. Her faith was stronger, her understanding greater and her peace deeper.

We sat on the concrete benches, with Cross Mountain in
the distance. The vineyards marked the edge of the graveyard
and filled the landscape towards the mountain. Old shade
trees blew, kissing our cheeks, and hope filled us. I felt a glow
coming from inside and saw it in Mom's eyes, Ed's expression, and Paul's well-being. Ed's wonderful grin spread
across his face, and it became contagious. Soon we were all
grinning as we prayed.

We entered the church for the liturgy. The faithful were
multiplying. The music radiated through my being. Paul was
singing. How glorious this was. My beautiful, wonderful

mom had done all she could do for her sick son. She was excited to go home. I could picture my six-foot-two father wrapping his arms around her petite frame and cradling her as she released all the emotions of this experience. She had come here for their son, their creation, their precious gift. She did her motherly duty to save their son, to put his life before hers and bring him here for a miracle.

Our last of everything was emotional. We were hanging on to the prayers, the Rosaries, the words of Our Lady through the visionaries. The sights, the sounds, the blanket of love over this pocket of the world was now in all of us and we wanted to remember.

The Miracle of the Sun occurred again that night. As the sun fell from the sky and swirled, the flares of radiant colors spiraled, spectacular, unbelievable, and exhilarating. The feeling of our smallness in this vast universe hit us. We were beginning to internalize the fact that all was possible with God. All is possible … that is profound. What my eyes had seen, my ears had heard. This was truth.

I needed to leave here, live in the truth, and surrender to Him. I gained more than I could ever have imagined in Medjugorje.

11

The Trip: Day Seven

"Dear children, today also I invite you to prayer, now as never before when my plan has begun to be realized. Satan is strong and wants to sweep away plans of peace and joy and make you think that my Son is not strong in His decisions. Therefore, I call all of you, dear children, to pray and fast still more firmly. I invite you to self-renunciation for nine days so that, with your help, everything I desire to realize through the secrets I began in Fatima, may be fulfilled. I call you, dear children, to now grasp the importance of my coming and the seriousness of the situation. I want to save all souls and to present them to God. Therefore, let us pray that everything I have begun may be fully realized. Thank you for having responded to my call." August 25, 1991

Friday, August 16: We were going home! Our tour guides announced they'd escort us directly to the airport. Yes, the same one we had arrived at; unfortunately, Dubrovnik was not in the plan. With the civil war heating up, it was good our journey was concluded. I remember feeling so relieved that we'd not have to deal with buses and directions.

I could not believe the transformation in just six days.

Before our arrival, my body and mind had been on the verge of bursting. A tug-of-war waged in my being, between anxiety, fear, confusion, and confidence, trust, and peace. The fear side was winning then. Now, six days later, a life was altered—actually, many lives: mine, Ed's, Mom's and, of course, Paul's. Who knows? Even others may have been touched or changed through our witness. Some watched from afar as we worked and searched for the miracles, the healing, the enlightenment.

So much had happened it was hard to wrap my mind around it. I felt reluctant and nervous about returning to the real world. Here, this mark on a map was a cocoon of peace to all who visited. I longed to see my husband, but here I felt a heightened awareness. Something had opened inside, and I did not want to go back to where I was before; whatever it was, I cannot label or define it exactly. There had been a shift in me.

Paul was remarkably better: his loss of breath improved, his weariness subsided, his jaundice skin replaced by a healthier shade of pink. Eager to sit in front of his doctors, he wanted to tell them what had happened and how he was feeling and then undergo all the tests. He wanted to hear them confirm that this miracle mission was a success. His faith had trumped all of ours. Whatever happened on Cross Mountain was so personal, transforming and life altering that his faith soared.

Ed was hopeful, yet ready to return to his home and comfort zone. He told me that his brain churned with all the events, and he was speechless. Only God knew for sure what had happened in Ed. Was the HIV gone? Ed changed too. He was more of a believer than on our arrival, that was for sure. He had a calm knowing confidence of the Blessed Mother. He was quiet and did not share with me the heart stuff. I so wanted to know.

Mom was definitely weary and at the same time revived. The faith of my mother had hit a new high and her relationship with the Blessed Mother was more precious, intimate, and solid.

As we rode towards the airport, the beauty of this country left us speechless. Six days ago, it was dark as we hugged the roads. On this day, the sun was shining, the sky that perfect shade of brilliant blue. The winding Adriatic Sea below the rich fertile mountains was breathtaking. The two-lane roads we traversed were narrow, snaking, and treacherous, but the views incredible. Ed's fears—when riding, days earlier, with only the headlights to guide us—evaporated in the daylight. The redeeming beauty he now saw went beyond the headlights. Our driver stopped at one point to show us a magnificent wonder. My curiosity piqued as we rounded a road and saw a merging of waterfalls. We had someone take a group picture: our arms linked, our grins big, hanging on with love, hope and anticipation. "Triumph" was the word that comes to mind as I reflect on that moment. We had done it; we came, we prayed, we asked, we saw, we listened, and we received. We said our goodbyes and thanks to our guides.

Our plane departed on time, without conflicts. We were heading home. Our first stop was Rome. We stayed overnight and took a flight to New York in the morning. I was reflective and quiet as I settled into my seat. Later, Paul and I talked at length about maintaining the praying once we got home. We agreed to support each other so we could keep it up. We knew and acknowledged that the farther we got from the holiness of Medjugorje, the greater the challenge would be. The goal was to remain devout. To pray, say the Rosary and follow the desires of the Blessed Mother—for each of us. I think there was a bubble around us that we did not want to pop, but we both felt it dissipating and thinning the farther we traveled. I looked forward to home, my husband, my stepsons, and the normal routines of life. Still, I wanted to keep this spirit.

We arrived at JFK on Saturday. As I laid my eyes on Michael, I fell into his arms. I reacted to his tight embrace, his scent, his kiss. I was home. We retrieved the luggage, loaded the rental car, and drove to our condominium. We were all talking at once on the ride home, nonstop chatter filling Michael's ears with Medjugorje. We had one more day together before Mom, Paul, and Ed flew to their respective homes.

We visited with Michael's parents, who lived in the neighboring town. We shared our experiences. Paul, Mom and Ed glowed. The more they talked, the more the spirit of Medjugorje overflowed.

That night, when I was in my husband's embrace, he whispered his love, his fears, his concerns, his passions, and his thankfulness that we had made it home. He shared his soul, and I was grateful for the abundant love and for my partner, my husband, my love.

The next morning, we said our tearful goodbyes and gave hugs that would last until we would see each other again. Parting was hard. Mom flew home to Myrtle Beach, Paul and Ed returned to Miami. Our miracle mission was accomplished—a story in each of us, told uniquely. We resumed our lives, looking through changed eyes.

12

Reentry

"Dear children, I am with you for so much time and already for so long I have been pointing you to God's presence and His infinite love, which I desire for all of you to come to know. And you, my children? You continue to be deaf and blind as you look at the world around you and do not want to see where it is going without my Son. You are renouncing Him – and He is the source of all graces. You listen to me while I am speaking to you, but your hearts are closed and you are not hearing me. You are not praying to the Holy Spirit to illuminate you. My children, pride has come to rule. I am pointing out humility to you. My children, remember that only a humble soul shines with purity and beauty because it has come to know the love of God. Only a humble soul becomes Heaven, because my Son is in it. Thank you. Again I implore you to pray for those whom my Son has chosen – those are your shepherds." February 2, 2012

"Dear children, Today I call you to a difficult and painful step for your unity with my Son. I call you to complete admission and confession of sins, to purification. An impure heart cannot be in my Son and with my Son. An impure heart cannot give the fruit of love and unity. An impure heart cannot

do correct and just things; it is not an example of the beauty of God's love to those who surround it and to those who have not come to know that love. You, my children, are gathering around me full of enthusiasm, desires and expectations, and I implore the Good Father to, through the Holy Spirit, put my Son – faith, into your purified hearts. My children, obey me, set out with me." July 2, 2011

The transition between a slice of heaven and the real world … we had to reenter. We had been beyond this world, and it was time to cross the threshold and dive into the atmosphere of our lives. It felt like being in a womb—the umbilical cord severed so we could breathe independently, with all graces Our Lady provided in Medjugorje.

Paul and Ed slid back into their Miami palace. I could not stop thinking about his encounters. Could their friends see the difference in Paul's health? Was it as obvious to them as it was to us? What did they think of his explanations? As Paul shared, was the incidence on Cross Mountain becoming clearer in his mind?

Paul had called me within a few days of being back. "Barb, you are not going to believe this. My friend Tom could not sleep one night while we were away on the trip. He told me that he woke up in the middle of the night, worried about us and filled with concern. To help quiet his mind he turned on the television. Barb, this was amazing, because on the screen was a documentary about Medjugorje. Tom said he blinked and blinked, focusing his tired eyes, all the time repeating, 'No way, no way.' The TV was on a network channel. He was mystified. He was stunned. He watched in disbelief as he heard about the apparitions, the happenings, the miracles, and the draw to this holy place. Barb, he never went back to sleep that night. Can you believe this?"

"Wow, Paul!" I sat with my mouth open in surprise.

Paul continued telling me how he was relaying the story to his doctors, colleagues, and friends. They listened to his miraculous journey and were astounded by the broadcast connections in Miami.

He began his rounds with the doctors. His primary care physician, after hearing the details, was hopeful. The initial blood work results were favorable. A healing was not conclusive, but the signs were looking that way.

Our conversations filled with enthusiastic optimism and cheer as we continued to keep each other focused on the praying and everything else.

"Don't let up, Paul," I repeated. "Keep saying the Rosary and remember what we heard."

We needed to be obedient with all our beings, but it was hard. Assimilating back, as a changed person, was challenging. I kept trying to cheer myself on: How could we not be thankful, prayerful and persevere in doing all that was required. In reality, it was getting harder and harder to stay in the spirit.

"Paul, we are so frail," I'd admit to him, and he'd agree.

We gravitated back into our own unique societal influences. I felt as if I was on the sidelines, not completely engaged as I had been before. Some of the old patterns of behavior resumed. One week had changed a lot, but it was unrealistic to do it all immediately, even though I tried. Inner turmoil preoccupied both of us. I reflected on a Bible passage from Exodus.

What did God think about His chosen people in the desert? After He parted the sea, He provided food from heaven, shade from clouds and delivered these people from slavery, towards the land of milk and honey. Yet those who witnessed great miracles complained in the desert. They were not satisfied or faithful, with all they had received. The chosen people questioned their faith and trusting obedience, as did we. We were struggling.

Content and grateful to be home with Dad, her partner of forty plus years, Mom was recuperating. She returned to her routines of retired life in Myrtle Beach: golf, gardening, and her bridge groups. However, Mom dutifully began each day with attending Mass. She was praying her Rosary and completely steadfast in prayer as she awaited the call that would confirm the miracle. Mom communicated with all my siblings—Kathy, Rick, Greg, and Joe—to share the details of the trip and all the astounding experiences. I believe she also instructed each to keep on praying for Paul.

Mom, the ambassador of this family, the one with the rock-solid faith, the one who did not back down, the one who, from the moment she hung up the phone after hearing of Paul's illness, pleaded, and prayed for his deliverance from AIDS. She marched forward, a soldier with unrelenting belief, a light for all of us to emulate.

What was the driving force? How did she stay so obedient to the request? Was it motherhood? Could it have been her grandmother whose unwavering devotion had made such a lasting impression on Mom? Was this the seed planted in my mother's heart? Was it her nature, her discipline to remain so steadfast? I admired her attitude and wished I had the same fortitude—a goal for me to strive to attain.

In Long Island, I gathered my stepsons, Michael and Matthew. They were relieved to have me home. It was comforting for us to be under the same roof once again. I was safe. Michael had said they were worried about the pending war and the unknown happenings in Medjugorje. I sat on the couch with them and told all that had happened about the miracles we saw. I said it through a few tears. These handsome boys with warm brown eyes had been our best men; they stood up for us at the altar as we pledged our love. My husband's children were so much like him: their mannerisms, their looks. With these boys whom I loved, I could savor the love between mother and children, the bonds so strong. I gave the boys some souvenirs and blessed rosaries from Medjugorje. I heard about their lives and what I had missed, and we regrouped this little splintered family. I stared at their impressionable young faces. They listened when I spoke. I tried to ease the intensity of it all. Once my story and theirs were told, we played a game of cards as the words dissolved into the air.

I made copies of my journal, which was raw. I tried to convey the details as best I could, reporting how profound it had been. Unfortunately, the words did not give justice to all the events as they played out, but I tried. I mailed the copies to my siblings in Ohio, Indiana, Michigan, and Virginia. That task completed, I went back to work.

On the elevator to the forty-second floor of my office on Broadway in New York City, I was hesitant, anxious about being back and the mound of work I would have to plow through. I was thankful for my bosses, the permitted time away and the support, but felt so different. They all wanted to know what had happened, the details, everything. As I shared, I felt transported back. It was a challenge to get motivated to the tasks that needed attention.

My soul filled with the supernatural energy of Medjugorje each time I relayed the story. My boss was Jewish. He had recently lost a son to cancer. His son was my age. My boss listened with a heavy heart and compassionate eyes. His second wife was Catholic. This was her stepson. Their hurt was still so raw. She listened with a tuned ear as I conveyed the story.

With much to ponder, everyone wished Paul would receive the miracle we desired. There was fragility as we waited. Nevertheless, life in the knitwear industry went on and I quickly caught up with my clients and responsibilities.

Regina, my sister-in-law, wanted to get together and hear what had happened. She lived in the city, so we agreed to meet after work. She was the one responsible for introducing me to her brother. She had a special relationship with Our Lady. Regina and I had gotten close while I dated her brother, sharing our spiritual journeys and discoveries. There was a kinship, a connection. She had prayed for our safety on this journey, and I had brought her back holy water and a rosary. I retold the story as we sat in a crowded restaurant, the hustle and bustle not disturbing the bubble around us. Her beautiful eyes focused on me with such sincerity and love. Regina believed all I was saying. I mean, she truly got it. There were those whose expressions showed their skepticism. Their eyes reflected the struggle to believe. They were trying to decipher the truth from the wanted desire of the miracle. In this mental exercise, they were not truly listening. Regina listened. It was a blessing to have her support as the weeks unfolded.

I met with Cindy, a friend from childhood, from Cincinnati, a comrade in grammar school and our adolescent years. She was my roommate for a short time in Manhattan and had, coincidentally, also pursued a career in the design industry. She participated in our wedding, our hearts united. She listened with tears and amazement in her eyes. We hugged halfway through the story. She knew Paul; he used to chauffeur us places before we had driver's licenses. She was another one praying for the miracle with all her heart. She was a grounding support for me.

Miami, Myrtle Beach and Freeport were joined by our tether of optimism while we immersed back into our schedules and waited. The telephone wires connected us as we anticipated and prayed for the final miracle to be confirmed.

13

The Call

"Dear children! In this time of grace again I call you to prayer. Pray, little children, for unity of Christians, that all may be one heart. Unity will really be among you inasmuch as you will pray and forgive. Do not forget: love will conquer only if you pray, and your heart will open. Thank you for having responded to my call." January 25, 2005

Paul continued to sustain good health and was doing remarkably well. It had only been a short time. The doctors watched him closely; they monitored his T-cell count. It had improved and he was no longer transfusion dependent, as prior to the trip. Feeling healthier, he returned to work. In September, with the school year about to begin, Paul was busy as assistant principal of South Miami Elementary, a role he loved. He focused his energy on the kids, and his body continued to progress positively.

Hope prevailed. We spoke often and hung on in the vast sea of faith, health, busy lifestyles, family, and jobs. Sometimes our conversations may have sounded mundane; we simply wanted to be close. I wanted to hear his breath, his voice. On other occasions, we spoke about the big stuff. He would extrapolate on how God was encouraging him, and he physically felt revived and could not believe that this was possible. He was invigorated in both body and spirit.

"What if this is it, Barb?" he'd say. "What if I am cured? Changes will have to happen. They have to." He'd go on to talk about the huge changes he'd make in his lifestyle. "What about Ed, Barb?" he'd whisper desperately. "What am I going to do? I know I cannot continue to live this way. It cannot remain the same."

I could hear the strain, the sorrow, the hope—his confusion in a myriad of contrasts. I listened but had no answers. He had to make these decisions on his own. I was there in support, my ear pressed to the phone, longing to touch him and look at him.

On Labor Day weekend, Paul went with friends to Disney World, the land of "make believe"—a reprieve for him and time for needed fun. Paul's medicine port line was still in place under the flap of skin in his forearm. It was still too soon to remove it. Long before our trip, the port line had been inserted for his varied medicines. He told me how excited he felt about the pending trip, especially of a new exhibit he wanted to see. He was thrilled to feel well and energetic; this excursion was reminiscent of healthy times.

Afterwards, he told me the details, and I could hear him smile. He even went on a water ride. A few days later, the nagging, anxious fear invaded. A low-grade temperature burst his bubble. Oh no, what's this about? He felt bad, took some fever reducers, and desperately tried to ignore the tidal wave he feared. He rebounded weakly into life and the school year.

On Friday, September 13, my birthday, I had spoken to him from my office in Manhattan. He sounded tired, scared, and sick. My heart pounded hard as I held the receiver.

He said, "Please come."

An urgent plea—he had never asked me to come; he always said that he was fine and not to worry, so hearing his voice say "come" made the hair on my neck stand and a knot form in my throat and chest. I told him I would get there as soon as I could.

"Hang in there, Paul. Pray, and I love you," I whispered, my throat tight.

When I hung up the phone, the emotional mayhem reeled my entire body and I cried. My co-workers saw my face. They offered support and listened to my fears. I quickly began to take care of business and make arrangements so I could be there for Paul. My birthday as well as my husband's was on this day. I felt torn leaving my husband so abruptly. I was able to get a flight out on Sunday.

Uncertainty on a daunting path was about to begin. Mike wanted me home. He was concerned for me. Paul was feeling so bad. On our birthday, Paul drove and admitted himself to the hospital. Then he waited for the ball to drop, the hope to banish, the sickness to win. The tether was being yanked.

I pleaded with Our Lady: Help my brother. I began reiterating Hail Marys and Our Fathers. Upon arrival I took a cab straight to the hospital. Paul's face softened when he saw me, relief etched on his brow. I touched his head. Poor guy, he looked lousy and felt so warm. Pure and simple, I love this man.

His temperature would not ease. They said an infection was present, but they could not find the source to attack it. I heard rumblings from the doctors, of an opportunistic infection—a pathogen had infiltrated.

Oh no! All the effort to make him well, and now this comes to pass. Why?

Mom and Dad arrived. More support. My brother was relieved.

Still, Paul was declining. Mom and I stood by with compresses; after one heated on his head, a cool backup followed. The fever could not be reduced. There was lots of activity, the doctors scurrying to figure out the reason for the fever. They wanted to help Paul fight this battle.

One doctor, with concern written on his face, said, "I *need* to find the source," while frustration labored his voice.

Visitors came, and Paul struggled. We sat. We hugged. We prayed, kneeling around his bed, loving him, feeding him with our words, appeals for improvement. He was on an IV antibiotic ... the fever pressed on. Ed sat like a lost puppy, so frightened and worried. Ed had traveled thousands of miles on a miracle mission. He had stood by Paul, medicated Paul, listened to his frustrations, soothed him, nurtured him and took Paul's wrath when he was tired of being sick. Ed learned to say the Rosary in Croatian and prayed it over and over—this Protestant boy. He loved, quite simply, and did what he had to do in the situation. Also, HIV-positive, he knew this would be his fate unless a cure was discovered. Now he sat watching, in this sterile hospital, the commotion swirl around him, and he was helpless.

"Barb, this is surreal," he said to me at one moment when Paul was groaning. "Can the inevitable be happening?"

I said, "Please do not go there."

We left the room in search of the hospital chapel. We clutched our rosaries and prayed with our entire beings. We hung on to each other with our eyes. I was petrified.

The days seemed to overlap, and my other family members began to arrive. Paul continued to have a constant flow of visitors; he had touched many lives here in Miami. Hushed exchanges took place in the halls and waiting rooms. Words were passed from ear to ear, some penetrating, others just floating in open space. We hugged people we barely knew, seeking comfort for the hole that was forming. The brother, the son, the partner, the friend was being hailed in the hallway, rippling good vibrations; he was lifted up high. He made a difference.

Our other brothers came at various times since they lived in different states. Rick, who was closest to Paul in age, seventeen months younger, a father of five, traveled from Georgia. Greg, the fourth child, lived in Virginia with his wife and four children. Joe, the youngest and father of four, arrived from Indiana. Each of the boys had their whispered talks. It was wonderful to see them and have strength in numbers, each of us feeling our own stuff.

My sister Kathy came from Ohio, leaving her two children with her husband. She was the one I turned to when I didn't want to talk to Mom or Dad. Kath, the oldest child who comforted us, now looked forlorn as her eyes fixed on Paul. She assumed the role as ambassador, of sorts, standing guard outside Paul's room. She talked to and informed his friends of the latest developments, but kept them out of his room, per his request.

He was scared. Paul felt horrible. He needed shelter from the eyes and voices of grieving friends and associates. Kathy was there to organize and keep up the wall for Paul.

His doctor took me aside in a small room on the same floor as where Paul was failing. The doctor was so disturbed that he could not find the source of the infection ravaging through Paul's body. He told me what a unique and special brother I had. He told me he desired a cure so profoundly for this exceptional patient. He talked about how inspiring Paul was after Medjugorje and how well he looked.

"He made me believe in the impossible," he said. "This man is too young and vital to go." This stoic man cried. He said, "I do not know if I can continue to be a doctor and watch these young promising lives extinguish."

We hugged; I could feel his tremendous pain.

He continued to talk. "Paul and I have worked for a long time battling this disease and we want to win," he said.

I knew for certain at that moment we were coursing downhill rapidly. Paul's counts were failing, and organs were shutting down. Oh God, help my brother Paul.

For hours, we took turns cooling his burning body with towels. No sooner would we lay them down, they would heat, and need exchanging for a cool one. He cooed at the relief of the refreshing, wet comfort.

He slept and mumbled. We circled his bed, praying the Rosary. Sitting at the foot of the bed, my father sat, grasping Paul's foot, hopeless but connected. This tall strong man did not weep, but gazed with love, his eyes translucent. I felt so blessed to have this man as my father. A man who did not agree nor could understand the choices his son had made; even so, he was a fortress. A father who gave, sacrificed, and would always love and protect his son.

Mom remained at Paul's side, stoic, standing guard over her child, her son. She prayed, she loved, she whispered words of comfort that only mothers can give, and she soothed his sick body. She held his hand and kissed it. She would tire momentarily and seek comfort in the arms of my dad. Then she'd return to her post at Paul's side. Mom and Dad clung to each other. She would look at each of us, quietly counting her offspring, as she'd done hundreds of times when we were young.

We rotated spending the night in the hospital. Paul was never left alone. One night Joe and I stayed; he slept in the chair in the room, I lay on a stretcher in the hallway. I was desperate to sleep a little. I could not believe what was happening. I tossed and turned, got up, paced, checked in on my brothers, exchanged glances with the nurses—who were awesome. I prayed. I volleyed from extreme sadness to uncompromising strength. I told myself, I know God's will is at hand and we are not in control.

The contrast measured in time between a few weeks ago and now was so extreme. Paul experienced greatness beyond his imaginings in Medjugorje and, hopefully, this gave him inner peace. I know it sustained us.

One day he said to my mom, "I want to go outside, please. I want to feel the breezes."

We called the doctor, who said, "What? He requested this ... he requested?"

"Yes," the nurse said, "Paul requested this."

The doctor could not believe it. He was not in the hospital at that moment. In shock, he replied, "This man should not even be alive. The blood counts are so low, this cannot be." He approved for us to take Paul outside in the sunny Miami weather.

The nurses moved his fragile body to a wheelchair. Mom pushed him out the door and a crowd followed. It looked like the Pied Piper circling the hospital grounds. Paul, a huge grin on his face, was leading. Mom leaned into him to listen and talk. The family followed at a distance behind Mom as she kept a pronounced lead. She wanted Paul by herself. Friends and family walked next in line, and then the nurses at the rear. He loved it. He was grinning and talking. It was amazing. We all smiled as we paraded. His face was peaceful and delighted. He "Ahhhed" as the wind danced around him. We circled a pond outside of the Italian Renaissance–designed hospital. It did not look like a hospital from the outside, but like a resort. Mom piloted him around three times, and then the nurses encouraged us to return him to his room. He loved the sun, the palm trees, the beauty of the manicured grounds, the sensations of the fresh warm air swirling around his tired body. We each cheered him on while he savored this outing, his joy pulsing. Mother Mary, thank you for this awesome moment.

14

The Rebound

"Dear children! Today I call you to love. Little children, love each other with God's love. At every moment, in joy and in sorrow, may love prevail and, in this way, love will begin to reign in your hearts. The risen Jesus will be with you and you will be His witnesses. I will rejoice with you and protect you with my motherly mantle. Especially, little children, I will watch your daily conversion with love. Thank you for having responded to my call." March 25, 2005

Settled back in his private room, he spoke with each of us. I wondered what was going on. Were we going to be taken so close to the end line ... then a complete healing? This rebound was amazing; he was laughing and carrying on. The doctor spoke to the nurses to hear the latest and, when informed of Paul's comeback, was baffled. The nurses relayed the messages from the doctor and commented again that this was not medically possible. Paul's body had been shutting down; his blood counts and his current stamina were in complete contrast.

Was it a miracle that he was so strong? He delighted in the simple joy of fresh air and sunshine. He was so grateful for the sensations he experienced. As we puffed up pillows, settled him back in a crisp, fresh bed, we chatted. Paul expressed his love and talked to our open hearts.

This was the last time we would see him so vibrant and energetic.

I can go back to sitting in the room, perched next to him on the bed, gazing at his delight and Mom's expression of relief. Then the door shuts on the joy, replaced by silence.

He was quiet, resting, we thought, then he was in a coma. No more communication. He was shutting down for real. The period from the stroll and elation to the deflation seemed suspended in midair.

Delight, then depression. The last hurrah before the close, not much suffering. Thank You, God. Just a decline and then quiet, expressionless attendance. At this point, were the angels present, guiding him on his next mission? Was he in a new realm? Was he on the bridge joining heaven and earth, being directed in the fog? Was the light beyond, shining, leading him?

I remember he weakly uttered to my mom when she got close to his face, "Grandma?"

He was not fully conscious, so Mom's tears began to fall; she took comfort in the fact that maybe her deceased mom was there.

Mom rubbed his brow, refusing to leave his side. She held his hand and whispered prayers into hushed ears. A mother's love ... the pain wrapped itself around her. Here lay her son. She asked for a miracle, she prayed for a cure, she did all she humanly could do to help her child. Now she loved and waited.

My brother Joe wrote this poem.

Light and Hope
for my brother Paul

by Joe Heithaus

Candle broke in two. I'm trying to light
one of those black snake pellets in the sand;
you know, that odd form of firework, once lit,
a black snake coils out ... the way
strung-tight handkerchiefs slide
from out of the magician's sleeve. It's 1974
and we're on vacation in Myrtle Beach.
I'm twelve, pyrotechnical, amazed by flames.

Picture all the light in the world, sun, Tara in *Gone
With the Wind* ... chairs on fire in the mansion,
and the drapes, the gorgeous windows in the old churches,
the blue stained glass like the bottom of a flame, Grandma's
old gas stove ... blue light under four boiling pots, klieg
lights,
flashbulbs, even this list someday burning in the burning
library at noon ... orange redundant flames alight in a summer's

midday, so bright you must close your eyes.

Mom and Dad away, imagine Rick carrying the burning pan

of grease out of the kitchen and into the yard. *Stupid,*

Kathy said, *you might have caught your shirt on fire,*

But all of us relieved, standing around the flaming pan

in the backyard's dark as if enacting an ancient ritual,

staring at what could destroy the house,

fascinated by its light and warmth. I love you, Paul, so strange

to say, as it is always assumed in our family, the pictures

from the latest wedding testament to how we hold

each other tough without thinking, our hands

on the children's heads or around each other's shoulders.

What we have in common is this light and I've always

believed that this is what will carry us through

the dark ... this old metaphor of life and death as Catholic

as they come: candles at every sacrament, on Holy

Saturday the whole church lit by the congregation,

hundreds of thin white candles flickering a few hours

before Easter. It is Lent right now and I'm lighting

a candle for you and I'm trying to be relentless about

hope ... remember Mom reminding us to think

about the heat of the sun when we are cold. If I can

do anything for you besides this, let me know.

We all hang on to hope.

15

Fight

"Today, with my motherly heart, I call you gathered around me to love your neighbor. My children, stop. Look in the eyes of your brother and see Jesus, my Son. If you see joy, rejoice with him. If there is pain in the eyes of your brother, with your tenderness and goodness, cast it away, because without love you are lost. Only love is effective; it works miracles. Love will give you unity in my Son and the victory of my heart. Therefore, my children, love." September 2, 2008

I hoped Paul was drifting quietly on a cloud. I prayed there was no pain. I felt I was invading something very private as I entered the room. Outwardly he was peaceful. The pillow cradling his head was white and crisp. Mom and Dad were erect but weary as soldiers on either side, loving as parents love, the umbilical thread taut among the three. I stepped back and closed the door.

The day prior, I had gone to his church to begin the funeral arrangements. Unfortunately, his departure was imminent. This horrible fact was hard to face, but it felt good to do something, to be useful. The people at the Catholic church comforted me and gently guided me in the choices of readings, music and all the other formalities, while I felt the impending pain like a knife in my heart.

My sister was due in from Cincinnati; I left Mom and Dad keeping vigil at the hospital and went to the airport to pick her up. Kathy had two small children that needed attention, so she had gone home and returned to Miami when the news turned. We hugged each other and went directly to the hospital.

She saw Paul, Mom and Dad, and then we gave Ed a ride back to the house. He was exhausted and needed a respite.

Kathy suggested we go to the church. Upon arrival in the rectory office, I started a review of what we had done the prior day. My sister ignored me. She talked over me. I felt as if I was not there.

She dismissed me, saying, "I do this all the time, and I know what needs to be done."

This was a fact. She was a principal in a Catholic school, so she was familiar with planning liturgies. Nevertheless, I had already started the necessary steps in the planning, and I was instantly frustrated. I was hurt. How could she barge in and take over without regard to my feelings? I should have let it go, but the tensions heightened. I was easily upset and, stupidly, I did not let it go.

We left the church and went back to Paul and Ed's home. In the chaos of in and out visitors, I showed her to the room prepared for her and then I went crazy. I told her I was hurt and started to go into detail. She dismissed me again. Well, I started yelling, and it included not only the present situation, but also every crazy hurt I could resurface from our childhood. I could not stop. I was out of control. She yelled back. It was a blowout—sparks were flying, words were lashed, hurling at each other with such a vengeance it was awful. Our faces were red, our veins protruding. In the midst of the yelling, the phone rang. Then we heard a scream.

Ed yelled out, "He is gone!"

Oh no! How could this have been going on the moment that he passed? Did he come to us to stop the fight? Kathy and I stopped, looked at each other, stunned, and grabbed each other with love as strong as the anger that had torn at us moments before.

How insane I felt in that instant. We were a team. We loved each other and Paul with all our hearts. He was our best friend. We ran to Ed and hugged, cried, sobbed, and then jumped in the car and drove to the hospital.

The waiting was over. Paul was gone.

16

The Miracle

"Dear children, today I extend my hands towards you. Do not be afraid to accept them. They desire to give you love and peace and to help you in salvation. Therefore, my children, receive them. Fill my heart with joy and I will lead you towards holiness. The way on which I lead you is difficult and full of temptations and falls. I will be with you and my hands will hold you. Be persevering so that, at the end of the way, we can all be together, in joy and love, hold the hands of my Son. Come with me; fear not. Thank you." Mirjana's annual message, March 18, 2008

We arrived at the hospital and raced in—an "out-of-body" experience, surreal to walk in the hospital knowing that the person we were visiting was gone. We knew this was happening, but now the moment was here. Actually, it had already passed. I think of the hospital TV programs when people die. We have heard them say so many times, "We did all we could." In this case, I know they did.

Kathy and I stood in the hallway outside the room. The door was closed. We entered. Our mom, strong and stable, stood on one side of the bed. Our dad, the protector, the provider, the tall man who loved his son, on the other. I moved to Paul's bed. He looked so different. Gone. Cold. Empty. I bent down, tears streaming down my cheeks, and I kissed his forehead. It was hard, not feverish, and supple, but cold and hard. He was gone. Really, really gone.

I took Mom's hand, and she said, "I did not want to be here when he died, but I am so happy that I was. Dad and I were sitting with him. He opened his blue eyes, looked directly at me, then closed them. He departed. He said goodbye to us. I carried this boy, brought him into this world, then saw him leave. It should not be this way."

"He was a good boy," Dad said, and touched Paul's head and tousled his hair. Dad's eyes stayed focused on Paul.

My chest heaved. I wished they could have found the cause of the infection and eradicated it from my brother's body. I wished we could have seen the miracle of his physical healing continue. That may be selfish. I wanted him here on this planet to grow old with, to give me advice, to see my child and share the mundane trivialities of our lives. But no, this was not to be. This was not the will of God. The will of God, on this day, September 27, 1991, was to take Paul to heaven.

He had tried so hard to heal himself: all the years of trial drugs and therapies to conquer AIDS. How hard it was to grasp that now. A void, a black hole present in my heart, empty and crying. I wouldn't be able to hear him laugh or say hello on the other end of the telephone. I wouldn't be able to call him and share a project I was developing. I wouldn't be able to hear him rave about the students in his school. This part was over. This was permanent. He was not getting up.

I could escape the hurt by remembering all our NYC/Miami adventures, like the time we drove around Manhattan in a rented Lincoln Continental and then escaped the mayhem in search of fall foliage. Laughing and enjoying the luxury. Or the times in Miami when we cruised the waters pretending to be in scenes of *Miami Vice*. Or when we cracked open a watermelon after a hike and let the juice run down our faces. I could remember all the times that brought me joy with Paul. Those thoughts were a comfort. I also saw that in this great, great sorrow, there was contrast.

Thank you, Our Blessed Lady, for the call. You inspired Mom to suggest Medjugorje. Thank you for the miracles we witnessed and the transformations of our own hearts. Thank you for the abundant love that carried us to this day. Thank you for giving Mom this beautiful son to nurture. Thank you for a brother to love. Thank you for helping him cross to heaven with Mom and Dad by his side. There was so much to be grateful for. To love and to be loved is the greatest gift. Paul had received and accepted this gift. The miracle Mom wanted for the here and now, his physical presence, was not what happened. The miracle we did get was his passing, prepared, and surrounded by love.

In Medjugorje we had participated in the sacrament of reconciliation. As I looked at him, so peaceful, I was grateful for the atonement. I have heard it said that sin in our soul makes holes. The confession of our sins closes the holes, which allows us to gain strength in holiness and bring God's light fully to us. It was critical to reconcile our hearts and clear them so our souls could be whole. Paul died with a healed soul. That was the miracle. Paul, for a time, experienced a physical healing, but the one that was remarkable was the spiritual healing, the everlasting healing. I believe that all the prayers, all the cleaning, the confessing, all the things we witnessed allowed him to soar into heaven. That was the miracle.

We love and we lose, but in the space between—the sweet, wonderful stuff, the memories—Paul will never leave my heart. He stays close, especially when my brain triggers something and I say, "Ahh, I remember when ...." Belief is a gift, a precious, wonderful gift. Because of this, I know that Paul and I will meet again in a heavenly place.

His loved ones sat outside his room, writing the death announcement. Tears stained our faces. What a productive life he had lived in thirty-nine short years. This was what we came up with, the final summary. "He spent his life in the pursuit of the education of children. His love of the Arts, as well as his compassion for youth, contributed to his leadership in the Dade County School System as an Art Teacher, Administrative Personnel and most recently as the Assistant Principal at South Miami Elementary School. He touched

Prayer to Saint Joseph

To you, O blessed Joseph, do we come in our tribulation, and having implored the help of your most holy Spouse, we confidently invoke your patronage also.

Through that charity which bound you to the Immaculate Virgin Mother of God and through the paternal love with which you embraced the Child Jesus, we humbly beg you graciously to regard the inheritance which Jesus Christ has purchased by his Blood, and with your power and strength to aid us in our necessities.

O most watchful guardian of the Holy Family, defend the chosen children of Jesus Christ; O most loving father, ward off from us every contagion of error and corrupting influence; O our most mighty protector, be kind to us and from heaven assist us in our struggle with the power of darkness.

As once you rescued the Child Jesus from deadly peril, so now protect God's Holy Church from the snares of the enemy and from all adversity; shield, too, each one of us by your constant protection, so that, supported by your example and your aid, we may be able to live piously, to die in holiness, and to obtain eternal happiness in heaven. Amen.

Prayer to St Joseph
after the Rosary

This prayer to Saint Joseph—spouse of the Virgin Mary, foster father of Jesus, and patron saint of the universal Church—was composed by Pope Leo XIII in his 1889 encyclical, Quamquam pluries.

The prayer is ordinarily enriched with a partial indulgence (Handbook of Indulgences, conc. 19). During the Year of Saint Joseph, however—which lasts from December 8, 2020 to December 8, 2021—the use of this prayer has been included among those enriched with a plenary indulgence (see Decree of the Apostolic Penitentiary issued Dec. 8, 2020, section E).

It may be said on any day of the Year of Saint Joseph, but especially on his various feast days or other devotional days dedicated to St. Joseph:

many lives and will be missed by all." That was an understatement.

At the end of this article, we wrote: "the Health Crisis Network in lieu of flowers." This was an AIDS organization. Interestingly enough, some of those who suffer from this dreaded disease cover it up throughout their illness and sometimes even after they pass. Paul's funeral booklet had this quote by Goethe, on the front cover: *"Treat people as though they were what they ought to be and you help them become what they are capable of being."*

Paul had accepted and loved people, especially any child who crossed his path. He wanted them to be their best. He showered them with praise when a gift of music, photography, sculpture, or drawing revealed itself to them. On one of my many visits to Miami, during healthy times, he stood in front of the school, coffee cup in hand, greeting each student by name. Most of them responded with a smile and a "Hello, Mr. Heithaus." If they didn't respond, he followed them, teasing until they smiled and exchanged hellos. The students loved him, and he loved them.

The first reading for his funeral was from the Book of Wisdom. It begins with: *The souls of the just are in the hand of God, and no torment shall touch them.* It ends with: *Those who trust in him shall understand truth, and the faithful shall abide with him in love: Because grace and mercy are with his holy one, and his care is with his elect.*

Trust was a tough one. Something happened to Paul on that holy mountain when he said, "I am not afraid to die." I trust that was true. He experienced inner peace that changed him, I trust that was also true. The mercy was always there for us; we just had to ask and be open to receive it.

A dear friend, Maria, whom Paul referred to as his Miami sister, got up to read. Maria was there geographically when I could not be. She was a dynamic art teacher who inspired creativity in any child she taught. She and Paul shared work passion and enthusiasm for all the children in their school. The two of them were a united positive force at South Miami Elementary. Sometimes when I heard him talk of Maria, I was jealous of the closeness. I looked at her now with such compassion as she read from the Book of Revelation, which began with: *I saw a new heaven and a new earth.* It ended with: *Behold, I make all things new. I am the Alpha and the Omega, the beginning and the end. To the thirsty I will give a gift from the spring of life-giving water. The victor will inherit these gifts, and I shall be his God, and he will be my son.* Maria and Paul created new things, and were a gift to the students they touched and to each other. Maria would miss the day-to-day encounters, and for her I was sad.

The Gospel was from Matthew: *"The Greatest Commandment." "Teacher, which commandment in the law is the greatest?" He said to him, "You shall love the Lord, your God, with all your heart, with all your soul and with all your mind. This is the greatest and the first commandment. The second is like it: You shall love your neighbor as yourself. The whole law and the prophets depend on these two commandments."*

That sums it up. We are called to love and to do our best with ourselves, our families, in our communities and the world. Just as in the church at this moment, the love was pure.

At the Mass of Resurrection for Paul, inspired words washed over us as we said goodbye to the son, brother, uncle, friend, and teacher. A friend of Paul's, who had won an award for her voice, then sang. The tears welled and the knot in my chest tightened, but there was beauty. He loved music, and she sounded like an angel.

During Communion, the children's choir from his school sang. The closing song was "Let There Be Peace on Earth," the song Paul and I had sung from the deepest depths of our lungs on our descent from Cross Mountain in Medjugorje. It was an emotional hour as I said my final goodbye to Paul. The chapter of Paul on earth is now concluded.

Once back in New York, I read the following announcement from the US Embassy in Belgrade, notifying all Americans to leave Medjugorje immediately. By the end of September 1991, sanctions against Yugoslavia would start and the borders would close within forty-eight hours. The flow of pilgrims diminished, but they did not stop. Faith moves at all costs.

I want to close with a prayer inspired by Mother Teresa: *For all those who are unwanted, unloved, uncared for, forgotten by everybody, and especially all those who have suffered and died without love from the disease of AIDS. In Jesus' name, we pray ....*

Below is the message from Our Lady of Medjugorje, two days before Paul died.

"Dear children! Today in a special way I invite you all to prayer and renunciation. For now as never before, Satan wants to show the world his shameful face by which he wants to seduce as many people as possible onto the way of death and sin. Therefore, dear children, help my Immaculate Heart to triumph in the sinful world. I beseech all of you to offer prayers and sacrifices for my intentions so I can present them to God for what is most necessary. Forget your desires, dear children, and pray for what God desires, and not for what you desire. Thank you for having responded to my call." September 25, 1991

17
Ed

"Dear children! I am with you. As a mother, I am gather-ing you, because I desire to erase from your hearts what I see now. Accept the love of my Son and erase fear, pain, suffering and disappointment from your heart. I have chosen you in a special way to be a light of the love of my Son. Thank you."
February 2, 2008

"Dear children! Also today I call you to have more trust in me and my Son. He has conquered by His death and resurrec-tion and, through me, calls you to be a part of His joy. You do not see God, little children, but if you pray you will feel His nearness. I am with you and intercede before God for each of you. Thank you for having responded to my call." April 25, 2006

I had a dream, the kind that never ends, the inspiration clear. Ed had been consuming my thoughts. I had been re-flecting about his role in the miracle journey, before and be-yond; we were bound together.

The dream began with a visit to see Paul and Ed. It opened with me standing before a beautiful wood-shingled ranch-style home. A perfect summer day, brilliantly sunny and clear, I stood on the threshold of this home, noticing the impeccable façade. When I entered the immaculate airy living room, it was spotless—a vacuum cleaner even stood poised in the corner. Crisp nautical shades covered the furniture and walls. Ed and Paul sat, smiling, in navy blue striped wingback chairs. Ed talked of cleaning and preparing for this visit. His warm smile drew me close. As dreams go, they are fragmented.

Next, Ed and I ensued in a sightseeing mission as we climbed to the second story in this fantasy single-floor home. Upstairs, the ceiling low, we stood in a large foyer with three white doors ajar. We sneakily peered in the first door: a pristine cozy apartment. The decoration was striking: clean lines, fresh in shades of navy, tan, and cherry red; light hardwood floors glistened. Sheer drapes danced in the breeze from the open windows. Beyond the door to this apartment was a miniature house on a pedestal of white. Ed and I stared at each other, our mouths agape.

The miniature Victorian had white clapboard siding, a front porch, and a red door. It was perfect. Within seconds of examining this little house, the doors in the foyer began to close. I felt uncertainty and immediately turned to watch the doors shut, as if by an invisible hand. Ed and I faced each other, joined hands and, with nervous eyes, began to giggle in that frightened kind of way. Suddenly the lights went out, darkness engulfed me, and Ed was gone. I was alone. My throat closed. My hands reached for something in the blackness … ah, softness, a couch. I lay down. Fear flooded me and my heart raced with anxiety. A door opened and a familiar voice said, "What are you doing in here?" I woke up—relief. The unconscious state was gone, and light poured into the room.

Contemplating this dream made me reflect. It had a lot to say. In the beginning, it was wonderful to be in the presence of Ed and Paul. Simple joy. To be back in time when the days were pleasant, healthy, and carefree, when hours unfolded naturally, when we shared visits in Manhattan or Miami. Their restored Mediterranean Revival–style home always looked beautiful. The smiles on their faces brought comfort. Slipping off with Ed to go upstairs was reminiscent of our exploits as voyeurs in New York, looking in lighted windows at night, discussing styles and interiors, or spending time antique shopping in Miami.

People affect us. Personalities enter a room, and we gravitate to them; Ed walked into a room, and he lifted the energy. Ed was easy to be with—no pressure or stress, just easy-going and comfortable. He was funny and sarcastic; he made me laugh. I was young when Ed entered my life. I wanted to see what Paul saw in him. I wanted to know him. There was a mischievous side to Ed, a glint behind the eye that he might be up to something. This was wonderfully appealing.

Ed had a friend, John, who owned an antique store in Miami. Ed was a frequent customer. On many occasions,

Paul described Ed sneaking into the front door of their home with yet another antique, and if Paul saw him, he ran. Imagine him carrying a chair, desk or small dresser and running with it. Paul would shake his head and laugh. Ed had the spirit of a child, which is why I think he made a good teacher. He could relate to his students.

When Paul and Ed got the horrific results of the blood work, identifying them as HIV-positive, Paul was proactive, Ed was not. Paul jumped into all the drug test trials, seeking out a cure. Ed slowly went the homeopathic route, drinking terrible teas and concoctions that made his face distort, but after the gulp, his grin would reappear. I witnessed this heart-wrenching discipline.

He'd remark, "How can something so horrible help me?" He watched and waited.

When we planned the trip to Medjugorje, Ed was supportive but skeptical, hopeful but uncertain of this miracle mission. Maybe he would get the wish he desired. He sustained Paul throughout the full-blown portion of the disease and beyond. He took care of the medicine, knew what to do and when to do it. He guided us on what to expect and served at attention when Paul needed him. Paul was a lousy patient at times and Ed often took his wrath. Ed was devoted, unselfish, considerate, and caring. He carried the weight that he also had HIV, all the while taking care of Paul, watching Paul fail and slide downwards. I marvel at the thought of this Protestant boy in Medjugorje, who said Rosaries, prayed and prayed, went to Catholic Masses, saw, listened, and heard of hope and love from the visionaries. Ed did not convert outwardly, which was Mom's prayer, but who knows what was happening inside his heart. In Medjugorje he was present for all the graces.

After Paul died, Ed went through a period of isolated mourning. He came to New York for a visit, and we did a road trip to Vermont. It was great to see him, but it felt strained without Paul. The loss, the void weighed heavy between us. We talked of life and the particulars of his health. He was still stable with HIV, without symptoms. He had closed lips about his spiritual life. It was private.

About six months later, maybe less, Ed called and told me he had met someone. He was feeling guilty.

We talked at length, and I told him, "Ed, you loved and sustained Paul through so much. Allow happiness into your life."

He told me he had shared the fact that he was HIV-positive, and this person was accepting of that truth. This man was healthy and not infected. I believe he came into the picture as a friend to aid Ed during this time.

I am not a person who studies dreams. Biblical Joseph, in the book of Genesis, read dreams, and his dreams saved his life and those of countless numbers in Egypt. Dreams appear throughout the Bible as messages to warn or save or to tell of the future. God works through whatever ways He can to teach us, to connect with us. I do know that my dream brought Ed and Paul back to me for a moment in time. I could see them, hear them; Ed and I held each other. Upon waking I told my husband how comforting it is to have people we loved and lost appear to us in our dreams.

Ed and I spoke often and continued to visit each other. He and his friend even joined the family for a reunion in Myrtle Beach. In April of 1994, we were planning a rendezvous in Myrtle Beach with Mom and Dad. Ed was going to meet my daughter for the first time—Julia Pauline, who was five months old. Unfortunately, Ed took an abrupt downward slide, and the disease took hold. He fell quickly. By April, instead of a fun trip to Myrtle Beach, I went to Miami to see him in the hospital. Poor Ed. He was in pain; he was weak and hurting. I remember reading to him. He was calm as I read. I desired to help him in any way I could; I wanted to make him better. I did not want to watch this again. I prayed to Our Lady and to Paul for help.

Mom and Dad drove down to Florida to be there for Ed, to offer support. Mom wanted Ed to remember Medjugorje, all the miracles, and wanted him to convey to her his change, his conversion. He remained quiet. Her prayer was constant. Ed knew death was imminent and wanted to be in his home. He was clear about that. My dad wanted to grant this wish. He transported the frail weak man, who had been his son's companion, into his waiting warm car for the ride home—to the home Paul and Ed had shared, the one they had devoted

their energy restoring and beautifying. Once they got Ed settled in his hospital bed, Mom, Dad and Ed's friend kept vigil.
They waited on his every need and whispered prayers.

With heavy hearts, they watched this vital young man depart the earth on May 16, 1994. Ed was only forty-three years
young. At his memorial service, a quote from Emily Dicken-
son was in the booklet: *"Because I could not stop for Death –
he kindly stopped for me –...."*

The years spent in Miami frolicking around, lounging on
beaches, eating Cuban delicacies, speedboating in the bay
and canals to view houses, going to art shows, finding adventures to explore, ended on this sad day. This day another
young man lost his life to AIDS—productive lives cut short.

When Paul passed, he was cremated, and a continuing
conversation ensued of what to do with his ashes. They
stayed with Ed, in his home, for this reason. The idea suggested that we put the urn in the casket with Ed. In the end,
the ashes of Paul rested in his arms. This was sad, but perfect,
which no words can describe. Paul and Ed laid eternally to
rest.

I wonder about the dream, all the details, the stripes, the
colors, and the clean lines, the open and airy feeling. The upstairs adventure, being side by side, then emptiness ... he was
gone. It was dark and I was alone. The three doors upstairs
could represent the supernatural elements of faith, the Trin-
ity or possibly our choices. The gentle wind moving the cur-
tains could viably be the Holy Spirit. The house perched on

the white pillar, heaven. The vacuum? Maybe Paul cleaning the debris of his life, then going up, forward but unsure. It was almost as if with me it was safe. We could go together. He looked happy and surprised and in awe. Maybe it was a sign for me, that he had gotten it. He wanted heaven. He wanted the promises. He had made his peace.

In Medjugorje we embraced the thought and reality that anything was possible with God! I hoped and prayed that Ed cleaned his soul, then walked through the red door of the white house on the pedestal and was moving towards heaven.

18

Journey

"Dear children! May your life, anew, be a decision for peace. Be joyful carriers of peace and do not forget that you live in a time of grace, in which God gives you great graces through my presence. Do not close yourselves, little children, but make good use of this time and seek the gift of peace and love for your life so that you may become witnesses to others. I bless you with my motherly blessing. Thank you for having responded to my call." September 25, 2008

My journey after the loss of Paul pushed me deeper into my faith: searching, seeking, reading. Attempting to grasp and make peace with all the unanswered questions swimming in my consciousness. I missed my brother; we had gotten so close through his illness. To be his cheerleader had given me purpose. After his passing, I immersed myself in work, marriage, my stepsons and finishing a master's degree in education. For a while I progressed but felt as if I evolved in a fog.

Our usual routine of married life ensued. On Fridays we'd escape our Manhattan jobs, meet at Penn Station, ride the train home, jump into our jeep, pick up the boys from their mom's home and drive north. In four hours, we'd be

skiing in winter and mountain biking in summer. It proved
to be a welcome respite for the four of us—quality time at its
supreme best. The boys, Mike and Matt, were in their adolescent years, full of adventure, and the car ride discussions
brought us close. It was the place where we grew as a family.
Before Paul's death and after, the boys invaded my heart, the
desire for motherhood palatable.

On what would have been Paul's forty-first birthday, in
1993, Mike and I had been traveling extensively for our jobs
and couldn't wait to rendezvous. We missed each other desperately, so our reunion was superlative. Nine months later
we were wonderfully blessed with a baby girl, Julia Pauline.
What a gift!

My purpose now was clear. My infant child opened a
door of love that was so intense. When the nurse placed her
in my waiting arms, I got it! I profoundly understood the
meaning of the word "love." She was so vulnerable, so tiny,
so perfect. Amazing! This little person looked just like her
dad. I was head over heels in love with this baby. The twenty-
two-hour labor and pain evaporated when I held her close
and kissed her forehead. A beautiful bald miracle. All I
wanted to do was stare at her little face as she wrinkled her
nose, yawned or when a furrow formed in her brow. What
was going on in her little mind? She consumed me.

We brought her home to Long Island on the day of the
New York City Marathon. We navigated detours, closed
roads and potholes. Her tiny head bobbed in the car seat as

my husband circumnavigated the terrain. My nerves were on edge, anxious of the responsibility for this little life. My parents arrived a few days after we were home—to advise, comfort and marvel at their newest granddaughter. My in-laws lived close. They came with dinners. Mike and Matt came and awkwardly cradled their newest sibling.

Maternity leave afforded me the space to get accustomed to this new role and absorb myself in the constant changes of Julia and the connections we formed. I walked a lot during this time, leaving the condo in the cool late November temperatures and strolling on the tree-lined streets. I observed the Christmas decorations slowly transforming the neighborhood. Often, we walked to St. Christopher's Church for daily Mass. Julia was strapped in a baby pack to my front. I could shield her from cold winds and loved the peace of mind that came with motherhood. Her first word was "light"; she loved staring at the stained-glass reflections. Her eyes, wide, would follow the light that danced around the church walls in rainbow shades.

I returned to work in Manhattan in the New Year. I appreciated my job with the small knitwear company and the team I worked with, but it was going to be hard. The tears streamed as the tug of leaving Julia with a babysitter for twelve hours was torturous. I missed her. She changed so rapidly. When she was sick, it took me an hour plus to get home on the railroad and get her to the doctor.

As the year progressed my company allowed me to try working from home a few days a week. Unfortunately, this didn't satisfy my bosses. I was grateful for the trial. So just before Julia's first birthday, Michael and I agreed. I resigned and decided to stay home for a while and figure out my next steps.

Our one-bedroom dwelling was getting smaller by the minute, so I focused on scouring the real estate market for a house. My stepsons were at the ages when college was imminent. We envisioned remaining in Long Island for them and my in-laws, but house prices were driving us farther east on the island, to the point where Michael's commute to the World Trade Towers in Lower Manhattan would be longer and longer. On a trip out to New Jersey to visit a client, Michael found a town that was affordable, quietly rural and had a Vermont feel. He stopped to pick up real estate booklets and made the suggestion to look. So, Julia and I drove across the bridges searching out our next move. Just before Julia's second birthday we moved to Warren, New Jersey. Mike enrolled at the State University of New York at Oswego, and Matt soon would begin college at Hobart. We sold our weekend getaway in Vermont to purchase our home in New Jersey.

Lives moved forward, each day bringing surprises or challenges that led me to a greater awareness of the immensity of faith and the presence of God. Julia and I grew together as I taught in a preschool art program with her by my side. We ventured to imaginary places, creating with paper, paint and glue—the discoveries endless. At the end of a session, we had a huge unconventional collage map representing each make-believe place. It made me think about life and the places that I had ventured to, both in my work, with my husband and of course with Paul.

Curiously, our lives are unmapped. From our birth to our death, an array of lines, sometimes straight, curved, jagged, all lead to a destination. But our routes are unique. Each stop on the map, each line drawn, marks something significant. I believe God's hand was present, guiding and watching, as I exercised my free will in tandem with his prodding.

Thomas Merton wrote: "Every moment and every event of every man's life on earth plants something in his soul." Each experience leaves a mark on our map. We develop and change constantly, just as geographical maps do. We mark the details, the unexpected moments, the coincidences that affect our souls. My husband said I was different when I returned from Medjugorje, and I was. I walked through a door on that trip, crossed a threshold and my life would never quite be the same.

I was open, attentive to the spirit; my journey was on a guided course. In the summer 1995, I found out I was pregnant. I was thrilled. Twelve weeks in, I sorrowfully miscarried. During this period, after much testing I realized what a miracle our Julia was as I listened to the doctors explain my fertility complications. This was not how I had planned my journey. I had assumed a second baby would be in our plan. I mournfully acknowledged this was not God's plan for me. Mike and I had three beautiful children between us. Now it was time to see where God wanted me next on this road map of life.

Mom had comforted me at the time by confirming my career change from fashion to education, by saying, "Barb, I know how difficult this is, but maybe you are meant to impact and inspire many children with your teaching. Just think about this."

In the fall of 1995, I had a few more miles to go to complete my master's degree. While student teaching, I had an experience which caused a specific shift in my perspective.

The school was under the Williamsburg Bridge in Manhattan. I taught second grade with an Orthodox Jewish teacher. Several students had troubled home situations. One child in particular had lost both parents: one from violence, one from AIDS. The child sat upside down on his chair. I tried to accommodate this boy by sitting cross-legged on the floor to work on a simple page of math. He physically could not right his world. It was heart wrenching; they were victims of their environment. These innocent little children came into the world facing enormous challenges beyond their control. They wanted love and compassion. I was empathetic for these children. I, as a student teacher, though, was hypercritical of the instructor.

In my prideful, know-it-all, student state, arrogance reigned. How naïve, how wrong. I judged this teacher from the moment I entered the classroom. My notebooks filled with dozens of criticisms and comments on what was wrong and how to improve.

I came across a book titled *The Seven Spiritual Laws of Success: A Practical Guide to the Fulfillment of Your Dreams.* Each day, I traveled by train from New Jersey to Manhattan and then via the subway to school. I started reading this little book and made a promise to myself to enact one law each day. The law that struck me on this one particular day altered my whole experience in this school. The law is called "pure potentiality." Within the law were three exercises. The first was to practice silent meditation: pray thirty minutes each morning and each evening. With the train commute, I found this easy. I could say my Rosary, contemplate the recent messages of Medjugorje and reflect. The second was to appreciate nature. This was also easy. I was commuting into a crowded, noisy, less desirable area of Lower Manhattan and arriving home to a green-grassed, rolling hills, suburban neighborhood. I was thankful for my home and the nature surrounding me. The last was to practice nonjudgment.

I acknowledged that I was judging everything about this teacher. I decided that very day to appreciate and support what she brought to the teaching profession and aid her in her mission. The energy in the classroom changed immediately. I was shocked at how this slight commitment on my part could alter the atmosphere. From that point on, we worked as a team to encourage and empower the students in our care. It was awesome. In the end, I learned a great deal from her, and I realized how my judgment had been a wall preventing me from seeing clearly. This moment in time, this mark on my map, instilled insight about judging others and opened my eyes forever.

In 1998, our family transferred to Hartford, Connecticut, with Michael's job. We found a home and settled in Avon. One snowy early morning, Julia and I dropped off Michael at the airport. On our way home I had an errand to run, so we stopped by the preschool she attended, where I taught. I needed to pick up supplies for a project. I let the engine run as I ran inside the school to grab the materials. I could see the car from the window. As I was turning off the lights to leave, the director, who had been in her office, stopped me with a question. We spoke and walked towards the car so I could watch Julia.

When I finally opened the car door and loaded in the stuff, I focused on Julia. Her big bright smile lit up her face. She said to me, in a clear, matter-of-fact tone, "Mom, Uncle Paul is so nice. He just visited me!"

Shocked, I said, "Could you see him?"

In her sweet little voice, she replied, "No, he just talked in my head. He told me that if I ever needed anything, I could pray to him and he would tell God, because he works for God. He told me that you should pray to someone who has died, and they will tell God. Mommy, who do you think Daddy can pray to? Maybe his grandma, and you can pray to your aunt Ruth because you talk about her." She chatted on, and I was stunned—amazed that God had given this extraordinary opening for Julia and Paul to speak to each other. I quickly drove home and called Mom.

I told her, "Mom, we just got a kiss from heaven. Paul talked to Julia." I relayed every detail, and I could hear her astonishment through the receiver.

"Oh, Barb, how beautiful. Paul spoke to Julia. He is OK." Mom then cried and could not talk anymore. We closed with "I love you," and each moved through our day in a wonderful haze about the closeness of heaven and earth. This brief time in New England marked a wonder with my brother Paul and my Julia Pauline.

In the summer of 1999, we moved back to New Jersey. My husband returned to work in the World Trade Center, and I began a new decade of my life. Julia started on her elementary school career at Saint James—a wonderful coincidence—the same name as the church in Medjugorje. I embarked on my teaching career.

I substitute taught in a public school not far from Julia's school. She was in the first grade. In this interesting role as a permanent sub, one has the opportunity to see the workings, strategies and discipline techniques of a variety of educators. I was taking it all in. At one juncture I was an art teacher and loving it. On the third day of this particular assignment, the principal asked me to take over a second-grade class. Unfortunately, this teacher would be out for the rest of the year on a sick leave. After twenty-four hours of deliberation, I accepted.

I met the concerned parents and wonderful children, and together we set out on a journey of three months. The teacher whose classroom I was assuming was dedicated and had many years of practice. She had routines well established. I did my best to guide these kids to the end of the year with as little change as possible. God gives us challenges and, wow, we can learn, love, guide, make mistakes, clean them up, move on and grow. The experience was like learning to dance, and who would lead? Sometimes it was the class, sometimes I did and eventually we settled into a well-choreographed tango. Faith was missing in this classroom, though, and I longed to talk to the students about God, trust and prayer, but it was prohibited. This was a public school. We were studying Native Americans, so I had a thought. Each day when we gathered, we closed our eyes and thought of their teacher, whom the kids dearly loved. She was fighting a fight physically, and we needed to send her our love and healing. It was not formal prayer, but we gathered as more than two, quietly requesting from our hearts and focusing on the teacher. How could we not? She missed them and they her, and she was ill. I prayed constantly for God's grace as I taught math, reading, social studies and science. He was so present with me. I also talked to Paul a great deal when I was in this classroom and asked his advice. Sometimes the answers appeared so clearly. God was and is ready for our call. All we have to do is ask.

Logistics was a hurdle, with Julia in one place and me in another. We rushed a great deal. At the close of the school year, I approached the principal of Saint James. I knew I desired to share my faith with children, to talk about God and Mother Mary. In the meeting, I told the principal I felt called to this school. She offered me a part-time aide and librarian position. Do you ever have the feeling when you walk into a place and know instinctively it is right? This was how I felt. I was at peace.

We began the school year together and were only a few days into the routine. On September 11, 2001, Julia and I chatted of the coming day as we rode to school. The skies beautiful and clear, the temperature warm, it was a magnificently grand morning. The principal pulled me from the library early in the day to tell me the shocking news of a plane hitting the tower. Immediately, I thought of Michael, who was safe in Texas on a business trip. His company was on the fifty-fourth floor of Two World Trade Center. My thoughts raced to all the people he worked with. Oh God, no, this cannot be happening! Was it an accident? I ran into the office to find out more facts, when a second plane flew into my husband's tower. *Oh no, what is happening? God help us!*

My boys were not aware of their dad traveling; I tried to get word to them but was unable to reach Long Island because of the cell towers. I was able to reach my parents in Myrtle Beach and asked them to call my in-laws and the boys. My father called my in-laws, and they then got in touch with Mike and Matt.

The principal canceled all library classes and asked me to inform the teachers throughout the day as this horrible attack on our country unfolded, while not letting the children know. When parents appeared at the school, the principal ushered them into the library. A few parents retrieved their children. One mother came and took her boys home, already aware of the fate of her husband. God be with the family. We had yet to find out the grave impact on this small community in New Jersey.

I was the designated informer. I walked the halls, alerting the faculty of a third plane heading to the White House. It was frightening and awful to be the bearer of such horrific news. We heard of the Pentagon, and I walked again. Then, as the towers tumbled. Next, we heard of the plane down in Pennsylvania. Our country was in a state of uncertainty, of chaos, of attack, and it was beyond frightening.

All planes were grounded and airports closed. The United States was experiencing a lockdown in the midst of this tragedy. Teachers were awesome and continued throughout the day, servicing their students and maintaining composure. I took Julia home and explained to her what had happened, as best I could, in a way a child of seven could manage.

She began to cry and said, "All the pictures I drew for Daddy in his office are gone, all the photographs in his office are gone." Then she sobbed. The television was off-limits in our home. It was too monumental for her to see. When she was calm and distracted, I called the boys and began the solemn task of finding out about Mike's co-workers.

We had been to a wedding a few weeks before. This reliable young man who worked for my husband must have been in the building. So many faces and names poured into my brain. The answering machine was loaded with messages. After Julia was in bed, I sat down and listened and cried. I heard one voice after the next, asking about Michael and telling me who was OK. Then I heard the young man's voice and really sobbed. He was safe. I called him and he told of others who were safe—one story after the next of why they were not there at the moment it happened. I heard of survivors and those safe but still trying to get home. I spoke to Michael. I think he was in shock. He listened as I told him about my conversations and who was OK. He was quiet and uncertain of when he would get home. I wanted to wrap my arms around him and not let go.

So many lives were lost. So many children lost a parent. A high school student in our community lost both her parents. Many parents lost young enterprising children, so many whose lives were taking shape. This day was clearly a tragedy of the grandest proportions.

I wondered what it was like in heaven on this day, when so many perished. Our Lady of Medjugorje gave the world this message on August 25, 2001, seventeen days before the attack.

"Dear children! Today I call all of you to decide for holiness. May it be for you, little children, always in your thoughts and in each situation let holiness be in the first place, in work and in speech. In this way, you will also put it into practice; little by little, step by step, prayer and a decision for holiness will enter into your family. Be real with yourselves and do not bind yourselves to material things, but to God. And do not forget, little children, that your life is as passing as a flower. Thank you for having responded to my call."

At the close of 2001, during my annual Christmas visit to Myrtle Beach, Mom said, "You are working with children. It is time to share what you know about Medjugorje, especially now, with what is going on in the world."

I returned home and met with a priest at Saint James Church, since the apparitions of Medjugorje were yet to be approved by the Church. The priest gave his consent for me to share, with the junior high students, my story of personal conversion. I talked with the students in May, the month devoted to Our Lady.

Over the next several years, I gave the talk each May. With every talk, I opened up the miracles of Medjugorje inside me and felt transported back. I gained a new awareness each time I presented the story of the apparitions of Our Lady and the depth of faith of that community. One of the students came up to me after a talk and suggested I write a book about it. That child planted the seed in me which led to this testimony.

In Myrtle Beach, there was illness. My dad was failing. He was only seventy-eight. My father lost his dad when he was two. Dad always jested that he was going to "croak" early, like his father. Dad had emphysema but stayed away from doctors. This was not his way—even after insistent pleading from Mom and friends.

The strain of Dad's illness took a toll and he showed significant weakness when I visited in 2001. By February of 2003, his doctor informed Mom that we should consider hospice. Up until that time, Mom was the only caregiver. Mom weathered while Dad deteriorated. Hospice provided a respite for Mom and an ear to share his symptoms and give advice. We took turns visiting; he cherished having us around, sharing memories. We laughed and cried.

At the end of March, I was there with my brother Greg and sister Kathy. We prayed the Divine Mercy chaplet from *Diary of Saint Maria Faustina Kowalska: Divine Mercy in My Soul*, in the room with Dad while he faded in and out of consciousness. He knew we were present and was soothed by our tender touches on his brow or holding his hand. He was withering away. In the early hours of April 2, while I dozed in the room with Dad, I heard a change in his breathing. I went near him and in my mind's eye I saw a sepia photo of his mom, waving her hand and saying, "Come on home, Bobby, come on home." He was the last of her nine children to pass.

I kissed his forehead while tears stung my cheeks. I prayed and said, "Dad, it is OK to go. We love you so much." In that moment he breathed his last. I was grateful to hold his hand while he went home.

I woke Mom and brought her to him. She cried at his bedside and showed relief to see his suffering end. Her partner of fifty-four years of marriage, rearing six children and sharing the bounty of hard work, now lay quiet. My memories were sweet: the songs he sung to me, the strong embraces, the words of wisdom, the proud glances, the walk down the aisle on his arm, and the joy of my little newborn Julia in his arms. How blessed I am.

Once back in New Jersey, my wounds still fresh, I was in church one Sunday, kneeling in the pew with my face buried in my hands before Mass began. Suddenly a vision materialized in my mind: My father, sitting on a park bench with Paul and looking right at me, saying, "Barbie, can you believe I am here!" He put his arm around my brother and gave him the Dutch rub on his head, a gesture so familiar to my eyes. The image disappeared as quickly as it had arrived; I was astounded and overcome with tears. How beautiful was that! I saw Dad and Paul together. What a gift. I called Mom again and shared this kiss from heaven. We shared tears of joy and the sadness of missing them.

Life moved on. My stepson Michael and his girlfriend, Barbara, married a year later, and stepson Matthew met Lauren and married in 2005. I felt extreme exhilaration for these two boys I loved. Each married a woman I admired, respected and in a short time they had my heart. The family was growing. When you see your children with partners who love them and they are happy, it's a beautiful thing. Barbara and Michael settled in Long Island, New York, and Lauren and Matthew lived in Atlanta, Georgia.

I continued talking to the students and received invitations to talk to various adult groups. With each talk I felt more and more compelled to document the story. I departed Saint James in 2007, to pursue writing this story, but found myself directed down a road which God was clearly marking.

I felt led to stoke my faith. A spiritual book club beckoned. Our first title was *Hail, Holy Queen: The Mother of God in the Word of God*, by Scott Hahn, and the second was *The Seven Storey Mountain*, by Thomas Merton. During this meeting, a member of the group suggested I attend the current Bible study being offered and invited me to join her. The study, *The Great Adventure: A Journey Through the Bible*, by Jeff Cavins, hooked me immediately. I was thirsty to know more.

Then the offer came to join a faith-sharing group. Investigating what this was about, I became intrigued. The gist was to be present to the question: "How is God working in your life?" After consideration, I joined the group and found the process inspirational—an additional highway of insight to the faith knowledge I was acquiring.

Wisdom was streaming in. On a retreat, feeling overwhelmed with pushes and pulls of the Holy Spirit, I was asked if I had a spiritual director. I did not. A woman was introduced, and she directed me on awareness and tuning in to the actions of God. She enlightened me on all the happenings occurring in my life. Some profound things were transpiring, like noticing that the links on my rosary turned gold. Someone pointed this out to me and told me this had happened to others who visited Medjugorje. We discussed the odd coincidences that happened on a retreat: of a blooming azalea when no other plants had begun to show signs of spring; the strong scent of roses in the presence of a holy woman, Annemariea Schmidt, as she ministered to another; the strange and intense waking in the middle of the night to record dictated thoughts into my journal. The more discernment I gained, the greater the awareness of miracles both great and small, the answered prayers, the hunger for daily Mass and the desire to serve in my church. So much was stretching me on the inside, and I was embracing my Catholic faith in extraordinary and exhilarating ways!

Over time, four of the five requirements of Our Lady in Medjugorje—to pray with the heart, to say the Rosary, to receive Eucharist as often as possible, to read the Bible and monthly confession—were becoming a part of my routine. Fasting was still a struggle. I was humbled by the changes, and grateful.

Below is what I recorded in my journal from the dictation mentioned above on October 5, 2008, the feast day of Saint Faustina. I was awakened in the night, and this is what happened:

Good morning, beautiful Mother. You are speaking to me in that space between slumber and wakefulness. You want me to write, I think, and the answer is yes. Thoughts are already coming into my brain as I venture out of my warm covers to grab glasses, journal and robe. I feel my way down the hall to the guest room, turn on the lights … the time is 1:35 a.m. I settle on the bed, open my journal and smile when my mind is quiet.

She called to me. So here I am, ready to listen. The first thing I hear … LISTEN TO YOUR MOTHER … I record in my journal … THAT MEANS YOU! OK, OK, I am thinking. I am here! The following are the thoughts that came, one by one. …

1. If you had the choice to improve your life now, as an investment in everlasting life, would you do it?

2. This life is temporary ....

3. If you exercise, eat right, maintain balance in your vices, you can possibly live into your eighties or even into your nineties.

4. If life ends abruptly or too early, from natural disasters, illness, accidents, then we must prepare ....

5. As an exercise, stand outside, look up at the sky on a clear night. See the brilliance and majesty before you. Do you truly believe, with that hugeness before you, that you live and die and that's all?

6. Your Mother wants what is best for you and she is saying "Wake up and make it right."

7. You come into this world innocent, trusting, lovable, dependent, vulnerable and clean. Your Mother wants what is best for you, so LISTEN ....

8. Love one another and treat everyone equally. We are all just skin, bones, blood, organs ....

9. Say you are sorry when you hurt someone.

10. Feed those who are hungry.

11. Lift others when they are down; have compassion.

12. Do not, and I mean, do not hurt others with words, or physically. THINK ABOUT THIS!

13. Help your friends and enemies to be better people. We all have it in us.
14. Remember your manners, please, and thank you.
15. Feed your mind with the stuff that makes you a better person, not something that makes you feel uncomfortable or pulls you down. When in doubt, walk outside and, in the quiet, look up at the stars and beyond.
16. Get to know each other; take the time to build relationships.
17. Laugh.
18. Do not sin.
19. Follow me.
20. Create beauty.
21. End wars.
22. Give yourself to one person only.
23. Value yourself; don't sell yourself short.
24. Do not kill.
25. Do not cheat on ANYTHING ....
26. Do not take something that does not belong to you.
27. Be honest.
28. Be trusted by others.
29. Do business fairly.
30. Work together for a greater purpose.
31. Know you are special.
32. Treat others with dignity.

33. Help your neighbors.

34. Leave Christ in Christmas; He is my Son.

35. Give joy to each other, with a smile.

36. Walk away when something is occurring which will pull you down. Do not do it; you have a choice.

37. Be quiet and listen to your heart.

38. You are unique, the only one exactly like you.

39. RESPECT YOURSELF.

40. There is a struggle inside each of us, between good and evil … try always to choose good.

41. Do not say "hate"; it brings you down.

42. Reach out to those in need.

43. Give generously … give till it hurts. You will be repaid.

44. Ask for help from above when you need it. I am here to help you.

45. Give it to me when you are burdened. I want to help.

46. You are my child, and I love you with my whole being.

47. Love my Son. He is the Way, the Truth, the Light. … Just try it.

48. I want you to be with me for eternity … beyond this life, forever and ever.

49. You are precious to me, and I love you.

50. Read the Bible.

51. Study, learn, develop your talents. You might save a life or two.

52. Do not abuse yourself in any way.

53. Watch out for others and take responsibility.

54. Be your best, one moment at a time.

55. Do not be selfish; GIVE.

56. Try harder.

57. Reflect on how you are doing, each night when you rest.

58. Can you do better tomorrow?

59. Do not abuse others. We have to love.

60. Know how special you are.

61. Look towards heroes who made a difference.

62. Count your blessings and say thank you!

63. Be ready to forgive.

64. You are not always right—think about that.

65. Be humble.

66. Love me, your Mother. Respect me. Know how much I care.

67. This is not all there is, I promise.

68. Make it better. Start small.

69. Read about the saints.

70. Honor your parents. They made YOU!

71. Turn away from anything that is dark. You will know what I mean when it hits you.

72. Be open for hugs from above.

73. Rise above when necessary; remove yourself.

74. I am always watching you.

75. CARE.

76. PURIFY YOUR CONSCIENCE; wash it.

77. Keep some things private; don't share it all.

78. LOVE.

79. Wipe your feet when necessary and shake the dust off.

80. Rest. Tomorrow is another day!

The thoughts ceased. I was stunned. I looked at my journal. I had gone through pages and written what I had heard.

On our drive to school the next day, I handed Julia my journal. I told her what had happened and asked her to read some of the statements.

She said, "Wow, Mom."

We talked about this list, and I gave her copies over the years to keep reminding her of what was written and to implement the messages into her life.

When I got home, I typed the words into my computer and questioned what I was to do with them besides adhere to what they said. A while later, while meeting with a priest for spiritual direction, I told him what had happened and asked for his thoughts. I gave him a copy, and he read while I waited.

He looked up, smiled and said, "These are good thoughts from a loving mom. May I keep them? I would like to use them to teach the children at the school." He also added that this happened on October 5, his birthday.

Over the years I have shared them with faith friends and tried to abide by them. For me, this marked a moment of consolation, when heaven and earth met.

In 2009 we welcomed our first grandson, Luke. Matthew and Lauren received this little guy with open arms. Matthew's brother, Michael, and his wife, Barbara, were the godparents. We all celebrated with awe and joy. Our second grandson, Mikey, was born in 2010 to Michael and Barbara—more joy and gratitude for this family.

My husband and daughter watched my expanding faith steps. Julia and I said prayers on the way to school. We prayed at dinner each night and together when we had serious intentions. But a family Rosary, and more, was hard to ease into my family.

In Julia's last year of high school, Michael's mom was on a steep decline after years of Alzheimer's. She had broken her hip; the healing was taking a long time. She was weakening. By December, my father-in-law wanted to bring her home from a rehab facility. My husband was there to help and support his father and mother in this huge change and be there for her ultimate passing in December.

On the morning after she passed in the wee hours, my brain flooded with thoughts from her. I ran for my computer and typed. The words poured as if she was dictating. She was free, dancing and thanking all who had loved her and helped her. She expressed words to her three children. The voice was not mine, but hers. It was astounding and beautiful, another kiss from heaven for a woman who was locked in her body without being able to communicate for years. She was FREE! What a gift—to sense and experience these words from her and share them with our family.

The significant journey of faith began in August of 1991, but I know it actually began on the day of my birth. My unique journey, my story. Now I try to walk in His light daily, mindful of the growth yet to be and knowing that one day Paul and I will meet again. Faith is indescribable. It is huge, all-encompassing, miraculous, and I am forever indebted to my mom for her conviction regarding my brother's healing in Medjugorje and for starting me on the road I now walk.

Over the last few years, we have experienced natural disasters with such force that towns and lives have been lost, in addition to other worldwide calamities. Our country is facing monstrous challenges. We cannot depend on what we have or on the assurance that we will live catastrophe free; it is out of our hands. I have learned that we must trust in God and Our Lady to steer us on our journey as individuals and as nations.

The influence of her appearances in the tiny village of Medjugorje and her call to us, all her children, is to look beyond and know that this life is but a glimpse into eternity and that she loves us. She wants us to cooperate with the Holy

Spirit, recognize the moments and act on the inclinations. Many years have passed since I began this writing, and it has been many years since my miracle trip to Medjugorje.

There have been so many surprises along the way. While my daughter was in high school, I worked for Scholastic. I encountered a librarian and told her about the story I was working on. Through this sharing of faith, she traveled to Medjugorje twice and is actively spreading the message. Jesus asked His apostles to spread the Word. Sometimes we are not aware of the seeds we plant when the Holy Spirit works through us; it is a gift, a moment of grace. This story is not finished. An invitation came my way and so the story continues.

19

Return in 2014

"Dear children, I call you all and accept you as my children. I am praying that you may accept me and love me as a mother. I have united all of you in my heart, I have descended among you and I bless you. I know that you desire consolation and hope from me because I love you and intercede for you. I ask of you to unite with me in my Son and to be my apostles. For you to be able to do so, I am calling you, anew, to love. There is no love without prayer – there is no prayer without forgiveness; because love is prayer – forgiveness is love. My children, God created you to love and you love so as to forgive. Every prayer that comes out of love unites you with my Son and the Holy Spirit; and the Holy Spirit illuminates you and makes you my apostles – apostles who will do everything they do in the name of the Lord. They will pray with their works and not just with words, because they love my Son and comprehend the way of truth which leads to eternal life. Pray for your shepherds that they may always lead you with a pure heart on the way of truth and love – the way of my Son. Thank you." June 2, 2014

Jeremiah 17:9-10 "More tortuous than anything is the human heart, beyond remedy; who can understand it? I, the

Lord, explore the mind and test the heart, giving to all according to their ways, according to the fruit of their deeds."

1 Chronicles 28:9 *"As for you, Solomon, my son, know the God of your father and serve him with a whole heart and a willing soul, for the LORD searches all hearts and understands all the mind's thoughts. If you search for him, he will be found; but if you abandon him, he will cast you off forever."*

"I cannot believe I am going back. Father Sean asked me to coordinate a group from our parish," I told my mom, who was now living in Cincinnati after suffering a stroke. "Mom, it has been twenty-three years since we were there." I could hear her crying on the other end of the phone.

"Barb, that is wonderful. When will you go?"

"I'm not sure exactly, Mom, but next summer is our goal. I have to call the travel agent and find out what's possible. We hope to stay with one of the visionaries, Ivan. I am so excited I am going back."

I could hear Mom's voice crack as she whispered, "It didn't work for Paul. He was not healed. We lost him. I thought taking him there would cure him ...." Her voice trailed.

"Oh, Mom, our trip worked. Your heartfelt prayers worked more than you can imagine. Paul was healed. He was given eternal life. He talked to Julia when she was four, remember? Our faith promises us eternal life. He is in heaven, Mom."

"Do you really believe that, Barb? I wanted him here with me. I miss him."

"He is there, and you will see him. You are almost ninety years old, and you will see him and Dad. It's real, Mom!"

"Well, honey, I am excited for you, that you get to go back. I wish I could go with you, but I'm too old and could not do it. When are you going?"

I repeated the information.

Mom had suffered a stroke a day after playing eighteen holes of golf. Her vision was now unstable, her hearing was affected, and her mind was faltering. The circle of conversations got smaller as repetition was required. She is my hero and will be forever. It was her faith that started this story; otherwise, who knows where I would be?

So now I am going; I am returning. The last time, I was shell-shocked. Paul was dying, and I considered myself the facilitator. Now I am organizing. How unreal!

It began in June of 2013, when the pastor of my church called my cell phone after returning from a trip to Medjugorje. He had been the invited guest of a parishioner.

He simply stated, "Barbara, I thought about you on this trip. Medjugorje is incredible, so much peace. Would you consider leading a group from our parish? I want to return.

In fact, I did not want to leave. It is a peace-filled place. You can think about it and let me know."

I smiled ear to ear, my heart raced; I was being asked to return to the place that inspired the book. The place that changed my life—the topic of the story I painstakingly plodded through with so many insights and spiritual growth. Incredible!

I ran to the kitchen and told my husband of the conversation.

Michael smiled and said, "I guess you are going back."

I said, "Are you coming with me?"

"I will think about it."

It's affirmative; those few words, "you are going back." His support was huge! What was next? Tell the holy priest. YES. Then arrange a meeting.

We met at breakfast—Father Sean, my husband and a friend, Mary. We listened to Father Sean recall his recent trip and express what he envisioned for the future parish trip. His smiles and wide eyes conveyed the joy of Medjugorje as he poured out what he had experienced.

He said, "What I think would be a good number for us, would be twenty to twenty-five people."

He also had some musts: to stay with the visionary, Ivan, and to have Ivanka as our tour leader. Father wanted to go at about the same time next year, in June. He asked me to talk to Rosemarie, who was the reason for his trip, and find out the details and more logistics.

"OK, Father Sean, I am on board and will do my best to make it happen."

A meeting with Rosemarie and her mom (the people whom Father Sean had traveled with) happened, as well as a phone call to 206 Tours and a shout-out to friends that a return to Medjugorje for June of 2014 was in the works.

I grabbed my journal, but before I began, I paged back to the first entry in the red leather-bound book.

May 16, 2013, the visiting image of Our Lady of Guadalupe. I wrote about the invitation to have this life-size traveling image rest in our parish for one day. Arrangements were made to have the image brought to our stone chapel. The perfect quiet place for her to dwell, in contrast to our main cavernous church. The blessed traveling image of Mary, who gave us this selfie, this miraculous image in the year 1531 when she appeared to a peasant, Juan Diego. The picture was positioned to the side of the altar for our nine o'clock Mass. I had written in my journal, the words of Blessed Pope John Paul II, who had this to say about the image: *I ask Our Lady of Guadalupe to visit every diocese and parish in America. May she cross this continent, bringing it life, sweetness and hope!*"

As part of my role in the spirituality ministry at my church, I had coordinated and committed to being present for the entire day with this visiting image: to oversee the Holy Hour, the Rosary, the Divine Mercy, a witness talk, and final prayers.

What she gave me in those hours as I sat in the quiet, watching people trickle in and out to venerate her image, was peace. As people put the stethoscope to the image, I prayed. On the image, Our Lady has a sash wrapped around her midsection, indicating that she is pregnant with Jesus. There were many miracle stories preceding this visit, of people hearing a fetal heartbeat, so we had the stethoscope available. A boy of twelve, dressed in his soccer uniform, nonchalantly placed the stethoscope near the proper positions and, miraculously, heard the heartbeats. He turned to his mom with the most incredible joy. One woman returned three times to kneel in front of the image, her eyes pouring tears of love to Our Lady. A young girl, who was very sick at the time, attended with her mom. I prayed hard, watching them kneel in prayer. I was present, watching intimate exchanges between them, and asked Mary to wrap all those who came and my family in her mantle.

Now that I was returning to Medjugorje, I could see the connection between the image of Our Lady of Guadalupe and the invitation to return to Medjugorje, where Our Lady was appearing. The invitation for my return came only one month after this image graced our parish. We never know which road our faith will take us when we cooperate. I inscribed my thoughts, my anticipation and plans in this bound journal.

That August our family gathered for a beach vacation in Duck, North Carolina, on the Outer Banks. We spent a week enjoying sun, surf, meals and family time together. Mike, Barbara and Mikey drove down from Long Island, and Matt, Lauren and Luke came from Atlanta. Julia and a college friend rode with us from New Jersey.

While on vacation, Matt showed us this strange lump on his right arm and explained that a puncture biopsy had been taken days before. Now he waited to hear the outcome. His leg was in a brace because of a basketball injury. The poor boy was hurting. His four-year-old Luke and three-year-old nephew, Mikey, were definitely the distracters for his discomforts. The lump on Matt's arm lodged concern for us all and we wanted news. The doctors called, informing him it was a fatty tumor and nothing serious. When he returned, he could make an appointment to have it removed. Relief!

In our week together we caught up with the details of our lives, and mine was the exciting fact that I was returning to Medjugorje.

After vacation, I scrambled to complete the arrangements for a parish ministry fair that would take place in September. As part of the Spiritual Enrichment Ministry, we would roll out the Pilgrimage to Medjugorje for June 22, 2014–June 30, 2014. The tour company supplied brochures. I had made posters to entice people to spur interest and instigate conversations about this holy place. I talked and told my story many times throughout the weekend and passed out many flyers. Now the people had to discern whether they were feeling the pull. We also passed out seven hundred books of the title *33 Days to Morning Glory*, to guide us in a parish-wide Consecration to Jesus through Mary that would begin November 6, 2013.

In late September, we gathered for an "information night" about the pilgrimage to Medjugorje. Those feeling a pull and interest came to listen. Rosemarie and her mother shared their experiences of profound peace. We answered questions, exchanged books and collected names of those considering the trip.

Christina Georgotas, a young film producer, came to our parish in early October 2013, to share excerpts of her film, *Queen of Peace*, a story about Medjugorje. Over one hundred children, some parents and those interested in the pilgrimage attended. They saw and heard this young vibrant woman talk of her conversion from work with Kelly Ripa, to spreading the messages through film and her magnetic attraction to this holy place. She told them what Our Lady is asking of us. Her testimony was engaging and powerful; the children sat in rapt attention while plastic rosaries dangled from their hands. Some adults considering the pilgrimage made their affirmative decisions that evening.

A friend called to see if I could give a talk in November to a group of women. I agreed and told her I would talk on the word "grace." It was the theme decided on for our pilgrimage to Medjugorje. What I read and shared was that "grace is favor, the free and undeserved help that God gives us to respond to his call to become children of God, adoptive sons, partakers of the divine nature and of eternal life" (Catechism of the Catholic Church, 1996). We have to cooperate with God and pray sincerely that grace is gifted.

After this talk, the principal at Saint James School wanted to meet with me. I strolled over to the school building and walked through the familiar halls and into his office. It felt good. He asked me to return as librarian to the elementary school; the current teacher had resigned and would be moving in a few weeks. A definite grace-filled moment.

It was at Saint James, back in 2007, when the inspiration to write this story had occurred. On the crisp day in November 2013, before returning to my post as librarian, we celebrated Mikey's fourth birthday in Long Island, New York. On our return drive home from this magical farm fun day, we received a call from our son Matthew, in Atlanta, telling us that the lump we were concerned about in August had been diagnosed as a rare aggressive cancer!

Oh no! This was a punch in the stomach. It would mean a battle to fight the growing tumor in his arm with chemo, for now. He proceeded to meet with oncologists and would begin treatment the Monday after Thanksgiving. Oh God, help this boy, this young father, husband and son. Prayer chains were enlisted as soon as we got home. On some of the Medjugorje websites there are places to send petitions. Matthew's name was typed and sent.

Work began with the beautiful children at Saint James, but with a heavy heart for Matthew. In regard to the pilgrimage, we had secured eleven rooms in Medjugorje for our journey, with nineteen of us going. My husband had not committed to the trip. With this new development we were unclear on what would transpire with Matthew. I booked the space in my room for my daughter.

Everyone was praying for Matthew as he endured the stays in the hospital, the chemotherapy and constant tests. Going to Medjugorje now, while Matthew fought this battle, felt huge. I could not help but think about Mom twenty-three years ago, taking her son for a miracle, and now I was going to pray for my stepson Matthew, or maybe even take him. That was a secret hope!

Each month I gathered the messages from Medjugorje, savoring Our Lady's words, meditating on them and then passing them on to those signed up for our pilgrimage. The Christmas message to the visionary Jakov read:

"Little children, today in a special way, Jesus desires to come to dwell in each of your hearts and to share with you your every joy and pain. Therefore, little children, today in a special way, peer into your hearts and ask yourselves if the peace and joy of the birth of Jesus have truly taken hold of your hearts. Little children, do not live in darkness, aspire towards the light and towards God's salvation. Children, decide for Jesus and give Him your life and your hearts, because only in

this way will the Most High be able to work in you and through you." December 25, 2013

There was comfort in these words—the clear task that we do our best, make the right decisions in our life, so that He can work in us. With His help and our cooperation, He can work in us and through us!

In my job at school, I strived to live the messages, to love unconditionally each little person who entered my door. I would try to forgive when necessary, be open to the workings of the Holy Spirit and pray that together with guidance from above, we could learn and grow. Some days were easier than others, but I found the greater my commitment to faith, the greater the revelations. On an average day over a hundred children crossed the library threshold. My role was to encourage, inspire, teach a new concept, share an author or a story, and hope the students got something from the exchange.

I began my day with Mass at seven, to pray for Matthew's healing and to say thanks for the gifts received. The list of thanks from small to great clearly altered the outlook for the day ahead. Prayers for patience and strength during challenges were also uttered. We are works in progress and we cannot do it alone.

In early March as we struggled with one of the snowiest winters on record, those who had registered for the trip met for the first time. We were now eighteen. My roommate would be Regina, a woman from the parish of Saint James—unfortunately, not my daughter Julia. Julia had secured a summer nursing opportunity at a camp in Massachusetts, which would begin during our trip. As an inspiration for the group, I copied the following words of Father Sean's, at the top of the agenda. *Everyone who comes to Medjugorje is invited by the Blessed Mother. We come with expectations and dreams. We need to be open and receptive. We as pilgrims walk a journey towards God. We are filled with faith, prayers and want miracles, but our miracle may come and be different than what we expect. It is God's will for us, not ours.*

We introduced ourselves and shared how we came to our "yes" for the pilgrimage. Father Sean, one other pilgrim and I had been to Medjugorje previously. The others were first timers. We created a circle of excitement, anticipation, and apprehension as we awaited the date for our journey to begin.

We met one more time in early June to cover last-minute details before our departure. School ended on Friday for our summer break, and we departed on Sunday.

We landed in Sarajevo, after a brief flight change in Munich, without any snags. We received the best welcome from our tour guide, Ivanka, who met us as we exited customs with our bags. The intimidation of leading a group kicked up my stress level, especially recalling the 1991 mix-up. As I walked out of the airport the sun was shining and, there, before my eyes, was not the dusty bus from my past pilgrimage but, a large, modern transport with an image of Our Lady of Peace painted on the side! Relief!

Ivanka welcomed us and proceeded to take over. On our two-hour drive to the final destination, she led a peace Rosary. This consisted of seven Our Fathers, seven Hail Marys and seven Glory Be prayers. Ivanka shared the history of the village and talked of the forty million pilgrims that had been drawn to Medjugorje.

She engaged our thoughts with conflicts of the past civil war and repeated messages from Our Lady concerning peace, stating that disharmony begins in the human heart. She emphasized peace to reign within ourselves first. From there, spread it to our families and beyond. The trip from the airport to the village took us on smooth, engineered, improved highways with views of rushing rivers, majestic mountains and quaint towns. We had our phones out, taking pictures. I was making this trip with two dear friends who had heard my talks over the years and were part of my faith-sharing circle. Their support was unprecedented. We laughed and pinched ourselves that we were together on this trip as we absorbed it all!

As my priest had requested, we would be staying with Ivan. Over the years since the apparitions began and the influx of thousands who came to this tiny village, the accommodations had changed drastically. My eyes took in the modern updates, hotels, restaurants, and street-side shops as we made our way to the guesthouse.

When the bus pulled up, there was Ivan, the visionary who still sees Our Lady every day, in front of a gated, coral-painted concrete, clay tiled-roof home. It was dotted with trees and a manicured garden. He smiled and stood ready to meet us. The visionaries are "holy celebrities" in Medjugorje and beyond. His gentle demeanor was humble and warm. He carried our bags, addressed questions, and led us on. He had aged gracefully since we saw him in 1991 and his joy was welcoming.

In the courtyard, outside the main entrance to the guest home was a replica of Michelangelo's *Pieta* sculpture. Pink and red blossoms in varying shades circled the carving. Opposite the guest home was a stucco-roofed, quaint framed chapel silhouetted by a background of lush green mountains. The air was different. I inhaled deeply at this eye-candy package. When I squinted my eyes, I could see in the faint distance the concrete cross on the peak, where Paul had had his transfiguration. My heart filled with emotion, gratitude, and relief.

The guesthouse was three stories of immaculately shining tile floors, a few couches in the lobby for gathering, a large dining area with family-style tables to the right and the stairs straight ahead. Our room was on the second floor. It was small: two single beds, a bath and closet. It was perfectly simple. We were located close to Apparition Hill, but I had yet to get a sense of my surroundings. We were directed to settle in and then to meet at the chapel for the Rosary and Ivan's meeting with Our Lady.

After Regina and I unpacked, we gathered the intentions we carried in envelopes from all those from home and walked over to the chapel. I was drawn to a beautiful statue of Our Lady perched to the left of the altar—the movement of her veil and folds of her dress fluid against the coral rounded wall. Her outstretched hand held a rosary. The crucifix of her Son was directly in front of me, the top of which touched the ceiling. A statue of Joseph was to the right. Below the altar, on a step, there was a basket where we could place our intentions. I pulled out the 8 x 12 picture of my Matthew, his wife Lauren and son Luke, and perched them so they were clearly visible. In the basket, I laid all the other prayers I had carried from the parishioners, to support this image so I could look into Matthew's face as I prayed. I also thought that Our Lady would appear directly above this basket. In front of the basket was a single kneeler for Ivan.

At the designated time, we met in the chapel and recited the Rosary, led by Ivan and Ivanka. Beautiful meditations were read, drawing me in deep. At the conclusion of the Rosary, Ivan made his way to the kneeler and began to pray. I had my eyes closed and, suddenly yet mysteriously, a blanket of silence permeated the room—as if all sound was vacuumed out. Everyone was on their knees in pure devotion. Ivan's back was to me, but I could see he was talking by his subtle gestures, his head focused upward. Wow, could Our

Lady see us as she spoke to him at this moment? What an amazing gift, to kneel before this moment where heaven touches earth.

After the apparition, he moved behind the altar table, his eyes closed. He told us how hard it is to see Our Lady with heaven open to him, and then come into the presence of this earthly plane. On this first night he told us that *"She blessed us all, our petitions, those who are sick, she blessed the priests present and spoke of her love for them and emphasized obedience."* On our first intimate encounter with Our Lady, I prayed, *Heal my son, Mary, please!*

In a jet-lagged stupor, several of us wandered the neighborhood and roamed to the base of Apparition Hill. I was getting my sense of where we were, and memories flooded back. However, the dramatic change of growth disjointed the landmarks I recalled. All I could say was the breath of heaven touching this valley illustrated that life was and is not static; it is always rebuilding, growing, changing. In the years between the two visits the religious shops, boutique hotels and restaurants blossomed and nestled into the changing landscape. There was vivid contrast between old stone homes and the fresh modern buildings.

Our second day was June 24, the feast day of John the Baptist. After breakfast, we met in the chapel for morning prayers with Ivan and Ivanka. She reiterated the history lesson from the day before, on the bus, adding more facts about the small community that existed here before the two world wars, the building of the church, the losses of fathers and the resilient villagers. Overwhelming faith persisted and strengthened. Later we ventured for an information walk leading us into town, about one and a half miles on a path. I had walked this way before, with my sick brother.

We strolled on a stone walkway behind the church, the outdoor seating now set on a smooth platform of concrete with refined borders. The vineyards I had run through in 1991, in desperation, were an open field lined by hotels, with a new brick walkway leading away from the church to the graveyard where Father Slavko was now buried. Along the walk, set back from the path about twenty feet, are five shallow alcoves made of stone, with images of the luminous mysteries created in colorful tile mosaics. We passed a corridor leading to the risen Christ sculpture which had been added in 1998, created by the Slovene sculptor Andrej Ajdič.

A line of people waited to climb to a perch to wipe at a mysterious liquid that drips from the knee area. Some people had a small white cloth, and some rubbed their rosary. We continued our information walk to the graveyard and listened to Ivanka talk about Father Slavko. I reflected back to what Father Slavko said to those gathered in the church in August of 1991, on my initial trip: *"Our Lady has called you here; be patient yet open to receive her message. She will let you know what she wants."* If anyone had ever said back then that one day in the future I would be a librarian in a

Catholic school and would lead a group to Medjugorje, I would have said they were crazy!

That night we met in the chapel for the Rosary with Ivan, and then the apparition. It was during this moment, with my eyes closed in prayer, that this vision appeared in my mind's eye.

My stepson Matthew was lying on something, not a cot, but narrower and hard, not soft, no blanket, and I was at his feet. Jesus was there by Matthew's head. He had His hand on his shoulder and His other hand on Matthew's arm, the one with the cancer. He looked at me with deep brown, loving eyes. Our eyes met, and without words He said, "I have got him." He kissed Matthew's head, then his arm. It was so peaceful. **Jesus had him!** Then it was gone. This private vision of Jesus with Matthew—wow! But what did it all mean? I will hold it in the depths of my heart, the fact that HE HAS HIM.

In our days following, we listened, meditated, prayed Rosaries, walked, hiked, confessed, shared stories, and witnessed revelations of our hearts. Of those in our group, some had strong movements of the spirit, or graces gifted. One woman encountered a statue of Our Lady becoming lifelike, her skin supple and she moved. Another saw the sun yo-yo from the sky, and one had revelations which drew her closer to Jesus as she fell going up a mountain. The experiences of each person astounded, and we heard of answers being given to questions they were seeking. Each person was on a unique faith quest, and, in a most miraculous way, each was being met in a private, surprising way.

Our priest returned to the guesthouse late one evening, after missing dinner, causing concern. We saw his face filled with radiant joy after spending hours hearing confessions. He was glowing; Jesus had led him to heal and forgive souls on their faith journey. Each day provided more revelations.

One night I felt a need to call my husband. We had just left the church and were getting something to eat. He reported the results of some tests Matthew had at Memorial Sloan-Kettering in New York—the worst-case prognosis. I could hear the heaviness in my husband's voice and my heart broke. My prayers had to be amplified!

My emotions surged. I needed to be alone and desperately wanted to return to the guesthouse. The woman I was with asked if I wanted to walk or take a cab. I wanted to clear my head, so we walked. Her son asked if I wanted to pray or could he sing for me. I asked him to sing. He was in our choir at home. He belted out a song in Italian. It reverberated off the mountains and filled me with immense peace. It was the most beautiful sound and perfect for the brutal fear raging in my mind. I will never forget the gift of his voice.

On June 25, 2014, Our Lady's 33rd anniversary message resounded for the world.

"Dear children! The Most High is giving me the grace that I can still be with you and to lead you in prayer towards the way of peace. Your heart and soul thirst for peace and love, for

God and His joy. Therefore, little children, pray, pray, pray
and in prayer you will discover the wisdom of living. I bless
you all and intercede for each of you before my Son Jesus.
Thank you for having responded to my call."

We were learning to offer everything and trying to allow
Mary to guide us in our movements. I concentrated on my
walks, desiring them to be prayer focused on Matthew,
thanksgiving, and wonder.

While climbing Apparition Hill I observed kindness
multiplied: members of the group aided each other in the
rain, on slippery rocks. I watched as others grabbed arms for
balance and some who carried supplies, offered rain gear,
and focused attention to the needs of others. All this was
done while silently praying a Rosary which was amplified
through the listening devices in our ears. At the top we saw
the statue given by the Korean family, and heard the miracle
story of unbelief, resulting in a miraculous cure. This mountaintop was where it all began.

One night a woman, Colleen Willard, came to Ivan's
chapel to give her witness talk. She held the packed audience
spellbound as she told her story of a brain tumor, metabolic
bone disease, myofascial fibromyalgia, connective tissue disease, adrenal insufficiency and more. One of the visionaries,
Vicka, prayed with Colleen in 2003, and she was cured completely. Her doctors were astounded upon her return and
confirmed all. Her restoration was miraculous. That night in
the audience was Immaculée Ilibagiza, author of *Left to Tell:*

Discovering God Amidst the Rwandan Holocaust. She survived the genocide and was bringing a group to Medjugorje. Miracle stories abound!

Matthew 7:24 *"Everyone who listens to these words of mine and acts on them will be like a wise man who built his house on rock."*

Father Stanko gave a talk at the church. His major recommendation was: "Help each other and exchange your testimonies. Go forth, pilgrims, and share what you have experienced." Each one in our group was having personal revelations which would be the ripple effect of this pilgrimage upon our return.

On the feast of the Most Sacred Heart of Jesus, this message from 1988 was shared with us:

"Dear children! My invitation that you live the messages which I am giving you is a daily one, specially, little children, because I want to draw you closer to the Heart of Jesus. Therefore, little children, I am inviting you today to the prayer of consecration to Jesus, my dear Son, so that each of you may be His. And then I am inviting you to the consecration of my Immaculate Heart. I want you to consecrate yourselves as parents, as families and as parishioners so that all belong to God through my heart. Therefore, little children, pray that you comprehend the greatness of this message which I am giving

you. I do not want anything for myself, rather all for the salvation of your soul. Satan is strong and therefore, you, little children, by constant prayer, press tightly against my motherly heart. Thank you for having responded to my call." October 25, 1988

Ivanka reviewed the schedule and let us know that the visionary, Vicka, would give a talk. One of the women in our group suffered from a major health issue. She had struggled for a long time and the pain was evident. We had spoken to Ivanka to see if we could make arrangements for Vicka to pray with her. Yes! It was going to happen. We were all connected as a group and wanted prayers answered for this woman. Vicka's home was a bus ride away, so we loaded in, and upon arrival Ivanka took this woman and her husband into the home. The rest of us, along with another hundred pilgrims, waited in the courtyard. The heat of the day was stifling. To get relief from the sun, we managed to huddle under one of the few trees.

After forty minutes, Vicka came out on a balcony about five hundred feet from the shade of the tree. She spoke through an interpreter. She recalled the first days, how she felt, the shock of the Mother of God appearing to them— simple children. The visionary told how Our Lady taught them gradually and the instructions she gave for them and for all of us. Vicka shared how she had watched herself grow more devout and how it spread to her friends, her community and beyond. She lived the messages; her smile radiated.

Her love radiated. When she finished her witness, she wanted to pray over us. She extended her hands, and silence fell over the crowd. Vicka began to pray. We had been standing a long time, but as she prayed I closed my eyes and extended my hands forward.

I felt a breeze blow through me … soothing, refreshing … and then I experienced my second interior vision:

Standing before me, several feet away, was the Blessed Mother. She was my height, a white veil covered her head, her brown hair fell over her shoulders, her pale skin was perfectly smooth. She did not look at me; her eyes were focused downward and in her arms she held my Matthew. He was not awake but lying limply in her arms as she stood holding him. I felt movement to my right, so my eyes moved, and I saw Matthew's wife, expressionless. No words were exchanged. She was with their son Luke. My husband and daughter joined Matthew's mom and her husband, his brother and wife, and his half-sister and her husband. With more family and friends, a crowd gathered. No one spoke; all eyes were forward, towards Mary holding Matthew. I looked around and more people joined, until I could not see beyond the multitudes of people. It was then that I had a profound movement in my heart. These were the throngs of people praying for Matthew. He lived in Atlanta, so many friends, co-workers, neighbors, those of his wife and his son's school were all praying. His mom and brother in Long Island, the community he grew up in, all had people praying. My family in Ohio, South Carolina, Virginia, Indiana—he was on prayer chains in New Jersey, in our school, church and beyond. All these prayers for Matthew, lying limp in her arms, one of his arms dangling. I felt the breeze, and the tears flowed. I opened my eyes from this clear, tangible vision and cried. It evaporated and was gone.

That night as we prayed in the chapel, I questioned what had happened and prayed about what I saw. He was limp in her arms. What did that mean? He was back in Atlanta with his wife Lauren and son Luke, living their life, going to work, school functions, and in treatment for his cancer. But all the people, all the prayers, they were tangible. I believe it all counts. Not one prayer is wasted. They are all used in some extraordinary way.

The woman from our group was prayed on by Vicka, and we continued to hope that something extraordinary would happen to her. That night in the chapel, Ivan asked that we extend prayers for priests and for Pope Francis. Our Lady asks repeatedly that we pray for our shepherds.

In the morning we set out to the base of Cross Mountain. At the base we plugged in our listening devices and walked silently, hearing meditations from the yellow book, *The Stations of the Cross,* by Tomislav Ivancic. This was the place; I was standing on the same rocky soil where Paul had experienced his transfiguration, at the seventh station. We climbed with sticks to balance our steps among the rocks. The memories flooded—Mom's weary face as she begged for her son, as Paul moved between the stones with Grandpa's cane and Ed watched. Now I was here with friends, sojourners in our walk, hearing what the Holy Spirit wanted to impart on us. My heart wanted to burst, it was so filled with gratitude and longing. I shed tears at the seventh marker and listened intently as Jesus falls a second time, his torn, wounded body crumbling under the weight of his cross. I prayed for Matthew and the cross he carried.

After Cross Mountain and Mass, we headed to a place I was not familiar with, Cenacolo, a residence for addicts needing to be healed. It was founded by an Italian nun, Mother Elvira. Her call from the Holy Spirit was to minister to those who live in desperation and hopelessness. We listened to testimonies from two young men and were struck by their raw, unnerving honesty of their drug-induced behaviors in contrast to their hope of recovery from the darkness. The men of the community work to rebuild their lives and literally build the buildings in and around the community. It is very impressive, and the recovery rate is astounding. This Scripture says it all: *"My grace is sufficient for you, for my power is made perfect in weakness"* **2 Corinthians 12:9**

On our last night we gathered to share our stories, our takeaways, what we will carry back to our loved ones and community. Many of us were lost in our thoughts, trying to comprehend deeply the significance of this pilgrimage. We'd return home with spirits raised and altered. I would see Matthew in a few weeks. Did he feel a change from the electric prayers, the kiss from Jesus? Did he sense the throngs of appeals for his survival? What was next for our Matthew?

"Dear children, I, the mother of all of you gathered here and the mother of the entire world, am blessing you with a motherly blessing and call you to set out on the way of humility. That way leads to the coming to know the love of my Son. My Son is almighty, He is in everything. If you, my children, do not become cognizant of this, then darkness/blindness rule in your soul. Only humility can heal you. My children, I always lived humbly, courageously and in hope. I knew, I became cognizant that God is in us and we are in God. I am asking the same of you. I desire for all of you to be with me in eternity, because you are a part of me. I will help you on your way. My love will envelop you like a mantle and make of you apostles of my light – of God's light. With the love that comes forth from humility you will bring light to where darkness/blindness rule. You will be bringing my Son who is the light of the world. I am always alongside your shepherds and I pray that they may always be an example of humility for you. Thank you." July 2, 2014

20

Matthew

"Dear children! Today I invite you to open yourselves to God by means of prayer so the Holy Spirit may begin to work miracles in you and through you. I am with you and I intercede before God for each one of you because, dear children, each one of you is important in my plan of salvation. I invite you to be carriers of good and peace. God can give you peace only if you convert and pray. Therefore, my dear little children, pray, pray, pray and do that which the Holy Spirit inspires you. Thank you for having responded to my call." May 25, 1993

Within days of our return from the trip, I received a call from a courier who was delivering some twenty books for our group. *The Stations of the Cross*, by Tomislav Ivancic, was the collection of meditations we had heard in Medjugorje but were unable to purchase. The woman was going to Express Mail them to me. I said, "Please don't. You can send them regular mail. We are going to visit our son in Atlanta, who has cancer." I don't really know why I said that, but I did.

She repeated the word *cancer*, and asked if I had some time, which I did. She instructed me to get a notebook and pen. I grabbed my journal.

The woman shared her story of being diagnosed with stage 3 breast cancer, which had spread to her lymph nodes. She had not wanted to proceed with the traditional treatments, opting for no chemotherapy. She outlined the ins and outs of her alternative treatments, the doctors and what she had done. She was two years out and healed completely, with no cancer in her system. She was still healthy, and her body was better than before, which she attributed to the nutritional guidelines of her healing.

Was this an answered prayer? I took all the information, and she offered to talk to our Matthew if he was interested.

We arrived in Atlanta. I told Matthew and Lauren all about the trip, the prayers, and asked if he felt anything supernatural or odd while I was in Medjugorje. He grinned and said he didn't recall anything specific. He looked pretty good except the chemo had left him bald and puffy. He said he liked his doctors at Emory Hospital. He listened politely to what I had heard from the courier but was content and confident to follow his doctors' recommendations. The visions I experienced remained buried in my heart; however, I did let him know that hundreds were praying for him.

While we were there, Michael and I took Luke on a field trip to Conyers, Georgia. It's funny that our daughter Julia had a friend from college whose grandfather had traveled to Medjugorje and, in a chain of events following his trip, became a Ukrainian Catholic priest. I had met him prior and knew he lived in Conyers. He was also praying for Matthew.

In his possession he had a second-class relic: a simple brown habit worn by Saint Padre Pio. My hope was to take all spiritual tools into a healing for Matthew. Matthew looked at me with love but great skepticism. He said many times, "I do not have your faith, Barbara." He did not want to join us, but did support Michael, Luke and I spending an afternoon in Conyers asking for and receiving prayers while praying with the habit of this holy saint.

As God would have it, we also met the artist who had painted an image that hung in my home office. It had been a gift given to me by the parents of Julia's college friend. She had joined us on our family vacation in the Outer Banks of North Carolina. When we returned home, her parents presented me with this print. It was a thank-you gift. I was overwhelmed by its message and beauty. I guess she shared what I had told her on our eight-hour ride to Duck. I spoke of my story and Our Lady's hand in my life. The image was of Mary, with the words: *Just Have Faith in my Son Jesus.* Now, here in Conyers, we would meet the artist.

He was an elderly gentleman, small in stature. We exchanged formalities and were invited to sit on the couch near him.

He began speaking and then, after a pause, said, "I have been to Medjugorje. I was there to escape the FBI, during the civil war." He laughed, saying, "I thought it'd be a good place to hide."

Long story short, because that was his story to tell. He encountered Our Lady, miraculously, while on Prodbrdo Hill; he saw her during an apparition. As a result of this vision, he returned to the US, faced an indictment, was imprisoned and, once released, returned on several occasions to Medjugorje. Each time sparked a happenstance that altered his life course. He had never painted in his life. While on one of the pilgrimages he was told he would paint. The print I had received was the result. He had numerous challenges that he mercifully accepted regarding his health, his business and his family. The result: he gave everything to God and trusted what would unfold for him. He lived humbly in Conyers, with the disposition of a joyful child. Over the years he had traveled extensively, sharing his witness, and spreading the message of Medjugorje. On our drive back to Matthew and Lauren's, as Luke snoozed in the car seat, Michael and I chatted about what we had seen and heard.

We stayed in Atlanta for a week while selfishly craving normalcy. The air was filled with the weight of Matthew's illness. It was in our guts and in his countenance. It was hard to leave them. I challenged myself to adopt the words of Padre Pio: "Pray, hope and do not worry." Worry was useless; it accomplished nothing. Prayer was useful. It was hard to do this but being conscious of it helped. The visions I had experienced presented an outcome I was not ready to face. Loving and playing with Luke, laughing, smiling, watching him cuddle with Matt and be a normal energetic little guy was wonderful and at the same time tough. *God, please take care of this precious family.*

After Atlanta I headed to Cincinnati to share the Medjugorje trip with Mom. Her memory and body were declining, yet she listened, cried, laughed, and believed it all! She was the one person in the family who truly got it. We had walked the same steps. I loved this lady so much. One day I went to daily Mass near her new home, an independent living retirement abode. After Mass, I had an overwhelming, invisible but powerful Holy Spirit pull. I was going to ignore it, but the yank was convincing. I went to the rectory and asked to speak to a priest.

An Irish priest heard the request, poked his head around a corner and said, "Let's talk." He ushered me to his office. I asked if there was someone who could bring Mom Holy Communion. I explained that I lived in New Jersey, and Mom had recently moved to Cincinnati and was not a member of the parish, but it would mean the world to her. He said that he could help, but he was leaving on a sabbatical to Myrtle Beach for a month. He stated that the deacon could come to Mom. As my mouth dropped at hearing "Myrtle Beach," I learned he was going to the parish Mom had just moved from in Myrtle Beach, where she had been a Eucharist minister. Then he told me the deacon had been to Medjugorje and would love to meet Mom. It was and is a very small world. I chose this church because of the Mass times, and now I elicited two more people to pray for Matthew and help Mom. It is wise to pay attention to directions from the Holy Spirit.

In September Michael was turning sixty. We arranged a small family celebration in Boston, near the college where Julia was a student. Matthew and Luke flew in. We waited for them outside the arrival door at the airport. As they came through the doorway and into the bright crisp daylight, my first thought was that Matthew's hair had grown back. He looked fantastic. My husband jumped out of the car and hugged his son in a long embrace of joy and relief.

Michael, Barbara, and Mikey drove up from New York. We picked up Julia and rendezvoused at the hotel. Time together was precious: an Italian dinner of celebration and then a Boston College football game. To witness Matt and his dad sharing Matt's beloved sport, in all the excitement and enthusiasm of the BC crowd, was awesome! It was a quick weekend, and then everyone returned to their jobs and lives.

In October, during a return trip to Cincinnati, Mom and I sipped coffee in our PJs when there was a knock on the door. I finally met the deacon who was bringing Mom Holy Communion. We had spoken on the phone a few times and were now face-to-face. He couldn't believe the timing of my visit. He told me he was giving a talk regarding Medjugorje in a few days and asked if I'd come share my witness. I hesitated for a moment and then said yes. Mom would hear our story being told to an audience for the first time. Even though she was fragile, she hung in there and traveled back to the holy village with me as I spoke to the small crowd gathered in St. Bartholomew Church.

On my ten-hour return drive to New Jersey, I prayed and detoured to the Padre Pio shrine in Barto, Pennsylvania. A fellow teacher had asked me to pick up some books. Padre Pio, a saint with the stigmata, was definitely instrumental in my spiritual growth. Unusual things occurred. For example, a book about the saint kept being pulled out of the stacks in the school library. One day it was on the floor. I read it and was inspired. I had also been invited to be part of a team to start a Padre Pio prayer group in our parish. A modern print of Padre Pio was given to my father-in-law by a cousin from Italy, as a random gift. It was not his taste, so he gave it to me; it is framed, in my home office. I was reading more about Padre Pio's life and even became a spiritual daughter through what I had learned. I believe the surprise talk in Cincinnati and the detour were moments to bolster me for what lay ahead. I walked the grounds, bought the books, and continued my drive home.

After Julia's twenty-first birthday in November, her brother's cancer was active again. I wrote in my journal … "Faith is … living and believing in God in the midst of uncertainty, it is eternal seeking, continuously growing, embracing the Scripture, and cooperating with the movements of the Holy Spirit." My heart was hurting for Matthew and all the family who was riding every wave with him. He was going to see specialists in New York, for surgery on his arm.

It was the season of Advent. In the Church of St. Catherine of Siena, across the street from Memorial Sloan-Kettering Cancer Center, I attended Mass and prayed. With uncertainty, Matt's closest fans waited with strangers in the poinsettia-decorated waiting room while Matt was being cut open. During the Mass I heard the reading from Matthew, the genealogy of Jesus. Matthew's high school football jersey number, fourteen, was mentioned three times in the Scripture. This was a time of joy. In this season of preparation for the birth of Christ, Matthew's surgeons would cut into his arm to remove muscle, tissue, and bone to eradicate what was left of the radiation-zapped tumor.

He would recover in New Jersey. Lauren was there for the surgery and planned to return to Atlanta for Christmas while Matthew recovered. Unfortunately, post-surgery, more cancer was detected on his neck. Lauren and Luke returned immediately, on Christmas Eve. At Newark airport we picked up Luke. A large gift-laden suitcase was transferred to our car. Lauren went directly into Manhattan to be by her husband's side. The operation would take place in Sloan-Kettering on Christmas Eve. Thank you, God, for all the dedicated doctors and nurses who would be present.

Once settled in New Jersey, Luke—this little boy—was awaiting Santa. In the rush, friends had packed Luke's gifts. Since Lauren stayed with Matthew, we did our best to bring joy into this strange out-of-body Christmas Eve. Lauren re-turned from the hospital after the surgery. Santa came. Luke bounded out of bed, unwrapped gifts and was a delighted in-nocent little boy. Lauren wanted to be with Luke on this Christmas morning. The pull between husband and son was so hard. She departed for Memorial Sloan-Kettering to see Matthew after the avalanche of presents and some nourish-ment.

Michael, Julia, Luke, and I cleaned up, and then drove to Manhattan after Mass, to see Matthew. Julia and I spent most of the day taking Luke around to see the sights of New York City while actively playing a game of counting Christmas trees. At a street vendor we bought him a black-and-white leopard hat with long side panels and pouches for his hands. We smiled for pictures and tried to be joyful on this Christ-mas Day for this little boy whose dad was in the hospital and would be waking to such uncertainty.

Matthew woke on that Christmas morning with the ina-bility to move both his arms. His battle was traumatic.

Fear, worry, panic, upset—contrary words for the joy of Christmas—but this was the wave of emotions. At the end of the day, as dinners were bringing families together, we met at a restaurant near the hospital. At the table were Matthew's mom, his stepfather, Michael, Julia, Luke, and me. After all the running around, Luke gulped down some pasta and fell sound asleep. Lauren remained by her husband's side. What a crazy time. Life as we knew it was being yanked out from under us. Love was key, Matthew center, his wife, child, then the rest of us. Everything was heavy.

Matthew was discharged from the hospital before the drop of the New Year's ball in Times Square. Lauren and Luke returned to Atlanta. Julia was off with friends to bring in 2015, amidst preparing for her semester abroad in Italy. We nursed Matthew as best we could. We managed a trip to Long Island to connect with family, before Julia left and specifically to see Grandpa, Michael's dad, a prayer warrior and widower. I am certain his rosary beads were worn down in his desperate pleas for Matthew's recovery.

Love, honor, courage, patience, humility, kindness, gratitude, honesty, compassion, and other virtues swirled during this time. Matthew's tumors were active, and it seemed that the doctors could not keep up with the battle inside him. But in the midst of the turmoil, Matthew was also teaching us. He showed tremendous courage, handling the information voiced in each call from doctors. More tumors. He shed tears for his wife and son. He listened as they were scrambling to ascertain which drugs to combat his specific cancer. Predominantly, his concern was for others. He honored his marriage and valued Lauren's opinions for the treatments and directions. The tears poured in quiet, gentle waves as he talked with his dad. Matthew's love for his wife and for Luke was profoundly beautiful. His politeness was stunning. In his position, would I be as gracious? As we fed him and aided with his physical therapy exercises, there was always a polite

"Please," a "Thank you" and a smile. He was patient, kind and loving as this rhabdomyosarcoma raged inside.

Life circled around Matt's battle. Julia was excited for the journey of her young lifetime, studying in Parma, Italy, for a semester, but filled with concern and anxiety about her brother. He encouraged her to enjoy, have fun and be safe. He watched and smiled as I assisted in the packing efforts as she evaluated what was necessary or frivolous to meet the suitcase weight requirements. How absurd: Matt, downstairs on the comfy couch, dealing with life and death, and Julia, upstairs, anxious about her pending departure. Julia and Matt's farewell hug was tough to watch; my heart hurt. Michael and I drove her to the airport, kissed our girl goodbye and sent silent prayers asking God to watch over her. It was January 12 of a new year for her adventure as uncertainty abounded.

One of Matthew's best friends from Atlanta flew to New Jersey a week later to be his hands, support, and journeyman to return to Atlanta. All that could be done with the doctors in New York had been concluded. Matt desired to be home with his love Lauren, Luke, friends and the concerned and committed doctors at Emory. In the background beyond were thousands of appeals in prayer being voiced for this dear boy. Lauren's parents had been a huge support in Atlanta, helping her with Luke's schedule and now were there to help with Matthew's appointments. Her mom, a registered nurse, was a blessing in his medical trials.

In my journal I recorded from something I heard. ...
Two men looked out beyond the jail bars. One saw mud, the
other saw stars. ... Always look up in the midst of trials. I was
learning this was easier said than done, but I was trying.

On Friday, January 30, a day marking my father's birthday, we had completed yet another Catholic school week.
This was a busy time; my library was rearranged to become
a temporary bookstore. I organized, ran, and met with the
visitors and students as they perused the carts and tables.
When it was over, I packed the cases, counted the money,
put the library back in order, prepared for classes the following week and made the necessary calls to complete the fair.
Thank God it was the weekend. I was exhausted. My dad had
been gone twelve years and on this day I recalled memories
and sent love and thanks to him for being a great dad.

On February 1, we were buckled in and on a plane to Atlanta. The call had come from Lauren shortly after my return
home from school, as I dropped my bags in the kitchen,
ready for a glass of wine. The phone rang. My husband's face
crumbled before my eyes. Oh no! Another strike, this time
in the brain! Surgery to remove a tumor was imminent.
There was bleeding too; he was confused and disoriented. An
oncologist, a neurologist and surgeons called; Matthew was
in the ER. Poor Matt, the blows to his arm, his neck, the surgeries and more tumors growing in his rib cage, his calf. Now
his beautiful mind! It was Super Bowl Sunday. The operation
had been scheduled to take place on Tuesday but was rushed

in on this day. Memories of this football boy rushed by: the runner, sprinter, wingback, halfback, the bulk of helmet and pads running, ball tucked in his arm to score, to a touchdown, to win!

God, what is happening? All these surgeries—how much can he take? I love this boy. L-o-v-e: four letters that cause the stomach to lurch, the heart to hurt, the tears to flow, the prayers to pour.

In retrospect, God's hand was always present in the details. As we were buckled in and seated above the clouds, the past twenty-five days played in the pages of my mind. We waited during the first surgery … a collection of loved ones present in force to be there for Matt. We were able to get Julia home quickly from Boston, without weather problems. I was out of school for the vacation when the second surgery happened and was available for Luke. Lauren and Luke were able to fly back quickly, and again the weather cooperated. Angels packed Luke's Christmas packages and Santa arrived for him. Julia and I could entertain Luke while Michael was at the hospital. From my perspective I could see these things, these momentary episodes strung together. But understandably, my husband could not; he was broken, crying more than I had ever witnessed. Lauren was watching these events unfold. Surreal. The man she loved was declining and her future dreams evaporating with each new scan.

At his Emory Hospital bedside that night, post-surgery in ICU, amidst the machines' beeps, the tubes, bandages and scars, Michael and I prayed through the tears. His mom, Jo-anne, came to stay the night in the room, and in her hands was the Medjugorje book, *Pray with the Heart!* I had given it to her years before, when her husband battled cancer and won. We exchanged a look—tenderness and compassion without words. I departed the room and headed back to the hotel so she could be alone with her son. I reached out to our Julia to give her the news. The surgery was successful. The tumor was like a clean perfect ball that was scooped from his brain. He would recover.

On February 2, the feast of the Presentation of Jesus in the Temple, I went to Mass at the Basilica of the Sacred Heart of Jesus, a historical church a few blocks from the hospital in Atlanta. This place was my refuge. I could silently pour my heart out. On this day, a priest from Poland shared a memory from his childhood. The tradition in his home village on this feast day was to take special candles to the church, to be blessed. These candles would be taken home and lit in times of trouble. It would remind the people that the light of Christ would be with them and protect them. He said that as a child this gave him great comfort. He then instructed us to look at the candle on the altar and told us to be a light to anyone we would encounter. I would carry this thought back to the hospital.

Matthew was bouncing back so profoundly from these surgeries, with a strength that shocked the doctors. His will to survive was extraordinary. Matt was pushing himself be-yond the limits and was grateful for all the enthusiasm and encouragement. The highs were amazing and the drops extreme. For her part, Lauren also was holding it together.

Matthew was discharged again, surviving with a horse-shoe-shaped scar on the side of his head, and looking remarkable—an incredible boy enduring and pulling through brain surgery! Lauren's generous parents had been managing Luke on the home front while this episode unfurled. Now they would stay and continue to help their daughter and Matt handle the various follow-up appointments and physical therapies which encouraged his healing and strength. This proved to be a balanced waiting game, as the other tumors remained quiet.

We returned, numb, to our life in New Jersey, temporarily. For a few weeks we went through the routines. Then we'd return to Atlanta to help and be with Matthew. A month or so before the brain surgery I had committed to participation in a Life in the Spirit seminar at Saint James. It had begun while we were in Atlanta. The sessions were recorded. I looked forward to the escape of writing notes and listening—anything to occupy my mind.

I journaled from the book of Ephesians. Saint Paul spoke about the burdens we carry and the need to put on the armor of God, to build and strengthen ourselves in life. Another statement that got my attention was made by Mother Teresa, referring to us as a pencil in God's hand. We must surrender to God's will and allow Him to work. There were so many Scripture passages and saintly quotes referenced that highlighted my family's hurting, desperate hearts. I read, prayed, and pleaded with all my being to cooperate with God for our dear Matthew, and begged for a radical miracle. Full healing!

For a short time, there was calm. Michael and I began planning our departure back to Atlanta. We'd take Matt to appointments and drive Luke to school and pitch in and help with whatever else was needed. Michael debated with me when I told him I had decided to drive so we could have a car there. I am notorious for making long solo rides; I enjoy audiobooks and quiet time and refer to these rides as a retreat of sorts.

My first stop was Lauren's alma mater, James Madison, to rendezvous with a good college friend from Virginia and her husband. We talked, walked the campus, had lunch and they listened to all of my heartaches about Matthew and were genuinely wonderful. Next stop was the home of my brother Rick, on Lake Hartwell in Fair Play, South Carolina. He and his wife Jan listened and showed tenderness as I rambled on and on. We enjoyed dinner and time together, catching up on their five children and families. I was going to stay a few days, but in the morning I got an alarming call.

Matthew was in an ambulance, on his way to the hospital. He could not move from the neck down. It was horrifying! Poor Matt, poor Lauren, and Luke! The tears began to fall. Rick, Jan, and I prayed together and then I left abruptly.

I was only two plus hours away and found my way to the hospital and his room in record time.

His trusted oncologist was telling Matt there was not much else they could do. My heart sank. Conversation ensued about more chemo, but the doctor did not believe it would work, so his recommendation was hospice in the hospital. Then his words of hope: to bring him home. With tears in his eyes, Matt looked at Lauren, her parents and me, firmly saying, "Take care of Lauren and Luke." Matthew's first concern was for them, his family. My chest heaved; this was devastating. I left the room as Lauren and Matt talked. I headed to the airport to pick up Michael.

He appeared within minutes of my arrival, and we drove back to Emory. Matt's brother, his wife, Matt's mom, his stepfather, and half-sister also boarded planes in New York. Having the car was helpful. These were Matthew Lorenzo's last days—unless God answered the prayers for a radical miracle.

Hospice nurses were—and are—a gift, soothing the patient and the family as hours turned into days. We moved in and out. Walking the same sidewalk, using the same elevator, the same cold hallway over and over to be with him to the end. We watched him sleep, chat, try to eat, talk sports and love. He was amazingly with it, even funny. Crazy timing: it was Lauren's birthday. Matt was not sure what to get his girl and suggested to buy her workout clothes. We decided otherwise. Lauren's cousin's daughter was sent off to buy the gift. Cards were purchased in the gift shop for Matt to choose. He dictated the note to me as I wrote the words to his partner, his wife, his love. He would give Lauren the gift when she arrived that night, after she kissed their son good-night at home. She slept in the hospice room with Matthew. Lauren had so much to juggle.

We talked about advice for his son, which expanded into some of his pet peeves. No close talking; personal space is important. Use plates! What is it with the crumbs? As a child, Matt hated the Hulk, and we smiled, remembering.

It was intimate as he stated advice about girls: "Run, child, run!" Then said, "Just kidding. Treat them with RE-SPECT!" When you try out for a team or whatever you want to do, "Go balls to the wall." Matt smiled as these words came out of his mouth. When you experience failure, pick yourself up, and again, "Go balls to the wall!" (From a dictionary, the history of the phrase comes from using maximum effort, energy, speed without caution or restraint. It possibly originated as an aviation term referring to the throttle levers of a military aircraft which had a ball on the top.) Matt continued. When driving a car, USE your horn. A little tap-tap to let them know. In the midst, he said, "Do not mourn me, celebrate me. Set a good foundation." He loved saying CAPICHE! and REALLY!

It had been a weirdly good day … days before he would pass. Selfishly, I wanted to make sure Matt had the proper sacramental anointing, so I called their parish in Marietta and asked for a priest to come. The basilica a few blocks away was also called for the priest to come and Lauren had already asked for a priest when she had met with the hospital administration. Much to my amazement, three priests arrived within minutes of each other, all giving Matthew the sacrament of the Anointing of the Sick. He received a trifecta of prayer!

One night my husband and I were in the room with a sleeping Matthew. We were the last shift before Lauren, after some time with Luke, would come to spend the night. Michael was sleeping on the couch, and I picked up the booklet from the New Jersey Life in the Spirit course. I read in Scripture, **John 17**, **The Prayer of Jesus**, which begins with these words: *When Jesus had said this, he raised his eyes to heaven and said, "Father, the hour has come."*

This was the end for Jesus, and here I sit, looking at Matthew. Bless this boy, my stepson. I read onward. … *Are you ready for death?* REALLY!

My eyes went from Matthew to the booklet. I read on: *God has a plan, for He loves us. Through sin we are separated from God. He sent His Son to die for our sins. Would you like to receive God's forgiveness?*

What matters most to Jesus is the attitude of our heart, our honesty. Matthew had a beautiful heart.

Lauren arrived, and we said good-night and left her with her husband. My heart was breaking for her.

In the waiting of the days following, Matthew was able to see Luke. They exchanged "I love you," "I love you more," a volley back and forth. He had told Luke that if he needed him after he was gone, to close his eyes and Matthew would be there. His son, his mini-me—they looked and acted so alike. Lauren's friend shared that Matt's recreational Atlanta basketball team was dedicating the court to him. They were honoring this boy as he lay here. He commented on his brother's pink sweatshirt. Then his brother put on a hospital gown, reminiscent of childhood when they were always dressed the same. At one point he insanely remarked … that he was sorry it was taking so long to die. So long! Matthew, how crazy, you are just thirty-six. We waited, and he wanted us not to be inconvenienced. What a guy!

Michael, my husband, had been keeping his father, Frank, abreast of what was happening with Matthew. Frank lived in Baldwin, New York, in the home Michael grew up in, from high school, onward. On this particular day, Matt was quiet; he only raised his wonderful eyebrows up and down to communicate; he slept most of the day.

A call came to Michael from his dad's neighbor. That was strange. Then the shocking news: Matthew's grandfather had a heart attack on the front lawn of his home after taking his garbage out. He had been resuscitated but was unresponsive. He was in the ICU at the hospital, and Michael's sister was on her way to his side. They had just talked the day before. Oh no!

I called Father Sean, the pastor from my church in New Jersey. He had been talking to me about Matthew and guiding my prayers. When I told him about my father-in-law, Father Sean drove out to Long Island to be with him. We were greatly amazed, comforted, and soothed at this gesture. We are forever grateful for the actions of this holy priest.

With this news, all we could do was pray, wait and love. As Matthew neared his end, we experienced a divine moment. His pulse slowed, eyes closed, Lauren's tears fell as she held his arm and hand. Her strong dad stood behind her to hold and brace his young, only daughter. Matthew's head began to move up and down, right and left, as if being questioned. We watched in quiet awe at this intimate exchange. All his loved ones surrounded the bed in a tight circle of love. There were tears, and a sense of surprise as we watched.

After a lapse of time, his eyes fluttered and opened and a small grin appeared as he asked, "What's for lunch!"

We all moved away from the bed, sighing with relief.

He said, "No, really, this is perfect." In a quiet voice he asked, "What do each of you want from heaven?" His gaze moved around the bed.

My dear husband, Matt's dad, said, "Matt, run free. Get out of this body. Run!"

There were other requests, but the best was the way his eyes took in each person, especially Lauren. He loved her profoundly. He told us that he loved us all so much, and again told us to take care of Lauren and Luke.

He looked up and said, "They want me in the middle."

We didn't know what he saw in the invisible space beyond the bed, but clearly there was a "they" directing him.

Matthew continued talking. He wanted to be celebrated and asked that we not be sad. It was amazing. It was his last exchange, and what a gift.

Matthew John Lorenzo passed on March 19, the feast of Saint Joseph. Saint Joseph is known as the intercessor of a happy death and for families. Matthew's funeral was on the first day of spring, at Holy Family Catholic Church. The crowd was large as we prayed.

Lauren had written, *All who knew Matthew can attest to his authenticity and integrity towards family, friends and career. Matthew was fearless and tenacious in every facet of his life.* I am thankful for the young boy who had stood at the altar as one of our best men and who will and forever be a testament of love and honor.

Lauren and friends carried out a tremendous event in tribute to Matthew, with the help of the Falcons football league. The backyard of their home in Marietta was transformed. It was a comfort to spend time with friends and family, sharing stories of this man as the sorrow swelled in our hearts at losing him. We watched his son Luke and the other children huddled over markers and paper, doing crafts, and then running and giving us stickers on our hands. Life was going to move forward with a missing piece.

21

Frank

"Dear children! My call for you is prayer. May prayer be a joy for you and a wreath which binds you to God. Little children, trials will come and you will not be strong, and sin will reign, but if you are mine, you will win, because your refuge will be the Heart of my Son Jesus. Therefore, little children, return to prayer until prayer becomes life for you in the day and the night. Thank you for having responded to my call." July 25, 2019

John, a dear friend of Lauren and Matthew, was serving a choice whiskey at the gathering for Matthew. In the midst of family and friends, sharing our love and stories of Matthew, my glass was refilled over and over. When I went to stand, I was completely unstable; I could not walk without assistance. It was clearly time to leave. My husband and my brother helped me to the car and back to the hotel to sleep and recover. I had lost it. I was worthless. I had drowned myself in this cocktail and now would slumber. I clung to Michael's hand in my restless, sleepless tumbling amid the tide of emotions, knowing that early the next morning we'd drive to New York, to Frank's bedside in the hospital intensive care unit.

It was the fifth Sunday of Lent. As we drove, I looked for Catholic churches and Mass times in the towns we approached. Finally, one coincided and we got off the exit only to drive through country roads. This Mass was not to be an easy on, easy off stop, as my dear husband preferred. When we turned into the parking lot it was crowded.

The church loomed large, modern and new. We genuflected and knelt. God, I am sorry for my sins and please help us in our travel and in the days ahead. Bless Lauren, Luke, our family, and Frank. Thank You, Lord. Michael and I held hands as we knelt, stood, sat listening and taking the words of Scripture to our hearts. Tears rolled. We leaned into each other with a bond, exchanging strength as needed. After Mass, the drive north ensued.

Unfortunately, I could not contribute to the drive; my heart was breaking. My husband, who had buried his son, drove to his dad. We talked of our various conversations with Matt's co-workers and laughed at some of the stories. Sharing this stuff lightened Michael's load. We cried, too, and talked of the plan once we got home.

We were exhausted after the more than ten-hour drive, so spent the night in our bed at 2 Providence in New Jersey, and then on to New York hospital in the a.m. Yuck, to be in a hospital once again, after all the weeks with Matt. I was bolstering myself for what we might see.

Thank God Frank recognized us and took our hands, but he was clearly confused and living in the past. He asked Mike to attend to the tenants from the Brooklyn apartment above the store that was run by his family more than sixty years prior. He talked of the war and covered his head with the sheet and cried when remembering things. The doctors had stabilized his heart and the plan was to move him out of critical care, but he was not well. My husband's two sisters were there, and they were an awesome united front. My husband desperately needed his family.

His sister from California and I were there to transition Frank from ICU to a regular room. Once he was settled in the bed, with the curtain drawn closed between his roommate and him, he pointed to the TV. My sister-in-law took the remote, turned it on, and to my surprise, the chaplet of Divine Mercy was being sung on the station in this non-Christian hospital. He loved this devotion and sighed. We joined in the chaplet. It was clearly a blessing.

I returned to New Jersey to create a semblance of order, pick up mail and food and take care of all that had been neglected while we were in Atlanta. Michael remained with Frank. Five days after our drive home, on the morning of March 27, Frank breathed his last. He was eighty-eight years old. How unexpected!

He was now out of the confusion and at peace. We were numb. His funeral was planned to be held in his beloved neighborhood parish of St. Christopher—the church where he had buried his beloved wife four years prior and celebrated weddings and the baptism of our Julia. He was a man of faith, a veteran of WWII, a Knight of Columbus and a man who shepherded his wife through her disease of Alzheimer's. Father Sean from New Jersey came to preside at the funeral and officiate at the burial. We were humbled and grateful in this time of loss.

What a Lent: the sacrifices, trials, tribulations as we walked through the past forty days. Frank was buried on the Tuesday of Holy Week. I took comfort in the fact that both Matthew and his grandfather would be in heaven for Easter, and I could only imagine what that would be like.

Life went on; we took a deep breath and moved forward. The home that Michael had lived in since high school was being cleaned and prepared for sale. All the stuff was sorted, packed, sold, pitched, treasured and labeled. I was reminded of the Scripture, **1 Timothy 6:7**: *For we brought nothing into the world, just as we shall not be able to take anything out of it.*

Through the losses, our Julia remained in Italy for her semester abroad, knowing her brother and her grandfather would have wanted it this way. I prayed, as she had to deal with this pain so far away. Thank God she had found a good friend who could be by her side. I struggled with thoughts of bringing her home, but after many conversations, did not. Lord, watch over her wounds and forgive me if I made the wrong decision.

22

Out to Sea

"Dear children! Also today I am with you and with joy I call all of you: pray and believe in the power of prayer. Open your hearts, little children, so that God may fill you with His love and you will be a joy to others. Your witness will be powerful and everything you do will be interwoven with God's tenderness. I am with you and I pray for you and your conversion until you put God in the first place. Thank you for having responded to my call." May 25, 2015

On April 2, 2015, Michael and I flew to Atlanta. We had decided to bring our girl home for Matthew's burial at sea. At the airport, anticipation and excitement mingled; I couldn't wait to see her. I not only missed her terribly, but worried about her. Soon we would all be together. She traveled from Parma, Italy, to Milan, to Paris for her flight to Atlanta. She had been gone since January 12.

Our reunion felt powerful—arms finally entwined. Tears of joy welled as I gazed at this girl. She looked incredible. Our precious independent daughter had been far away, dealing with the losses, amidst adventures to magical European cities.

We rented a car, drove to Lauren's and retrieved our grandson Luke. We wanted to give Lauren some time with her parents on her own. We began the five-hour drive south to Ponte Vedra Beach, Florida. This was where family and friends would stay for a week and Matthew's ashes would rest in the sea. This was his desire and the place they chose. On the ride we basked in the details of Julia's travels—the cities, her studies and how she navigated and managed all she was experiencing.

Our son Mike, with his wife Barbara and Mikey, drove from Long Island, New York. We rented a house on the beach. Lauren, her parents, and friends were in a condo not far from us.

It was the Holy Triduum, the three days before Easter. I found Our Lady Star of the Sea Church in Ponte Vedra Beach, my respite to grieve and pray alone. I did my best to attend the services, with all that was going on. On Easter Sunday, we arrived at a standing room only, packed church. It was the Resurrection. We had made it! We could stand as family and celebrate with Jesus, knowing that our Matthew and Frank were at rest.

During the week we rested, cooked in our funky 1970s rental, and went between Lauren's condo down the beach and the house. Then came the day for the burial; only five could go on the fishing boat. So, Lauren, Luke, my husband, his son Mike, and Julia boarded in Mayport. They went out three miles to deeper waters. Lauren spoke of how much

Matt loved the water. At the set time and distance, Matt's ashes were placed in the water, words were expressed, champagne opened, love voiced. On the return to the dock, surprisingly, two dolphins swam near the boat. The collective sorrow and mixture of feelings stirred with the wonder of this sight. The family talked of Matthew and his grandpa Frank. When the five joined us at the restaurant where we waited, they talked of their amazement of the dolphins swimming alongside the boat.

Dear Matthew, rest in peace. Thank you for being my stepson, my friend, my first teacher in parenting and for marrying Lauren and giving us Luke to watch grow up. I still ask, Why? Why did you have to go so young? I look forward to conversing with you about this one day when we meet again. I am confident of that.

Life was and is not stagnant. I was constantly reminded to be grateful for the days I had because we don't know what tomorrow will bring. Sometimes we cannot make sense of the chaos of cancer, heart attacks, diseases, or accidents; they just are, and we must love through it all.

23

New Normal

"Dear children, I am calling you to be courageous and to not grow weary, because even the smallest good—the smallest sign of love—conquers evil which is all the more visible. My children, listen to me so that good may overcome, so that you may come to know the love of my Son. This is the greatest happiness—the hands of my Son that embrace, of Him who loves the soul, of Him who has given Himself for you and is always giving Himself anew in the Eucharist, of Him who has the words of eternal life. To come to know His love, to follow in His footsteps, means to have a wealth of spirituality. This is the wealth which gives good feelings and sees love and goodness everywhere.

"Apostles of my love, my children, be like the rays of the sun which with the warmth of my Son's love warm everyone around them. My children, the world needs apostles of love; the world needs much prayer, but prayer spoken with the heart and the soul and not only pronounced with the lips. My children, long for holiness but in humility, in the humility which permits my Son to do that which He desires through you.

"My children, your prayers, your words, thoughts and actions—all of this either opens or closes the doors to the Kingdom of Heaven for you. My Son showed you the way and gave

you hope, and I am consoling and encouraging you because, my children, I had come to know pain, but I had faith and hope. Now I have the reward of life in the Kingdom of my Son. Therefore, listen to me, have courage and do not grow weary."
October 2, 2018

Have courage! I was reading a fictional story, *The Invention of Wings*, by Sue Monk Kidd. A character in the book says, "We are all yearning for a piece of the sky, aren't we? I suspect God plants these yearnings in us so we'll at least try and change the course of things. We must try, that's all."

We were on our flight home. We had hugged our Julia goodbye and separated once again. She was returning to Parma, Italy, to finish the semester. She had matured in this European adventure, this time abroad. I missed her. I was thankful she shared this time with family. But honestly, I wanted to take her home and cling to her, knowing she was safe in her room.

I read the last pages of the book and then attempted rest, but this was not happening. I looked at my Kindle E-reader and referred to the books I hadn't finished. Ah, there was *The Life of the Blessed Virgin Mary: From the Visions of Ven. Anne Catherine Emmerich*. I had thirteen percent left to read. I open it and to my wonder, I was on chapter fifteen, "The Death of the Holy Virgin." Timing was everything. The words that made my soul soar instead of sink, in this plane above the clouds, was the following thought. The Blessed

Mother, knowing the end was near, gathered the apostles one by one from distant evangelistic missions. In her peacefulness, she gave directives for her death, appointing who got her belongings and where she wanted to be buried. The apostle Peter said the prayers and gave her Communion. Several apostles, vested in white garments, set a table, an altar, and a service was conducted. She was anointed and covered in a white coverlet. They prayed around her. It was serene. These scenes were from her visions. Catherine Emmerich elaborated on every detail. The Blessed Mother gazed upward, her arms raised. Then the ceiling of her home disappeared, and clouds of light appeared and the faces of angels. A path of light poured down upon Mary. She left the bed and her soul moved to meet loved ones. It was so incredible to read this after losing Matthew and Frank. To think of the unseen happening around them the moment their eyes closed. Their heart ceases and an invisible light shines on them as they leave their body and the soul moves towards heaven. Granted this was about the sinless, immaculate Blessed Lady who was assumed into heaven, but there was hope for our loved ones in the promises of faith!

The blessings, the white sheets, the words of Matthew as he gazed attentively into the invisible, "they want me in the middle" … all soothed my soul. I closed my eyes in thanksgiving for this book at this moment in time. Tomorrow would be Divine Mercy Sunday; I had tried to stay faithful to the nine days of chaplet prayers. Jesus, I trust in YOU!

I recorded thoughts in my journal about inspiration, awareness of life, death, purpose. When we get back, I have my job, the library, the kids. When I left for Atlanta, at the time Matthew was declining, the principal canceled the classes and closed the doors to await my return. No need for subs or for me to leave plans. The students and teachers would wait. They were welcome to bring in a class to read, drop off overdue books, but no exchanges. The circulation desk did not circulate; it collected piles, creating a wall of books waiting for me to check in and classes to resume. There was much to do, and the distraction would be welcome.

Sometime after our return, I was out to breakfast with a friend. We were in the midst of our conversation when a stranger politely interrupted, handed me a torn piece of paper and walked away. On it was written: "Angels watching over you, from **Psalm 91:11–12**, which reads *For God commands the Angels to guard you in all your ways. With their hands they shall support you, lest you strike your foot against a stone.*" Wow, interesting and something to ponder. My friend and I sat in awe and curiosity.

Dreams frequented my slumber, and on the eve of Matthew's birthday, my dreams took me into Manhattan ... a dark, dreary street ... I was walking aimlessly. My feet were so heavy, and I was walking crooked. A man yelled at me, and suddenly Julia was there, and we were frightened and had to keep moving away. When I woke and turned on the TV, there was a minister speaking, who said, "You just have

to get out on a limb with God. He will show you the way."
Strange it was not the news, not an advertisement, but a minister. I did need to trust in the way I was being led.

Some new books arrived at the Saint James library. One
had received a Caldecott Honor: *Sam & Dave Dig a Hole*, by
Mac Barnett. I was waiting for this one and excited to read it
to the classes. It was funny, light, and simple. We had all
probably dug a hole, hoping for buried treasure at some
point in our life. I read the book and engaged the classes in
discussions. I found they were commenting on it and going
deeper: an adventure in which we strive for goals, sometimes
they are before us, but we don't have the patience to keep
going. We may see the world differently. Sometimes the students gave such fresh perspectives.

I picked out a book for myself on my Kindle: *The First
Phone Call from Heaven*, by Mitch Albom. I was a little ob-
sessed with heaven at the moment. I was on my way home
from Cincinnati after a brief visit to love Mom and give my
sister a break. Mom was declining, and I was missing the lady
who I could talk to about anything. Today would have been
Lauren and Matt's tenth anniversary—so tough for Lauren.
A quote from the book that I had noted: *"We desire to set our
compass, real life sets the course."* So true. Who would have
imagined all that had transpired when the two of them said
their I do's. Another quote was: *"No soul remembered is ever
really gone."* So accurate!

Julia returned home after the semester in Italy. Sitting side by side to look at pictures of all her excursions and hear her stories was refreshing. She would begin an internship in a clinic this summer. I had one more month of school.

It was also Michael's and my twenty-fifth wedding anniversary. We had initially planned on going to Italy and meet up with Julia, but instead—with all that had transpired—we decided to return to the place where we had exchanged our vows, Vermont. It was quiet, peaceful, and perfect. We hiked up the ski mountains we loved to descend and ate at our favorite places. We returned to the Hermitage for dinner, the place where we had dined, danced, celebrated, and gathered with our loved ones.

Once the school year came to a close, we made the rounds to visit family in California and Atlanta and had some fun in New York. By the end of the summer Mom was declining further and it was decided for her to move into assisted living. My awesome sister, who was her primary caregiver, arranged all the details. I drove to Cincinnati to assist in the transfer. On the way I detoured to Franciscan University in Steubenville and as I walked the grounds, I was briefly introduced to the author Scott Hahn. We shook hands, and he proceeded to a meeting he was rushing to attend. I got in my car and laughed. I was a big fan of his writing; meeting him was very cool! When I arrived in Cincinnati, Mom was confused, especially about the move. It was upsetting for her, but it was best—nonetheless, very hard. It was heartwarming for the week that I was there to hug her, love her and comfort her, but as I departed, I sobbed. Mom was moving closer to the finish line.

At the end of the school year, Saint James had hired a new principal; the other had retired. I had introduced myself to the new principal and met with him before returning to Cincinnati. I had a pitch to make and wanted to get it off my chest before my departure. I requested an increase in salary for the year ahead, as contracts were in the works. He responded favorably—quickly, actually—and agreed to the request. But he had to speak to the board before it was official. Disappointingly, while driving home from Cincinnati I got a message that there would be no change in salary for the coming year. Then, surprisingly, I also received a call from the principal of another school. He asked me to interview for the position as media specialist. I prayed and then talked to a spiritual director for a few hours as I drove, considering the options.

When I returned to New Jersey I went for the interview and was offered the job. I accepted. I returned to Saint James, resigned, and collected my things. It was surreal. Saint James had been my home. I had automated, weeded, refurbished, and reconstructed the library with the help of devoted parents, resulting in a thriving hub of the school. Julia had been down the hall from second to seventh grade. It was sad to walk the halls for the last time. As my daughter had matured, so had I: as a teacher, speaker, and devotee of my faith.

Now things were changing, and it was a mix of sadness and excitement. Only several days remained before the school year would begin and, as a self-taught computer person, I had a lot to grasp, absorb and learn. I'd be creating lessons for instructing technology. The school year began with a full schedule of library classes and computer instruction. I was determined, trying to grasp the ins and outs of Google for Education, having a sixth-grade homeroom, and learning the routines of this pre-K to eighth grade Catholic elementary school. I spent much time after hours, when the school quieted, to think, get my act together, plan, read, learn, and try to advance my skills.

Julia returned to her last year at Boston College. I rolled up my sleeves and dove into school. Everything was going well. I felt the stress, but the students, faculty and support were fantastic and to my aesthetic temperament. The space was beautiful. It had been an addition to the school several years prior. The wraparound windows looked out to a tree-lined field which was often a spot for grazing deer. The library needed much weeding and organizing to update and function for the students to thrive. With the help of another school media specialist, I was figuring it out.

In December Lauren and Luke visited for an early Christmas. With heavy hearts we were experiencing our first Christmas without Matthew and Frank. So many firsts in that year with the huge void. Our Lauren was doing her best and being strong and courageous for Luke. She was required to maintain a happy face in the midst of missing the love of her life, as she did her best raising their little guy. I admired her tenacity. It was humbling to all be together and thank God for the love surrounding the family, and especially for the kids. They helped turn the tears into laughter and joy.

We had a blizzard in January. It was blinding, beautiful … and I was ecstatic because the forecasts indicated we'd have many snow days! It reminded me of being a kid, and I loved the feeling. When the snow ceased blowing, I grabbed the shovel and began clearing the driveway. It was a beautiful day, the sky a perfect shade of blue. The day before, as Michael shoveled to keep up with the drifts, I had lazily stayed in my PJs and watched out the window to capture the exquisite beauty of the storm. He had worked so hard, his back was aching.

Prior to this, we had always hired a snowplow for the season, but in hopes of selling our home, which was on the market, we had overlooked renewing our contract. The sky was a brilliant blue and the scenery spectacular—a white blanket and drifts of snow so high it was magical. I shoveled, sang, and enjoyed the exercise and the fresh air, but it was daunting. Michael came outside and surveyed my efforts; for all my hours of shoveling, he pointed out that I was not making much progress. At any rate, the clearing of the snow opened a door of unknown bone issues that would challenge me for a long time. I strained my back severely, only to learn that I had a compression fracture.

After the many days of school closures and doctor visits, the doc recommended that in my job I avoid bending over. Ha-ha! And the recommendation was to squat in the movements of my work. So, to accommodate the lifting of books, my bending over computers to assist children and the shelving of books, I squatted so as not to further injure my back. By April my legs started to hurt, and I returned to the doctor. The answer: my pain was likely attributed to the nerves stemming from my back injury, which sounded reasonable.

We congregated with family to pay tribute to Matthew on the first anniversary, and his brother Mike strategized the creation of a legacy. The Matt Lorenzo Scholarship Fund Golf Outing was established to support an athlete from his high school alma mater. The first event would take place that June.

It was a success. Their childhood friends gathered to celebrate and raise funds. Luke was growing up without Matthew and this was sad, but this incredible little guy, a mini-me of his dad, gave us all a part of Matthew. Luke thrived in his own uniqueness yet was imprinted with characteristics and traits like his father. Thank You, God, for Luke to carry on the Lorenzo name, for this legacy to be created and all the other beautiful tributes in Atlanta being aired for the man, husband, father, son, beloved friend, and colleague. Matthew Lorenzo lives on in our hearts.

Two days after the first anniversary of losing Matt, my brother Rick called to tell me he had been diagnosed with esophageal cancer. Oh God, no! Please, Lord, help! This news and his treatment plans sparked heightened prayers, pleas and a newer depth of intimate conversations on life that he and I had not shared before.

Julia graduated from Boston College in May, and it was a grand celebratory weekend. Her hands were blessed as she earned her nursing degree. Wow, seventeen years of education completed—she had done it! I was grateful for the answered prayers of protection, of solid friends, outstanding teachers, awesome grades and the skills to work as a nurse. We wished her future success. Then we moved her home.

Throughout the graduation celebrations I was on megadoses of over-the-counter pain relievers. By June, the pain in my legs was increasingly worse. I went for a full body scan and learned I had bilateral femur stress fractures. There was a concrete reason for my pain!

The treatment recommendations: non-weight bearing and use crutches. As I had the fractures in both legs, crutches helped, but it was clearly not enough. Weight was always being applied. Lying in bed worked and relieved the pain. With a computer on my lap and a list of tasks, I rationalized that this time was going to be productive. This injury was going to give me a summer to strategize for the next school year. I could write goals, get lessons planned and grow in my skills for the digital world.

Interestingly, my focus from school shifted to all things spiritual. I became a YouTube groupie. I was addicted, listening to talks on saints such as Saint Ignatius; and *The Discernment of Spirits: 14 Rules for Discernment,* by Fr. Timothy M. Gallagher; and to Fr. Donald H. Calloway's amazing conversion story. I journaled, read, worked on this story, found that the direction of my originally planned focused recovery time was moving further away from my media center and technology instruction and more into the depths of the divine.

We vacationed in Charleston since this was planned before my diagnosis. It was a struggle with the legs, but great to be together. On our way home we stopped at my brother's lake house. Rick was undergoing chemotherapy after having an operation on his esophagus. He looked good, considering this unexpected shocking development in his early retirement. He was outgoing, healthy, and active. I would never have guessed he'd have been in this situation.

His goal was finding a new perspective and turning inward, paying greater attention to faith. His wife, a spiritual beacon, supported and joined his prayers. Being involved with the Knights of Columbus had inspired him to ask us all to pray for intercession through Michael J. McGivney, the founder of the Knights. Venerable Father McGivney needed another miracle on his path to sainthood. Rick and I called each other more often, checking in and conversing—the God stuff and life drawing us closer.

Our New Jersey home continued to be on the market and the prospects of selling, slow. The market was tough, and we had to wait it out. All the while struggling with my health. I was not feeling stronger or improving to the degree I had hoped, and worried about my return to school. I went to school to survey the library I had abruptly left behind when I learned about my legs. There were piles of books needing to be cleared from the system, piles of books the students had returned in that last week and ones that needed cataloging. I was overwhelmed! Hoping to feel the energy to dive in and work, I sat in a chair and cried. I did not have it in me. The principal was willing to work with my health struggles. We discussed a substitute until I felt better. But, in reality, I did not have my mojo. I was considering this, but my motivation lacked. The thought of writing appealing lessons felt heavy, not exciting. I was clearly in a slump. I shifted my perspective to the kids and what they deserved: it was a teacher who was enthusiastic, presenting lessons that inspired and encouraged learning. My uncertainty for delivering this created more stress as August loomed. My desire to resign felt stronger and stronger. On August 15, I resigned via email and then headed to Mass at the church next to the school. It was the feast of the Assumption of Our Lady. On this day in 1991, I had been with Paul in Medjugorje. I knew the principal would be there. As he saw me walk towards him on the crutches, he understood. With sadness on both our parts, he accepted my resignation and offered me the position back as soon as I felt stronger. I was relieved and grateful.

At nine o'clock that same night, as Mike and I reclined, reading in bed, both our phones dinged with messages. It was the realtor telling us that an offer had been made on the house. Wow! I felt that the Blessed Mother was clearly watching over us. I guess I was not supposed to return to the school; this was in the divine plan for us. Our daughter, on the other hand, was happy, but now felt the pressure of getting a job and finding an apartment. I enlisted prayers from my faith-sharing friends and an absolutely amazing outcome occurred. Within a week, her brother had contacted a friend and Julia got an interview at Memorial Sloan-Kettering. On the feast day of Saint Monica, they offered her a job, and by August 29 she got a confirmation on an apartment she had looked at in New York City. Funny thing: Her realtor's name was Michael Matthew Fine. Our sons' names! How crazy, and, on top of it, our Matthew used to tell his dad over and over, "It is going to be fine." We were all starting new chapters. We were clearly being helped!

The buyers wanted us out in a month, so we scrambled to pack, sort, sell and strategize our plan. We would store in New Jersey and rent in Florida. In the past few years, we had discussed where we would relocate and, with Matthew's burial in Florida, that solidified it for my husband, and I agreed. We also knew we could not fathom buying a house that quickly.

Julia was a superstar. She arranged the yard sale. I was the bubble wrap queen, packing boxes while sitting with crutches propped nearby. Julia's job at Memorial Sloan-Kettering would begin in October, so she had the time to help. Thank You, God! She would move into her apartment on October 1, and we would begin our drive to Florida on the second.

Once the house closed, we spent a few weeks in Long Island with our Mike, Barbara, and Mikey. They took furniture we did not want to move to Florida. A win-win for all. We crowded their garage with Julia's things before her move. It was hectic and nerve-racking, but mission accomplished. Our sixteen years in our home at 2 Providence was packed with wonderful memories. Now we moved forward and south to embark on a new quest.

24

Our Lady Star of the Sea

"Dear children! Also today I call you to be like the stars, which by their light give light and beauty to others so they may rejoice. Little children, also you be the radiance, beauty, joy and peace – and especially prayer – for all those who are far from my love and the love of my Son Jesus. Little children, witness your faith and prayer in joy, in the joy of faith that is in your hearts; and pray for peace, which is a precious gift from God. Thank you for having responded to my call." September 25, 2014

Really? A flat tire! Our cars packed to the brim, a bike on the roof. Sunday morning was cloudy and cool as we began our drive south. We had left Long Island early, having packed up the cars the night before and said our farewells. Our dear kids had been hosting us, our stuff and Julia's long enough. My husband and son had moved Julia into her sixth-floor walkup apartment on Saturday. We said our goodbyes to Julia; this was strange and a mix of emotions.

Exciting for sure, but also melancholy knowing there would now be miles between us all. Only about an hour into the ride, Mike's car hit something on the road and—oh no, a flat! Not on a side road, but on the George Washington

Bridge which links New York and New Jersey. We pulled off after the bridge, and lo and behold, we were so lucky. We made some calls, located a place close by that had the one special tire he needed and a garage. Mike emptied the stuff off my passenger seat to be able to load the tire from another location, and off he drove. I sat in a dingy waiting room and couldn't help but smile when I looked up and, on the small TV, the Jacksonville Jaguars were playing. I had a horrible cold and sat with a box of tissues on my lap, questioning this interesting hurdle. In about two hours we were back on the road to a halfway destination. South of Richmond, a hotel would be waiting for us.

Praying and listening to spiritual stuff was my thing on the road, and not feeling so good, I felt lifted by the Rosary and various talks. My nose was turning a nice shade of red. Praying for others over the miles felt purposeful. We pulled into the hotel parking lot, got soup, slept and were back on the road in the morning.

We crossed the Florida border late in the afternoon. The palm trees and downtown of Jacksonville lay ahead, the picturesque St. Johns River interwoven in the cityscape. We were almost at the place we would call home. It was warm, sunny and I was feeling the stress melt. We settled into our rental condo in a community called Sawgrass. We were exhausted but relieved. Tuesday, October 4, the feast of Saint Francis, I thought of Mike's dad, Frank, and his love of his name saint. I went to Mass to say thanks that we had made it and Julia was settled, and Michael, Barbara and Mikey were thriving once again. With a heart full of hope, I knelt in a pew at Our Lady Star of the Sea Catholic Church. When I got back to the condo, I poured my coffee and turned on the news. Hurricane reports flooded the broadcasts. The hurricane's name: MATTHEW! Really, God?

Mike and I unpacked and set out for the grocery store and to register our names and cars with the homeowners association. I continued to watch the TV news. Not good. The storm was huge and heading in our direction; we would probably be in the zone for a mandatory evacuation. Oh no! The hurricane fever was completely new to me, and it was freaking me out. I turned off the TV and willed the storm away. I made lists, sent emails, and made dinner, drank wine and we took a ride to the beach. This was supposed to be good for us, here in Florida. Then the dark clouds came, and rain began. As I drifted to sleep, images of crowded highways and the storm flooded my sleepless night. I woke early, as did Mike, and we started looking for hotels. There was nothing; everything was booked. After several hours we secured a room about a three-hour drive away. We decided to leave on Thursday. We stored our stuff on the beds in case there was flooding and put Mike's car in a secured garage away from the beach and began our evacuation.

We stopped at several closer exits to see if we could get a room, but no way—all booked. At one point I read a review of the hotel we had reserved; there was talk of a prison nearby and non-hotel guests in the pool and lobby, and it had only two stars. We pulled off at the exit and began driving, but both of us were uneasy. We turned around and drove back towards the highway. There was a hotel. We pulled off. It looked nice and, as a matter of fact, was brand-new. I called our daughter-in-law, Lauren. Mike went inside to check on availability.

Lauren answered, and I explained about evacuating, no hotels, stress of hurricane Matthew, just arriving … and asked, pleaded … "Could we come and stay with you in Atlanta?"

She uncharacteristically paused. It was quiet, and then she said, "I was not prepared to tell you this, but I am dating, and he is taking me away this weekend …."

"Lauren," I said, "we love you and want you to be happy. You have been through so much, losing Matthew, and we want you happy."

I could sense some release in her voice. She said that of course we could come, and could we watch Luke? She explained that she had arranged for a babysitter and would cancel if we could stay with Luke. By the way, the new man in her life was John, the dear friend of Matthew's, and we liked him.

Lauren asked, "Why was the HURRICANE NAMED MATTHEW? Is this a sign? Should I go away with John?"

I did not know the answer, but suspected she needed to know it was OK by us, that she open her heart to love again.

She got our support, our yes to stay with Luke. Only God knows the answer, but we evacuated, spent a weekend loving Luke and she got to experience some freedom and joy. There was hope and mercy.

We returned to Ponte Vedra Beach—all was OK post hurricane—and set up appointments with the realtor, secured doctors with Mayo Clinic, established ourselves at the church and Mike with the golf schedule. One morning, after daily Mass I saw several people gathered for a teaching. I quietly took a seat and listened. This young priest was inspiring and informative. I decided to set up a meeting to talk to him a few days later.

While waiting in the church office for the appointment, a woman came in inquiring about a program called Walking with Purpose. I chuckled since my crutches were resting on my legs. I inquired also and signed myself up. The course of study was called *Opening Your Heart*. Perfect!

Walking with Purpose proved to be an abundant gift. The dialogue within the group was insightful, honest, provoking and caused us all to look deeper into our motivations and ponder what we were created for. In the first week of Walking with Purpose came an invitation from one of the ladies to join her in a Rosary prayer group at a couple's home. I accepted, and the beauty was in the heartfelt intentions, thanksgiving prayers and voices joined in a scriptural Rosary. The couple welcomed me, and the answered prayers resounded. One of my intentions was for a home that fit the criteria.

In November, I volunteered Mike and me to help at our first Thanksgiving in Florida. It was a dinner at the church. Prior to the feast day, I went to Mayo Clinic to get myself established with the orthopedic doctors. We met the doctor, who took X-rays of my legs. Then he stated there had been no healing since the original bone scan done in June of 2016. His treatment was to be back on crutches 24-7 and to meet with a surgeon. Needless to say, I sat on the beach on Thanksgiving Day—not a horrible hardship, but disappointed—while Mike went and served at the church. I was learning yet again I was not in control, but God was, and I was now to rest and move gently with crutches. My routine was daily Mass, Rosaries and Bible study.

It was a time of quiet, patience and thanks for all we had been through. The sheer beauty, warmth, salt air and no stuff. We were living in a furnished rental and all the stuff was in New Jersey. There was freedom in this! I had time to heal—forced rest. We met with our realtor and continued looking for homes. We were not finding the "one," so we moved to a second condo in December. This one had a view of the golf course and was updated and larger. Mike set up his work space and I set up mine in a spare bedroom. I worked on this manuscript, putting the story down, getting distracted in my journals. The one thing I did feel necessary to bring with us was my collection of twenty or so journals.

Seriously, prized possessions, the spine of my story and my personal references. Over the years I had attended many retreats and talks and participated in Bible studies. I always had my journal by my side, taking notes, recording pearls of wisdom and growing deeper.

We celebrated our first Florida Christmas in this condo. Since we were without our stuff, we bought a few lights, a small potted fern and decorated sparsely, yet it was good. Julia, Michael, Barbara, and Mikey came for the holiday. Surprisingly, Lauren and John got engaged. Hope surged for this dear daughter-in-law and Luke. Families were joined: John and his daughter Mollie, with our Lauren and Luke. They came to Florida for a visit, and we got to congratulate them in person. Luke and Mikey got to see each other and just be kids. It was a blast to be surrounded by family.

In January, I learned that a spiritual director in the parish had a healing ministry, so I made an appointment. My thinking was being present for whatever I needed: divine healing as well as physical. There were two of them to pray with me. They led me through prayers and a cleaning out of past hurts, always asking for the Holy Spirit to guide and show me what needed to be healed. I reviewed my life, in this sacred space where we gathered in belief, trust and love of the divine. Time stood still as we were engulfed in an overwhelming swirl of tears, clearing and beauty. This was different, revitalizing and heavy all at the same time. I thanked them, exited, and sat in my car, dazed.

The next day I had planned to drive to Clearwater, Florida, to attend a healing Mass at Our Lady of Divine Providence House of Prayer. The school of spiritual direction was on the grounds. I had heard about this school from a friend in New Jersey, who had gone there for her training. The woman I had met for healing had also attended this school, as well as numerous others who had crossed my path. The word "providence" always brought a smile as I recalled my New Jersey address, so blatant, 2 Providence. Our Lady and Our Lord were clearing and directing my paths. I had inquired about the school and exchanged emails with the director, but with the move, legs, and other life situations, it had been on the back burner.

So, as I drove south, I thought about a friend who had been my roommate in Medjugorje in 2014. She was having a mastectomy in New Jersey at this exact time. I offered Rosaries for the doctors, nurses, for healing and was taken back to 2014, remembering her joy and laughter as we walked the holy ground in Bosnia. Another friend who had been on that pilgrimage had relocated to southern Florida and was meeting me for the healing Mass. We planned on staying overnight for a visit, at a spa in Safety Harbor. I could not wait to be reunited with this woman, who has a heart of gold.

I had arrived early and after the four-hour drive I longed to stretch my legs. I grabbed the crutches, and my first impression was completely different than my imagination had conjured. Before me was a small house with additions, and other small houses along a street. It did not look like a school at all. It looked like a small retreat center. At the end of the street, only about a third of a mile away, was Clearwater Bay, and it was breathtaking. The water was so close, the breeze refreshing my weary body.

Standing near my car, I looked around. A woman approached and asked if I needed help. I inquired about the healing Mass, and she pointed to the church. I told her I had exchanged emails about the school. She asked if I wanted to look around inside, and I said yes, that would be great. As we entered the building the director happened to be standing there. I introduced myself and she unexpectedly asked if I would like an interview regarding the spiritual direction program. I was thrown off guard. My mind reeled for a few seconds since I was not prepared. I had just driven four hours and felt surprised by the request. Still, I enthusiastically said yes!

We moved into her office, and she closed the door. I mentioned that I had been praying, on my drive, for a woman who had graduated from the program.

She said, "I just heard from her husband. She is out of surgery, and all is well."

Amazing! I did not expect that, but I guess the director and my friend were close. What a relief to know.

The director pointed me to a cozy couch and, once I was settled, she asked me why I would want to be in the program.

It all spilled out. My faith explosion, Medjugorje, the children, my ministry, the move to Florida. She told me what the schedule looked like and how the first two weeks of the three-year study began. I felt like a bobblehead dog resting on the back shelf of a car. The topics, the study, the prayer, no tests, but groups, observations. I was thrilled; this was right up my alley. My heart raced, adrenaline surged, and I was in awe. We shook hands. I toured the one main room where all classes took place, saw the stained glass of Our Lady with outstretched arms … and my spirit soared.

Back in my car I was stunned by what had transpired. I drove the short distance to the church and waited for my friend. After hugs and greetings, we ventured into the church for the Mass and healing. Everything was from a place of heightened awareness. I don't know how to explain it, but it was extraordinary! Lord God, I trust in you!

February marked the month of my sister Kathy's and Paul's birthdays. As kids, my mom used to make a heart-shaped birthday cake for her first two: his was on the twelfth and hers the sixteenth. Valentine's Day fell in the middle; hence the heart cake. Kathy, her husband Dennis, my brother Rick and his wife Jan came for a visit. We toasted Kathy's birthday, told stories of the past, remembered Paul and celebrated Rick's wellness. He was doing great after his major surgery to remove the tumor in his esophagus. The guys played golf and walked the famous hole at the Tournament Players Club at Sawgrass. I have a picture of the three with huge smiles, holding glasses high.

Visits quieted, and we were back looking for a home. We had become enamored with the Sawgrass community and made the decision to look within and stay closer to the beach. We patiently waited. The condo was being rented; we moved again, to the third condo.

One day after Mass, a religious sister was introduced to me and, as she walked away after a short chat, she turned with a big smile and said to me, "Sign up for chirp?" I wondered what that was and went over to the church office to enquire. It was a retreat for women, at the church, an overnight and faith lift. It was called, Christ Renews His Parish, CRHP, not chirp. The timing worked and it would help me to meet more people, so I signed up. It was just before the weekend we planned to be in Atlanta for Matthew's second anniversary.

I had to borrow sheets for a twin bed. A blow-up mattress would be provided. When I arrived, I chose my space for the night, under a neon-signed exit door, a spot marked for escape. The anxiety was evident. The weekend began with a breakfast, introductions, and movement to another building. I was doing this on crutches, but I was skilled; it had been a long time. We were assigned a group and directed to tables. We introduced ourselves. A young mom was next to me. She said her name. Then she said that she kept hearing about a place called Medjuju ... something, where the Blessed Mother was appearing. She was from New Jersey and excited to meet people. I smiled inside. Wow, Medju something. I can tell her all about it and more. This was the launch of an intimate time spent with twenty-seven strangers on a faith dive deeper into the vastness of my Catholicism. It left a lasting impression and forged a bond with these women I began to call friends.

A week after, on March 19, the second anniversary of Matt's passing, we drove to Atlanta. Friends gathered in Lauren's home for an Italian celebration as she welcomed a new decade and a new life ahead with John. We missed Matt terribly, but this was a welcoming to remember and share stories.

The next morning, I got a call from my sister. OH NO! Mom had suffered another stroke and was BLIND! My heart and stomach lurched. I told Michael. His attentiveness was soothing; my heart was aching. Michael was scheduled to go from Atlanta on a business trip. We had driven to Atlanta, and I had planned on returning home. Plans were changing quickly. The magnetic pull to Cincinnati was strong; I wanted to be with Mom.

We agreed: I would drive to Cincinnati, he would fly out the next day, as scheduled. We went to Mass. As I knelt in Saint Joseph's Church, with Luke by my side, I prayed with all my heart. I said goodbye with tight hugs and began my seven-hour drive to Mom's bedside in Cincinnati.

25

Changes

"Dear children, My Son was the source of love and light when He spoke on earth to the people of all peoples. My apostles, follow His light. This is not easy. You must be little. You must make yourselves smaller than others; with the help of faith to be filled with His love. Not a single person on earth can experience a miraculous experience without faith. I am with you. I am making myself known to you by these comings, by these words; I desire to witness to you my love and motherly care. My children, do not waste time posing questions to which you never receive an answer. At the end of your journey on earth, the Heavenly Father will give them to you. Always know that God knows everything; God sees, God loves. My most beloved Son illuminates lives, dispels darkness; and my motherly love which carries me to you is inexpressible, mysterious but real. I am expressing my feelings to you: love, understanding and motherly benevolence. Of you, my apostles, I am asking for your roses of prayer which need to be acts of love. To my motherly heart these are the dearest prayers. I offer these to my Son who was born for your sake. He looks at you and hears you. We are always close to you. This is the love which calls, unites, converts, encourages and fulfills. Therefore, my apostles, always love one another and above all, love my Son. This is the

only way to salvation, to eternal life. This is my dearest prayer which fills my heart with the most beautiful scent of roses. Pray, always pray for your shepherds that they may have the strength to be the light of my Son. Thank you." January 2, 2017

I love my rosary because when turmoil strikes I grab the beads and pray. I drove, declaring out loud each mystery, pleading, thanking, loving, commiserating with Our Lady and overwhelmed with sorrow for Jesus. I sang, cried, laughed, called Julia, checked on Michael, called my sister to get updates and learned that two of my brothers were in Cincy as well. I arrived in the dark, at a hospital named after a healing pool in Jerusalem, Bethesda. I liked that. Her room number, 4114. REALLY. I could hear my stepson, Matthew; this was one of his words. So, the number fourteen twice was Mom's room number. And having this stroke on Matthew's second anniversary of his passing … connections abounded.

I crutched the long hallways; it was far from the entrance. My heart pounding, I was getting closer to Mom. In the hall I heard my sister's and brother's voices. I was home. Familiar voices echoed in the sterile environment.

Mom cooed when I bent over her in the bed and kissed her forehead. Four of her six children were gathered. She looked so frail, tiny, and confused. Kathy and Joe were heading back to my sister's house. As they said their goodbyes, my mom felt Joe's beard and told him to shave. We all laughed. She was with it! Rick and I stayed. I wanted to pray, so together we said the Divine Mercy chaplet. I held her hand. The tears streamed; I was here with my hero. I recalled a Saint Ignatius prayer that I said daily in Our Lady of the Mount Chapel in Warren, New Jersey. *Oh, my Jesus, take all my freedom, my memory, my understanding and my will. All that I have and cherish You have given me. I surrender it all to be guided by Your will. Your grace and love are wealth enough for me. Give me these, Lord Jesus, and I ask for nothing more.*

So much had been taken from her and yet she joked. She was not in pain. She loved and showed it in her gentleness. She was jumbled, confused, and now could not see. Our Lady of Peace, be with Mom. She fell deeply asleep.

Rick and I left. He looked good, considering this was the first anniversary since his cancer diagnosis. He had been in Cincinnati for a reunion when the stroke happened. Rick's oldest daughter, husband, and their six children were staying with Kathy. My sister's home in Ohio was always welcoming. She had a house full of guests. With my unexpected arrival, all the beds were full, but the kids had cleared one of the twin beds in the dorm-like room she had set up for her four grandchildren. I was exhausted. Following the anniversary of Matthew, a drive to Ohio, arriving to see Mom at the hospital, I fell asleep before my head hit the pillow.

In the next days, Mom was released and moved to a nursing rehab unit within her assisted living complex. Kathy was making the arrangements while I stayed with Mom in the hospital. In the confusion of the stroke, hospital and change, she was missing one of her front teeth. She looked so different from the energetic golfer in her cute attire, always smiling, only several years prior. But she was ninety years old.

It was tough to see her moved into a nursing home, eating in a dining room, bent over in a wheelchair, with other weary elderly patients near the end of their earthly journeys. Frankly, it was awful. The place was dreadfully depressing.

During my time in Cincinnati, the following message from Our Lady was given to a visionary, on March 25, 2017.

"Dear children! In this time of grace, I am calling all of you to open your hearts to God's mercy, to begin a new life through prayer, penance and a decision for holiness. This time of spring moves you to a new life, to a renewal, in your thoughts and hearts. Therefore, little children, I am with you to help you to say 'yes' to God and to God's commandments with resoluteness. You are not alone; I am with you through the grace which the Most High gives me for you and your descendants. Thank you for having responded to my call."

The words soothed, and the line that caught my attention was: "open your hearts to God's mercy." That was what I needed for Mom, Kathy, and myself. Our dad always said he was glad he had two girls. Kathy was amazing—arranging, caring, bringing Mom here to Cincinnati to attend to her needs. I came in and out. Kathy carried the day-to-day and she was tired, worried, and anxious as the days unfolded.

The Gospel that Sunday was John 9:1–41. Sometimes my ears perk up and I hear a passage that seems meant directly for our situation. On this day, the words were about being blind. Jesus anointed the blind man's eyes. He came into the world so that those who do not see, might see. That if you were blind, you would have no sin. Was Mom so close to her reunion in heaven that her sight was stripped? Was Mom made clean in all her suffering? What could I learn from this as I sat and watched her sleep? When she stirred, I gave her a sip of water, covered her, helped her to the bathroom, put salve on her chapped lips and loved her. I couldn't help but think of the unseen as she lay here. Her roommate had no one visit and she was quiet and sweet. It saddened me. So many in the hall, all with stories, but waiting in silence for the end. At one point Mom's roommate lay back in her recliner near the window and began a lengthy prayer, out loud, her eyes closed, resting. She prayed to the Lord for everyone here, her children, those hurting, the world, the leaders, for everyone. It was a constant prayer and felt deep, as though being poured from the recesses of her heart. I felt privileged to hear this dialogue with God.

The next day would be my father-in-law's second anniversary of death. As I looked around the facility, I thought how lucky he was to have a heart attack while taking out the garbage. He was in the hospital for a short time—long enough to see his kids and say goodbye. He never moved from his home and was taking care of himself at the end. That seemed better to me than this. But we aren't entitled to anything; it will play out as it does. I watched her robe rise and fall, taking her hand when she woke, confused, it was all I could do. Some of the nurses were so compassionate as they reassured, helped, and cared for these residents. They were the true givers. It had to be hard to face this every day. I listened to some of Matthew Kelly's meditations and heard the words, *become the best version of yourself.* I liked this phrase. Always work towards being better.

I stayed a few more days, and then began my drive home to Ponte Vedra Beach. Lauren and John were getting married on April 3, my mom's ninety-third birthday. I was happy to be going, but tearful to leave. On to happy times, to witness our widowed daughter-in-law begin again. They were getting married just miles from where we were living at the beach, her happy place!

Life is constant, as the cliché goes; we just move forward between the joys and tribulations. Look at all Lauren had been through as a young woman. So much unexpected heartache. Now she stood in an elegant white ensemble, her arm looped through her father's, our Luke on the other side, holding his mom's hand. She was beautiful, elegant, strong— no wonder our Matthew loved her. John and Lauren exchanged their vows in a dark-paneled room. They had hoped to say their "I do's" in the open air with the ocean behind them, but the weather did not cooperate. In this room of hope, they asked the children, Luke and Mollie, to say yes to the union, to commit to this newly formed family. With smiles they gave their yesses.

Michael and I felt honored to be there to celebrate and be a part of the young couple's future. At the dinner there was a toast to Matthew and their love for him and for our being a part of this day. I was happy John was the one Lauren gave her heart to. Our Matthew loved him, and John's compassion is huge.

With all my heart I was happy for them and, as Michael and I left to return to our condo, the tears rolled. I selfishly wanted our Matthew here, not gone, and we missed him. It was heartache. I prayed for the newlyweds, Luke and Mollie and our Matthew above. God bless us all. Help us to navigate this new normal and continue to love and grow as they find their way and settle in as a family.

Julia had scheduled a visit for the next week, so I was staying in Florida while my sweet sister managed everything with Mom, who continued to decline back in Ohio. Rick and Jan had gone on a cruise out of Tampa, so they stopped for dinner on their return home. Julia got to see her uncle. He was thin, yet happy. It was pleasant to see him and Julia at the same table. Over the next few days, she and I got to catch up on her New York life and the day-to-day expectations of the hospital. Both of us relaxed and enjoyed the sun together.

On the last day of Julia's visit we got a call from the realtor. He had a house to show us that had not yet gone on the market. Julia, Mike, and I met at the house and before we even went in, we acknowledged the attractiveness of the street. We met the realtor at the front door and saw the view of the pool and pond. This clearly was the one! I had to keep a straight face and suppress my enthusiasm, but as I gazed into each room, the better I felt. It was falling into place. After all the homes we had looked at, this one fit the criteria and I could see us here. Julia and I moved to a room upstairs, a bonus room, and she said, "This is mine!" We hugged with excitement.

Then it was time to get Julia to the airport. The buzz while we drove was exciting—about what we could do—and an offer was made. By the time she was home in NY it was accepted. Everything moved forward.

Meanwhile, Kathy was dealing with Mom, who was weakening. Kathy called and told me about a mysterious instance. Mom was whispering and, as Kathy got close, it was as if Mom was in a church with her own mother. In this dreamlike moment in this church, there was a priest, and Mom whispered, "A rosary was lost." How cool, Mom was communicating with her mother about this. Kathy relayed to me how tranquil Mom was in this dual time exchange. The fact that her mom, our grandmother, was there in the invisible was consolation.

We were entering into the holiest week of our Catholic faith. It was Holy Thursday, and I had an appointment at Mayo Clinic for X-rays on my legs. As I waited, I thought of Mom at the end stages and me with a new home, Lauren in a new marriage and, hopefully, my improved legs. The images confirmed that the right leg looked good and the left was almost healed. The added time on crutches worked as well as a new drug I was on. This was fantastic news!

This triduum would mark deep invocations of gratitude and strength for my sister and what lay ahead for Rick, Mom, and the concerns in my heart. To be able to spend the three holiest days on my knees, meditating on the suffering of Our Lord, was deeply moving.

My childhood friend and her son came for a visit the week after Easter. During their stay, my sister called. Mom was moved to a hospice facility. I booked flights to return to Cincinnati as soon as they departed.

I rented a car and went directly to the new place where Mom would spend her last days. Kathy was exhausted and the time had been draining. Mom's new place was opposite from the nursing home. It was brightly lit, peaceful, calm and she had a room to herself. I had desired Mom's death to be holy, so I started praying Rosaries, saying Divine Mercy prayers, playing music on my phone that she liked. She was sleeping a lot but had short bursts of lucidity. I told her about the house and our future. She smiled. She asked with clarity at one point, as my brother Joe and I sat on either side of her bed, if she was dying. We exchanged glances and said yes. Then she asked if we thought she would get wings. We smiled at that thought. Joe looked out the window and miraculously saw clouds that resembled an angel. He confirmed it with a picture on his phone.

One morning I was going to get coffee, bent down to kiss her and told her where I was going.

With her eyes closed, she said, "That sounds good."

When I returned, I fed her a little taste with a straw, and she cooed.

She also wanted her teeth brushed; I was told to be very gentle. Funny, what she was thinking of as she waited for death. Mom periodically raised her arms. Joe and I smiled, held her hands and lavished her with love. Rick called and spoke to her, as did Greg and his wife. We held the phone to her ear; she was very weak but smiled at the sounds of their voices.

I was spending the night with her and wanted to hold her hand as she made her way through the final breath and to what lay beyond. Another night, the nurses thought the time had arrived. It wasn't. She asked where she was going, what's happening, and she had moments of agitation. I played music and whispered to her, which seemed to help. I wondered about the unseen around her and Mom's love for the Blessed Mother. I was calling myself "a cheerleader for heaven." My brother called me a "midwife of death"—which made me smile.

The priests came, and she received the anointing of the sick. One priest was a neighborhood friend. When we were kids, we played church at his house. He baptized our dolls, married us, had Mass, all in play and he was eventually ordained a priest. I prayed the prayer of Saint Gertrude, for holy souls. I was pulling up prayers from memory, from friends and websites. Mom called out to our dad at one point and asked if he was asleep. She was seeing through the blindness.

On what would have been Matthew's thirty-eighth birthday, Kathy and I sat on either side of the bed, the room drenched in the afternoon sun. Mom sat up and clearly declared that she would like a piece of chocolate cake with candy on it. Then she lay back down to sleep. We giggled, not sure exactly what was happening.

At 3:00 a.m. on April 29 she woke, and her breathing was different. She slept most of the day, and at one point my brother-in-law came and suggested I go out. Maybe she didn't want me there at the end. I left and took a drive with the windows open. The air felt so good. I drove back to the hospice center and walked into the room.

My brother-in-law looked up from his paper, smiled and said, "No change."

Kathy came by with some wine and snacks. What a great girl! I poured the wine and sat in a chair at the side of Mom's bed. I rested my crossed ankles near her blanketed feet, toasted her, talked of good times. I chatted, watching her chest rise and fall. Then ... a change in the breathing. I quickly moved from the chair, sat on the bed, took both her hands, locked our fingers, and recited the Our Father. I smiled through the flowing tears. She was leaving. She was going to heaven, to her family, to Our Lady, to Jesus and to our dad. It was over. I love you, Mom. I thanked her for my life.

My phone rang; it was my priest friend from New Jersey. How did he know Mom had just passed? We talked. He consoled me, his voice so tender and soothing. He was a support through this chapter too. What a blessing, what a shepherd. I called Kathy, my husband, and my brothers. It was finished.

In the days that followed, family flew in, and we arranged the funeral plans. Everyone participated—all who could be there. Mom left this world, having six children, eighteen grandchildren and twenty-one great-grandchildren. We were blessed to have this incredible woman who had loved and encouraged all with abiding faith and conviction. What a legacy!

Rick and Kathy went through the will with us. It was shocking how skinny he was, and jaundiced. The cancer was raging again. His decline in the last month was drastic. Rick had managed the funds for Mom after Dad had passed, and now he had completed this task. He had faithfully carried out the last wishes as a competent steward, and now we were fearful for him and his wife for what lay ahead.

We all departed and returned to our respective lives. My dear sister Kathy could now rest.

Julia had flown in for the funeral, so we got a short sweet visit to love, mourn and be family.

We drove to the airport together and parted once again. We were headed to Atlanta and Julia went back to New York City. Luke was making his First Holy Communion. Our Luke received Jesus in the Eucharist for the first time—he was getting the foundation of his faith. It was the greatest gift Luke could receive, in my view. Thank You, God, for this joy, this celebration because of You, Jesus.

Mike and I returned to Florida and prepared for the closing on our home, which would be in a few days. A new beginning—a dwelling after the year of waiting and searching. The closing went smoothly. We ordered takeout and sat in beach chairs by the pool, our first dinner to commemorate this day.

Daily, I was checking in on my brother. Rick was not doing well; he was declining. The hospice nurses were called, and they were now visiting and guiding his large, tight, assembled family. The joys and the crosses of life and death continued.

I prayed unceasingly for Rick and his family. I took direction from Rick. He was asking for a miracle for himself—however that might unfold. We prayed for intercession from Fr. Michael McGivney, the founder of the Knights of Columbus, who needed miracles on his road to sainthood. This was the process I found on the Internet at FatherMcGivney.org: http://www.fathermcgivney.org/mcg/en/sainthood/index.html.

> For a person to become a saint .... A reported miracle must be presented to the congregation in Rome and judged favorably if there is to be a beatification, with the bestowal of the title "Blessed."

> Medical and theological experts must carefully examine the evidence in order to pass judgment on the case. If judged positively by the Congregation for the Causes of Saints, that judgment will be passed to the Pope, who alone makes the decision about beatifications and canonizations.

> It is for this reason that Reports of Favors attributed to the intercession of a candidate for canonization are so important. For Father McGivney, a healing through his intercession was reported early in the process, but in 2011 the Vatican Congregation judged it to not be miraculous in nature. Another possible miracle was reported in January 2012 and was currently under investigation by the postulator.

I thought of Rick's early retirement, his permanent move to the lake house—once termed the vacation retreat—his contribution to the Knights at his parish and all the visits and trips made nationwide to see his kids and fifteen grandkids. He always welcomed us, time and time again, to enjoy Lake Hartwell, to splash, waterski and make ourselves at home. It was one of my favorite places. How boundless and freeing it was for a moment in time, to have no cares, wrap arms around a pastel-colored Styrofoam noodle and float for hours. Their grandchildren would be in life jackets, jumping off the dock, and the older kids and adults conversed about jobs, world problems, reminisced, brainstormed new ideas and laughed in this body of water. We took boat rides to small islands and buried time capsules with news articles, letters, and trinkets, only to try desperately to find them the next summer. Our joys: to feel the sun, water, and breeze, to hear the laughter and see the bright bathing suits, baseball caps, huge smiles, and family bobbing on the ripples of dark water—what bliss! This was coming to an end.

Rick lost his battle twenty-nine days after Mom at the hour of divine mercy, 3:00 p.m. I love to think that she was there to welcome him into the heavenly realm. As his illness unfolded, I couldn't help but think of this Scripture, **Romans 5, *"offer our body as a living sacrifice."*** When I saw the line of people wrapping around the funeral home, I was in awe. He had expressed to me many times that he desired God's will in his battle with cancer and gave his suffering as an offering for loved ones. In conversations I marveled how God was transforming Rick through illness and suffering. He was open, willing to discuss faith and saw with such clarity.

He had encouraged me to serve and be a voice of faith to others. He'd say, "You never know how God is working."

Another funeral and gathering of family, to love and remember, and then a time of healing.

Once we were back in Florida, someone in passing mentioned that a pilgrimage to Medjugorje was in the works for late October. Wow! My heart leapt. I could use a respite. I wanted to return with all my spirit to where Our Lady still appeared daily. I asked Michael if he wanted to join me. He declined. My friend Fran came to mind in prayer. She said "Yes!"

26
Full Circle

"Dear children! Today I am grateful to you for your presence in this place where I am giving you special graces. I call each one of you to begin to live as of today that life which God wishes of you and to begin to perform good works of love and mercy. I do not want you, dear children, to live the message and be committing sin which is displeasing to me. Therefore, dear children, I want each of you to live a new life without destroying all that God produces in you and is giving you. I give you my special blessing and I am remaining with you on your way of conversion. Thank you for having responded to my call." March 25, 1987

Our grandson Mikey from New York and I were coloring at the dining room table during summer vacation in Florida, in our last condo. Our future home was still under renovation. Mikey and I were taking a break from the sun, coloring and chatting. My phone rang. It was the pilgrimage coordinator. She informed me that the trip to Medjugorje I had signed up for was canceled. They had not had enough people interested. She directed me on who to call for the refund. I could not talk; my emotions were brimming. I hung up. My heart lurched and I felt as if I was about to cry. With the sweetest look of concern, my sensitive grandson asked what happened. I told him about my looking forward to this trip and the cancellation. We talked about disappointments and continued our artwork.

My friend Fran and I had already paid the full amount to the tour company. Later that day, I called and told her the trip had been canceled. We agreed to talk in a few days and sleep on this setback and disappointment. We also agreed not to call the tour company yet for our money back.

That night I had a dream. I don't recall any details, but when I woke, I thought of Wayne Weible. It was strange, but I felt prompted to check out his website. My gaze jumped to pilgrimages and I saw he was coordinating a Medjugorje trip that would leave a week later than the scheduled trip we had signed up for and, miraculously, it was through the same tour company. The difference in cost was about thirty dollars. I called Fran, called the tour company, and switched our names to Wayne's trip. A Holy Spirit intervention for sure. I had met Wayne in 1991 with Paul, then in Princeton, New Jersey, when he gave a talk. He had written in his books about meeting Paul, and now I would return with Wayne. After so many losses and with the house renovation almost done, this would be a wonderful healing retreat for me. I loved how this had played out!

In September the moving van arrived from New Jersey, and we officially moved into the house. There was still work to be done, but the end was near. Unfortunately, the day the countertops were installed in the kitchen, another hurricane was bearing down on Florida. This one, called Irma, was huge! Again, we were in the "zone" and evacuated. This was distressing. We moved all the newly purchased outdoor furniture into the house and watched the news reports continuously. The hurricane was immense and threatening all of Florida.

We departed, only to meet with the thousands of others who were leaving the state. It was insane: cars lined up at rest stops for miles. I had never seen anything like this. It was surreal. After a grueling eleven-hour drive to Atlanta—which typically takes five—again we were stupidly late on securing a closer hotel. We arrived and tucked ourselves into bed. I was beyond exhausted, and my head was pounding. I prayed. The news coverage was constant since these storms are unpredictable. Finally, it was reported that Irma had passed our area without too much damage—a relief, but it was heading inland and to Atlanta.

We bolted and began driving on deserted highways as the winds picked up and howled. At one point I was loudly praying the mysteries of the Rosary and pleading as we drove south. We witnessed trees toppling on the northbound side of the highway. It was frightening. We insanely drove through the winds and rains of the outer belts of the hurricane. The memory still fresh of crowded highways and the eleven-hour drive, my determined husband was focused on getting us home. We raced to reach the south side of this beast. Finally, the wind died down; we had made it safely to the other side!

Instantly we became keenly aware that every area had suffered major power outages and there were no gas stations open. We pulled off at exits. It was eerie. No cars. Nothing. And everything was boarded and closed. Our gas gauge dropped, but we pushed on and crossed the WELCOME TO FLORIDA sign with a few gallons left. Thankfully, we found an open station. The eastern coast's north curve of Florida had survived again, but the St. Johns River had flooded, and a significant level of damage was being assessed.

In the last several miles to our home, we hit a line of stopped traffic at the bridge spanning the Intracoastal Waterway. We were waiting for the US Army Corps of Engineers to evaluate the safety of the bridge because of the hurricane's sustained winds. We finally were allowed to cross after a two-hour plus wait and in a short time drove through the gate of our community. Thankfully, we found only branches down, but no other damage.

Julia came for a visit a month after, to see the renovation and enjoy a Florida reprieve. Being together was great! When our time was over, we headed to the airport together—she, back to New York, and me, to Medjugorje. I'd be traveling with two women from the parish. I had met both on the CRHP retreat weekend. One had a history with Medjugorje and had made many pilgrimages. The other woman was making her first trip.

We were flying from Jacksonville to Atlanta, to Munich, to Split in Croatia, and then a bus to Medjugorje. In flight, I was journaling prayers and desires for this healing trip: to return with thoughts of tenderness for Matthew, Frank, Mom, and Rick. It had been a crazy few years and with the bone enhancement drug I was on, my legs felt strong. I journaled that the word for this trip would be OBEDIENCE, and that my ears, eyes, and heart would be open for my future path: God's will, not mine. I was excited to rendezvous with my friend Fran from New Jersey, in Munich, and curious to see what would develop with Wayne. When we arrived in Split, Wayne was there with his wife, Judith.

I had prayerfully, wishfully carried with me a prepared folder with my book synopsis to give Wayne if the opportunity arose. Years previously, in 2009, I had sent him a very rough stream-of-consciousness account of my 1991 pilgrimage and life, to the present. He told me that it required intense editing, but within there was a story which he would consider if I could clean it up. After eight years of rewriting, editing out the excess and painstakingly attempting to put this story on paper, I hoped he would be receptive. I wanted to surrender this all to God, but also found the whole ordeal—of the trip being canceled, the dream and traveling with this author who I had encountered in 1991—providential!

The group boarded the bus and off we were for our several-hour drive. We began with a Rosary, led by Wayne.

Thank you, Our Lady, for allowing this to unfold so that I could come on this trip. My legs were cooperating so far, and I knew adrenaline was going to fuel this pilgrimage.

Fran and I settled into our small simple room. We were eager to walk around, find out where the other hotel was located, since our group had been separated, and then explore. Past the lobby, we found Wayne outside. We introduced ourselves. Then I explained that I was the sister of the guy with AIDS whom he had written about in one of his earlier books, and about Mom in Myrtle Beach, recalling our first meeting in 1991.

With both hands, he grasped the sides of my upper arms and said, "I cannot believe you are here!" He repeated this a few times as his hands grasped my arms. He said, "You do not know the impact of that meeting. You can ask Judith about it too."

Wayne had the spark in his eyes that I remembered; even at eighty years old he still had enthusiasm. He had led many pilgrimages here over the years and spoke around the world. We asked him to direct us to the other hotel, and he agreed to show us. We spoke as we walked. It was cordial and informative, about Mom and Paul. I hungered for more, but my tongue was tied. I wanted to pull Wayne aside and sit quietly in a café and talk. Also, I couldn't wait to show Fran around this miraculous place. Wayne left us in the front of the other hotel and moved on. I was a jumble of emotions.

Fran and I connected with the others, and then crossed the street to St. James Church, the center of Medjugorje. It was wonderful to be back and show Fran this extraordinary place. After my two prior trips I was surprisingly comfortable navigating my way around.

As the days unfolded, we followed the schedule that was posted on a white board in the lobby of our residence. We walked to the home of the visionary Vicka, waiting as she finished with one group and then attended to us. Before each group presentation, she met with the visiting priests. The Blessed Mother was always asking us to pray for our shepherds, so Vicka gave them special attention.

A multitude of us crammed in on a front garden patio, waiting to listen to her speak. With all the travelers worldwide, the visionary met with the various nationalities and spoke through interpreters. As we anticipated her arrival, we prayed Rosaries and sang, smiling and chatting to strangers bonded by faith and belief.

When Vicka came into view she positioned herself on a stoop so we could clearly see her. She smiled with exuberant, explosive joy. She recounted the history, the first apparitions and then shared what Our Lady was asking of us. Vicka talked of seeing heaven, hell, and purgatory when Our Lady showed her by physically being carried to each place with the visionary Jakov.

"These places are real," she said, "and we need to think about our choices."

She repeated the five consistent messages: prayer from the heart, the Eucharist, fasting, confession, and immersing ourselves in Scripture. She blessed us and prayed over us with words given to her by Our Lady. It was beautiful. When the crowd eased, I found Fran, and her smile said it all. She had met a couple from Canada and hoped to see them again. It was Vicka in 2014 who was praying over us when I had the vision of Our Lady holding Matthew. On this day, gratitude of being in this place at this time filled my heart.

Wayne was scheduled to give a talk in the seating area behind the church. We gathered with the friends from Florida and others from the pilgrimage. About a hundred congregated to hear his story of conversion and how his life mission had been directed by Our Lady. He spoke of encounters that held significance, and soon I was hearing my own story: of his meeting me, Mom and praying with Paul. Wayne also said something that jumped out at me. HE HAD BEEN GIVEN THE GIFT OF HEALING! He went on to say that he had been nervous about it and was not embracing the gift back in 1991. It was new. My mind began to flash with WHAT IFs. What if: Wayne had said YES immediately, when Our Lady asked him to go to Paul? What if: he placed his hands with courage streaming from the Holy Spirit, and Paul had been healed? I began to cry. Not subtle, gentle tears; I let out a robust snort and then sobbed.

In my crying fog, I heard Wayne say, "The sister is here." He repeated, "The sister is here!"

He caught my eye and asked me to come up front. As I was walking up front, I was mentally getting my act together and pushing the tears deep inside. Event organizers suited me with a microphone and ask me to tell part of the story.

I started with Wayne meeting with us and planting a seed of hope. I then told the part of Paul's story, his desire for truth and the request at the base of Cross Mountain before our ascent. My brother wanted me to tell the fellow pilgrims the truth that he had AIDS, not cancer. I told the story of his transfiguration at station number seven, when he stated that he was not afraid to die. I concluded with, "The truth will set you free."

This was emotionally draining. I followed Wayne and Judith afterwards, wanting to talk further, but they were leaving to meet someone. He did not have the time. This left me in a strange state of mind, and I had to go off alone to recollect myself and shed some tears.

I repeated over and over, "It was the will of God that Paul died."

I went into the church and wrote this in my journal:

Blessed Mother, I sit in your church. You are the Queen of Heaven, Our Lady. You have summoned all of us to this holy place to pray, to honor and to draw us closer to your Son. To draw us closer, deeper in our union with Jesus.

Mary, joy is the gift, the prayers, the love, the people you have given me. I am beyond grateful. I can only imagine, as you watched your Son with the apostles, the joy you must have felt as you observed, but then the intense suffering. Loving while you witnessed the events unfold. You saw the belief rise in the disciples, the faith set ablaze by the miracles of healing and the followers growing in number each day.

You were told by Simeon that a sword would pierce your heart as you held your infant in the temple. I wonder, when your own mother and father died, how much suffering you endured. When Joseph died and left you a widow at such a young age. Watching at the foot of the cross as your bloody, lacerated, precious Son breathed his last, the horrifying anguish you must have felt. You were created, clean, uncorrupted—without the stain of original sin—so you loved purely, deeply, profoundly.

You witnessed the Resurrection: your Son walking, restored and opening the gates for us to heaven. I can only imagine that precise moment when your eyes met and you surveyed His handsome face perfectly clear of the wounds, blood, cuts ... oh, how your soul must have soared!

So, Mary, I am here in this church where you have appeared. I was humbled by Wayne as he told his story, but my humanness makes me upset, sad, frustrated. Paul suffered so much, and I know we will all experience hardships and each life has a purpose. Cancer robbed Luke of his father, our Matthew, and Rick of the joy of his many grandchildren. The will of God is hard to accept at times like these, but I believe we will meet again, and I will hang on to my faith and seek joy.

Please guide the rest of my days here, grant me confidence about the future and guide me to be obedient to your Son. I give you, my heavenly mom, all my concerns and ask you to bless the family I have lost and those whom I have.

On November 2, the visionary Mirjana would be experiencing her monthly apparition at the Blue Cross. We joined the throngs of faithful crowded on the streets and packed on the mountainside, waiting as she received the vision and the message. I couldn't get that close but managed to find a shop wall at the base of the hill to lean against as we waited. It was an amazing sight to see the thousands packed, the huge crowds. Fran and I were separated again and would meet up later. The people joined their voices in Hail Marys, in a variety of languages; it was soothing and remarkable. I couldn't help but think of God watching this from above as He looked on the seekers of truth. Was it similar to the crowds Jesus drew in His earthly walks?

When the time came for Mirjana to see Our Lady and her eyes focused upward, the crowds became still. Not a whisper. The quiet prayers to and from were palatable; it was hard to explain. I was grateful for this moment, this instance. I offered up my own prayers of thanksgiving.

Afterwards, an interpreter announced the words given to Mirjana from Our Lady, in three or four languages. I heard the words and let them marinate. What a precious gift!

"Dear children, as I am looking at you gathered around me, your mother, I see many pure souls, many of my children who are seeking love and consolation, but no one is offering it to them. I also see those who are doing evil, because they do not have good examples; they have not come to know my Son. The good which is silent and is spread through pure souls is the strength which sustains this world. There is much sin, but there is also love. My Son is sending me to you, the mother who is the same for everyone, that I may teach you to love, to comprehend that you are brothers. He desires to help you. Apostles of my love, a living desire of faith and love is sufficient, and my Son will accept it. But you must be worthy, you must have good will and open hearts. My Son enters into open hearts. I, as a mother, desire that you may all the better come to know my Son – God born of God – to come to know the greatness of His love which you need so much. He accepted your sins upon Himself and obtained redemption for you, and in return He asked that you love each other. My Son is love.

He loves all people without difference, all people of all coun-
tries and of all nations. If you, my children, would live the love
of my Son, His kingdom would already be on earth. Therefore,
apostles of my love, pray, pray that my Son and His love may
be all the closer to you; that you may be an example of love
and may help all those who have not come to know my Son.
Never forget that my Son, one and triune, loves you. Love your
shepherds and pray for them. Thank you." November 2, 2017

There was much to contemplate in these words. *He loves*
all people, all nations, we are all His children. To truly live
with purpose and help those to know Him.

Afterwards, we navigated the crowds and located the
large colored flag carried by our tour guide. We walked back
towards St. James Church as a group, and I rendezvoused
with Fran along the way.

An extraordinary thing happened to a young adolescent
boy who was traveling with our group. He was there with his
dad and grandparents. During the first few dinners I noticed
his head droop. He looked sad. He always wore a hooded
sweatshirt with the hood up. His body language revealed a
discontented young man. He politely answered questions
with one-word answers. There was something concerning
about him. As I was making my way towards the flag, I saw
him and he had a huge smile, his head raised, his hood down
and his demeanor radically changed. He said that Mirjana
had come right up to him, kissed him on the cheek and

handed him a rosary, saying, "Our Lady wanted you to have these." We walked back towards town, and he talked the whole way, with excitement in his voice, and couldn't wait to share this with his mom via a phone call. It was beautiful; he was transformed in this brief encounter. He remained talkative, engaging, and enthusiastic for the rest of the trip. Amazing!

After the English language Mass, we climbed Apparition Hill, praying the Rosary as we went. It was so reverent. The tour guide also shared stories of radical conversions on this mountainside, some of which I had heard before and some were new. She recalled the beginnings and fresh stories of miracle happenings and healings in this holy bubble. All of it saturated my mending heart.

A day later, we gathered to hike up Cross Mountain. The meditations were read from a small book, *Cross Examinations: Stations of the Cross*, by James E. Adams. A young priest read at each of the fourteen stations as we made our way to the concrete cross at the top. Some of the words hit me personally, as if written for me; for example, the thought that our crosses are our credentials for being human, and we strive to learn the wisdom of triumphing through our crosses, rather than in spite of them. Good thoughts. The higher we walked, the harder it got—symbolic of what Jesus encountered. At the seventh station I could feel Mom, Paul, and Ed around me, or was I wishing or considering the idea that they were there in the invisible, walking with me?

At the top, after taking in the breathtaking views, one of the women from Florida and I decided to stay behind and enjoy the peace. We'd make our own way down the mountain. We sat, talking and taking in the vista, sharing the moment. At the same time, above us we noticed a cloud formation of a veiled woman in profile, with hands together in prayer. It was very clear. We stared, smiled, and sat in momentary amazement. I will forever remember that time.

We attended the daily Mass in English and joined the multitudes for the international Masses in the evenings. We listened to the talks, all of which inspired a renewed depth of faith and belief. Fran was elated, absorbing it all, her enthusiasm contagious. We walked, discussing revelations of understanding, as we breathed in the air and wrapped ourselves in this mantle of tranquility. Someone from the group initiated a Rosary each evening, so about ten of us gathered— sometimes more—to pray. Wayne also joined; it was humbling to watch.

One day, I said to Fran that I'd like to deviate from the schedule instead of getting on the bus for an excursion. She agreed, and we stayed behind. I craved time to naturally allow the day to unfold. The only thing I had wanted to do was to see if I could locate Christina Georgotas. Back in 2013, I had invited her to speak to the confirmation candidates at my New Jersey parish. At that time, she was a young filmmaker who had previously worked in New York City with Kelly Ripa, before a profound transformation. Christina mesmerized about a hundred kids, sharing her story of conversion, her career and her film production. Then she showed excerpts of her movie, *Queen of Peace*. She magically captured their attention as each cradled a pastel plastic rosary in their hands. Coincidentally, I met up with her a second time, in Bosnia, in 2014. She was staying in the same guesthouse as my group. It was great to reconnect. In 2016, she married someone from Medjugorje, in St. James Church, and I had watched her wedding on my computer through Mary TV. I was laid up in bed, with pillows under my legs, after receiving the initial diagnosis of the stress fractures. I was hoping Christina was now living here but was uncertain.

We wandered through town and located the Mary TV studio, where I thought Christina might be working. This would be the place to inquire how to locate her. In 2013, over dinner, she and I discussed filming a witness talk from my 1991 episode. That had never happened and had been the motivation stirring in the back of my mind. When we got to the studio, a young man showed us around and then he said Christina was not there, but we'd need to go talk to Rosie at the tea house. I had never been to the tea house, but had heard of it, and kind of knew its location. Fran and I laughed as we followed the directive and ventured to the tea house on the main street.

We located Rosie and introduced ourselves. Then, the craziest thing: there was the couple from Canada that Fran had met while waiting to hear the visionary Vicka. They exchanged surprised hellos, and Fran sat to talk to them. This was the couple she had encountered in the cold, and Fran had given the woman an extra pair of gloves she had in her pocket. Here they were! The tea house was a meeting place; come in, have tea, and gather with others. Rosie was originally from England, came on a pilgrimage to Medjugorje, met the love of her life and stayed.

I told Rosie about wanting to connect with Christina, our New Jersey encounter with the youth and meeting again in 2014. Rosie stopped me and laughed.

The second crazy thing: Rosie said, "Christina married my son, and now they have a baby."

Another wow!

She filled me in. They lived in New Jersey and Rosie had just returned from a visit. Small world. She showed me pictures of the baby and family. Rosie proceeded to ask if I wanted to film a witness talk, and I said "Yes!" So, we scheduled it for the next day. All the while I was chatting with Rosie, Fran spoke to the couple. We exchanged phone numbers, emails and took pictures.

When we left, Fran said, "You know, all you have to do is 'just be,' and things are put into place."

So true!

After this, Fran and I strolled, smiling at the encounters. We were stopped by a woman from Romania. She introduced herself as Veronica and asked us a silly question about an English word. This was her way to get a conversation started. She was on her own and shared that her tour group had returned home, and she wanted to stay in this holy place. So, she did. Through her Hungarian accent, her enthusiasm for her faith oozed out, her eyes so clear and captivating. Because it had begun to rain, she directed us into a store that she loved. She showed us a collection of small meditation prayer books stacked neatly in a corner. She was like a librarian in the stacks, trying to entice the patrons with the stories inside the jackets. While we were there, the earth shook! We held our breaths, looked at each other … it was a strange few seconds. An earthquake, confirmed by the shopgirl. We laughed nervously. We bought some of her treasured recommendations and then said goodbye.

We heard it said from one of the priests that Our Lady invites us here to be broken open so that Jesus can work in us. She will do whatever it takes to get us closer to her Son. Hearing and seeing people's reactions and conversions was clearly evident; Our Lady's apparitions here were changing people for the better.

Father Leon, the priest for the English pilgrims, presented his story of traveling to Medjugorje in 1991, with his mother and a group from Singapore, when he was a teenager. He shared his encounter with Our Lady. He actually saw a vision of her on Cross Mountain while climbing to see the sunrise. He was with a friend who witnessed the same thing. Father Leon spoke with palpable awe and wonder and of the perplexity that stirred inside him. He shared his life after that event, his medical career and call to the priesthood, followed by his position in Medjugorje. Our Lady's plan for him played out, as he looked in retrospect. His message from her was to tell everyone these words that he heard:

"I am your mother, and I want you to tell everyone you meet that I am their mother and that I love them."

He said the love he felt being in her presence was overwhelming, as if he was the only person in the world and it was the most immense love, personal and direct.

Hearing all he said solidified again what I had been taught, and his no-nonsense way instilled a heightened obedience and responsibility on our part, in this walk of salvation. His talk had left thoughts reverberating in my mind.

I'd be meeting with Rosie at the Mary TV studio in a few hours, to give my "Fruit of Medjugorje" witness. I had filled my journal with the key points of my story. Then I went to the adoration chapel to pray and ask the Holy Spirit to intercede so that whatever needed to be said was expressed. At the TV studio I met with one of Rosie's sons, who set me up with the mic and explained how it would work. Rosie came in, and her warm personality calmed my nerves. We began our conversation and my story poured out. I loved my brother, and retelling this story brought him close. The recounting always illustrates the movements of my faith unfolding through each challenge, hardship, joy and sorrow. It was refreshing and conclusive to give my story, to let it flow. It was done. *My talk is #301 in the Fruits of Medjugorje segment on Marytv.tv.*

Now I hoped to talk to Wayne privately.

The rest of the pilgrimage, the gatherings, the moments with Fran, strolling through the fields, the peace, prayers, and comradery of the group from our guesthouse gelled and it was good. One evening a few of us were lagging after dinner, and Wayne sat with us. It was intimate as each shared a story or encounter, and he listened, commented, and agreed with the miraculous happenings. It was pleasant to see this; he was like a celebrity and at times it was challenging to connect with him. To experience the man whose curiosity led him to an encounter with Our Lady—which would change his life forever—was a privilege. For a moment I saw his humility and an eagerness to talk and share. It had been roughly twenty-six years since his first book and hundreds of talks around the world. I was one of many wanting to connect. How exhausting that had to be for him over the years.

At the conclusion of this intimate gathering, I approached him about my story. He actually brought up the manuscript I had sent him in 2008 and its rough quality. Did he actually remember? I told him I had a synopsis to give him.

He said, "Not here. Don't give me anything. Contact me when we get back, and we can discuss it."

This was hopeful.

He had recently completed his last book, which was still being printed, and copies would be sent to us after we returned. It was his life journey, from childhood to the present. He said it was the toughest thing he had ever written because it was the most personal of all his titles. Many childhood wounds were reopened, but ultimately he was pleased with the outcome. It was titled *The Joy of Medjugorje.*

When I returned from the trip, it was a time to dive into our new home and get prepared to host our first Thanksgiving and Christmas. We entertained family from New York and California. I shared my pilgrimage with anyone who would listen.

In January, Wayne and I began an email exchange. This was my last email comment from him, on February 6, 2018.

Dear Barbara,

Well, I think I need to explain why I have not been in touch with you over this past month. Unfortunately, I became quite ill and ended up in the hospital with pancreatitis and have struggled simply to survive. It has been a rough month, but the good news is I am progressing and getting better.

Barbara, I have just watched you in a review on Mary TV and wish to commend you for a job well done. Your story and that of your brother Paul will always stand out in my heart as one of the critical moments of this mission. I have not had an opportunity to re-review what you have written, but I promise you, I will. Please give me a couple days and your telephone number and we can talk direct.

Thank you, Barbara. May God continue to bless you.

Unfortunately, Wayne continued to decline in the hospital. He went into hospice and passed weeks later, with his wife Judith by his side. He left a legacy of words drenched in tenacity, hope, and perseverance in faith and the messages of Our Lady in Medjugorje.

I had read his last book as soon as I got it and could not help but feel this work was his final summary.

He had been a good and faithful steward of Our Lady. In the pages, I also read a retelling of his encounter with Paul. He had changed the names, but the story was the same.

His obituary read as follows:

Celebrating the life of Wayne Weible – 1937–2018
Wayne Weible, born in Long Beach, California, in 1937, died on Saturday, April 21st, 2018, after a three-month illness.

For the past 33 years, Wayne has made it his life's mission to spread the messages of Our Lady of Medjugorje, bringing hundreds of thousands of people to conversion to God. Wayne has traveled the world, speaking about Medjugorje, and he has written twelve books which have sold worldwide. In addition, Wayne has led dozens of pilgrimages to Medjugorje throughout the past thirty plus years.

Nearly thirty years ago Paraclete Press first published *Medjugorje: The Message,* a personal testimony from a journalist named Wayne Weible, whose life was changed by what he experienced in that little town in the hills of the former Yugoslavia. The book became a bestseller, and over the next decades, Wayne continued to spread the message of Medjugorje, writing ten more books, conducting pilgrimages, founding charities, and changing thousands of people's lives.

Over time, I continued to work on my manuscript, often procrastinating, putting it away for months at a time, never really comfortable as a writer but desiring to get this story completed once and for all. It has been a work of love.

As I was working on this final chapter, I felt compelled to reach out to Wayne's wife and see if she could provide insight to his comment about "the impact of that meeting" with Paul. We spoke. Her thoughts were that Wayne's up-bringing had left scars that made him lack compassion. He was a driven businessman, a reporter. Somehow, in that brief moment in time, a window of compassion opened that grew as his mission continued. In his earlier book he mentioned Mother Teresa and the comparison of AIDS being the leprosy of this time. He recalled acquiring more empathy for the disease. Judith said he spoke about the meeting with Paul in many of his talks, as one that was profound. God had created the happenstance for Wayne, for Paul, for Ed and for us. I also told Judith about Ed seeing halos over Wayne's head, and she said that many had seen that light while he gave his talks.

Our lives are a mystery.

I am typing my last words on a beautiful Saturday, while we are quarantined during the COVID-19 pandemic.

On March 2, 2020, Mirjana received her last second-of-the-month message. It is below.

"Dear children, your pure and sincere love draws my motherly heart. Your faith and trust in the Heavenly Father are fragrant roses which you offer to me—the most beautiful bouquets of roses which consist of your prayers, acts of mercy and of love. Apostles of my love, you who sincerely and with a pure heart strive to follow my Son, you who sincerely love Him, you help; you be an example to those who have not yet come to know the love of my Son—but, my children, not only

with words but also with acts and pure feelings through which you glorify the Heavenly Father. Apostles of my love, it is a time of vigilance, and of you I am asking for love, that you not judge—anyone. Because the Heavenly Father will judge everyone. I am asking that you love, that you convey the truth; because truth is old, it is not new, it is eternal, it is truth. It testifies to God's eternity. Bring the light of my Son and keep breaking the darkness which all the more wants to seize you. Do not be afraid. Through the grace and the love of my Son, I am with you. Thank you."

Medjugorje marks the longest apparition in history and is still ongoing—until when, only God knows. We do not comprehend the future but know it will be a "new normal" as we reenter life after this worldwide pandemic event. Thousands have perished alone, thousands have tested positive, others have been sick, struggled and survived; many are gripped with anxiety and fear as they mask up to go to the grocery store; schools are virtual; businesses are closed; jobs have been lost; weddings canceled, graduations postponed, sports silenced; and more, as we wait. Doctors, nurses and medical staffs are caring for the sick and racing to find a vaccination or drug cure.

Our Julia is one of those nurses in New York City. We wait, pray, speak words of love to our family and ask God to save us, to forgive the sins of humanity, my own sins and for Our Lady to intercede for us. Thousands are praying with greater piety and getting on their knees in intercessory prayer for what lies ahead.

The message below came out today.

"Dear children! May this time be an incentive for personal conversion for you. Pray, little children, in solitude, to the Holy Spirit to strengthen you in faith and trust in God, that you may be worthy witnesses of the love which God bestows upon you through my presence. Little children, do not permit trials to harden your heart and for prayer to be like a desert. Be a reflection of God's love and witness the Risen Jesus by your lives. I am with you and I love all of you with my motherly love. Thank you for having responded to my call." April 25, 2020

I am reminded of this passage in Scripture, as I believe we need to depend on Him in this trial and beyond.

Dependence on God: "Therefore I tell you, do not worry about your life, what you will eat or drink, or about your body, what you will wear. Is not life more than food and the body more than clothing? Look at the birds in the sky; they do not sow or reap, they gather nothing into barns, yet your heavenly Father feeds them. Are not you more important than they? Can any of you by worrying add a single moment to your life-span? Why are you anxious about clothes?

Learn from the way the wild flowers grow. They do not work or spin. But I tell you that not even Solomon in all his splendor was clothed like one of them. If God so clothes the grass of the field, which grows today and is thrown into the oven tomorrow, will he not much more provide for you, O you of little faith? So do not worry and say, 'What are we to eat?' or 'What are we to drink?' or 'What are we to wear?' All these things the pagans seek. Your heavenly Father knows that you need them all. But seek first the kingdom of God and his righteousness, and all these things will be given you besides. Do not worry about tomorrow; tomorrow will take care of itself. Sufficient for a day is its own evil." (Matthew 6:25–34)

May all who find this book in their hands, pray and know God is with you, and your heavenly Mother loves you. May God protect and inspire you in your walk of faith.

As of January 2021 I completed the program from the Cenacle of Our Lady of Divine Providence School of Spiritual Direction, virtually, and have begun practicing. With God, nothing is impossible.

27

The Story of Medjugorje

"Dear children, today I call you to live the messages which I have been giving you during the past eight years. This is a time of graces and I desire that the grace of God be great for every single one of you. I am blessing you and I love you with a special love. Thank you for having responded to my call." June 25, 1989

"Dear children! God sent me among you out of love that I may lead you towards the way of salvation. Many of you opened your hearts and accepted my messages, but many have become lost on this way and have never come to know the God of love with the fullness of heart. Therefore, I call you to be love and light where there is darkness and sin. I am with you and bless you all. Thank you for having responded to my call." October 25, 2007

    Our Lady had beckoned us to Medjugorje. Mom was inspired to appeal for a miracle cure. Prior to our quest in 1991, so much had happened in this little hamlet of the world. I had much to learn and comprehend. Neither Mom nor I had ever traveled to the other holy places of apparitions; this was a first for us. The story of Medjugorje is an extraordinary one.

Across the Adriatic Sea from the boot of Italy, in former Yugoslavia, is the village of Medjugorje. It means "between the mountains." It's a village surrounded by hills, dotted by small clay-tiled homes, vineyards, and a beautiful patchwork of farms.

In the heart of this rural farming community is St. James Church, named for the patron saint of pilgrims. The structure is questionably larger than the community it serves. God's preparation unfolded for this church at the start of the twentieth century. Amidst many trials, faulty plans, world wars and devastation, the current grand church opened its doors in 1969.

In the early evening of June 24, 1981, on the feast day of Saint John the Baptist, two children traveling by foot, towards their homes, came upon a vision. They called to their friends to come and see. They stood together to witness an image of a lady, in a simple dress and veil, holding an infant in her arms. She appeared before them. The six children, amazed and frightened, stared, frozen in their spot. The lady did not say anything. She disappeared as profoundly as she had materialized. Excited and astonished by what they had seen, they ran home to tell their families.

The following day, the children: Ivanka Ivankovic, fifteen; Mirjana Dragicevic, sixteen; Vicka Ivankovic, almost seventeen; Ivan Dragicevic, sixteen; Marija Pavlovic, sixteen;

and Jakov Colo, ten; followed by a small crowd, were drawn by an internal magnetic force back to Podbrdo Hill, the same spot where they had seen the lady. She appeared to them at the same time as the day before, but this time without the infant. The children all fell to their knees simultaneously and began reciting the Our Father, the Hail Mary and the Glory Be. The onlookers saw nothing—no vision—but they did see the changes taking place on the faces and postures of the children. Something was happening.

On the third day, the children, drawn there again, heard her say, *"I am the Blessed Virgin Mary, Queen of Peace."* She told the children that she had come to convert and reconcile the whole world. She said, *"Peace, peace, peace and only peace. Peace must come to reign between God and man, between man and man."*

Word spread rapidly throughout the community and more and more people gravitated to Podbrdo Hill to see and experience for themselves. The children returned each day, praying on their knees. Our Lady appeared to the children, saying, *"Have no fear, pray the Rosary."* She gave messages for them, the community, and the world. The children were in a state of ecstasy during the visitations, staring upward, eyes not moving; sometimes their lips moved, but no sound could be heard. On the fifth day, when hundreds were gathered, she said to the children, *"Let the people pray and believe firmly. Let them believe firmly and help others to do the same."* In answer to the question of why here, she responded, *"There are many devoted believers here,"* and as to how long she would stay, the response came: *"As long as you want me."*

The children described Gospa (the Croatian word for Our Blessed Lady) as beautiful, wearing a gray-blue dress and a white veil. Her eyes are blue, her hair dark, and her face radiates love and joy. She appears, standing on a cloud. The humility, integrity, and love for Gospa poured forth from the children.

The Communist authorities felt the opposite. Distressed at this outpouring of faith-driven believers, the government had no control. The news of the appearances was alarming. Instability was shaking the strict foundation of forty years of Communist rule. With the crowds multiplying daily, the police decided to take the children to a police station in Mostar, for intense questioning. The children were separated, and the results analyzed. Physicians were ordered to examine the children; they were declared healthy and of sound mind. This did not satisfy the authorities. Fr. Jozo Zovko, the pastor of St. James, was brought in for questioning. They wanted him to control and prevent the crowds pouring into Medjugorje. He could not obey their request; this extraordinary happening was not in his control. The authorities wanted this stopped.

The children asked the Blessed Mother for signs. On August 2, 1981, in the evening, with hundreds present, the sun began to dance across the sky and then fall towards the earth.

Colors sprayed from either side as it rotated. The people witnessed and saw images of crosses and the Madonna in the sky. The word "MIR" appeared in the clouds. Mir means peace. The crowds, now more than ever, continued to increase at an alarming rate. There were reports of miraculous healings: a paralyzed child walked, and sight returned to a person who had been blind.

The Communist authorities needed stronger measures to combat what was occurring. They looked for help from Sarajevo. Special police were dispatched to the area. Apparition Hill was barricaded. Limitations were placed on worship at St. James Church. For almost two years, restrictions were placed, and people were fearful. Father Jozo was arrested for his support of the children and sentenced to three and a half years imprisonment. He was freed after eighteen months, but the soldiers and police continued to be everywhere in the community. However, this did not stop the faithful. Devotion increased and hundreds of people came to this miraculous place.

Little by little, the government began to acknowledge the happenings at Medjugorje—but continued to observe closely. They saw the economic potential of all the pilgrims, so they permitted them to come. St. James began to have Rosary recitations and Mass twice a day, to accommodate the number of faithful flocking to the village. The messages of Our Lady were shared. Harmony pervaded for a time. The impact of this phenomenon on the children and the community was immense.

Our Lady chose these ordinary children to be her messengers, adolescents involved in their own simple lives. Family, chores, school, and activities filled their hours. Like all of us, the visionaries had dreams and hopes for their futures. They were all Roman Catholic, went to church on Sundays and prayed, but none, in their words, was exceptionally holy.

These events took them completely by surprise; the visions startled and astounded them. In the first few days, they were frightened and taken aback, but Our Lady's response to them was so genuine. Her hand profoundly touched their hearts. The children began to long for her visits. She prayed, guided, and sent messages for the mounting crowds. She instructed the visionaries by using Gospel truths to lead them and all to her Son Jesus. Gospa entrusted each with a prayer intention. She also told them of future happenings in Yugoslavia, as well as for the entire world.

Ivanka Ivankovic was almost fifteen at the time. She was the first to see the Virgin. Ivanka led the other children to the place where the vision had occurred. Her mother had recently died from an illness and her young adolescent heart was raw. She asked Our Lady about her mom. Gospa revealed to Ivanka that her mom was happy, and in time allowed Ivanka to see her mother. She looked beautiful and told her daughter she was proud of her. When I saw Ivanka during a visit to a parish in New Jersey, she told this story through tears. She said that when it happened, she could not believe that she was looking at her mom, seeing her in perfect health. Ivanka's prayer intention is for families. She lives in a town close to Medjugorje and has three children. She does not travel as much as the other visionaries do. Her daily apparitions stopped in 1985. She now has an apparition once a year, on the anniversary of the visitations.

Mirjana Dragicevic was sixteen when this all began. She was living in Sarajevo and was visiting her grandparents at the time. She is the most educated visionary and studied at the University in Sarajevo. Through her initial talks with the Blessed Mother, she gained a deeper understanding of the state of the Church. Mirjana is married and has two children, and lives in Medjugorje. She also travels, spreading the messages. Her prayer intention is to pray for those who have not come to know the love of God. Her daily apparitions stopped in 1982; however, in 1987 she began to receive visitations and a message on the second of every month, for her intention. Her second-of-the-month messages ceased in March of 2020.

"Dear children! As I call you to prayer for those who have not come to know the love of God, if you were to look into your hearts you would comprehend that I am speaking about many of you. With an open heart, sincerely ask yourselves if you want the living God or do you want to eliminate Him and live as you want. Look around you, my children, and see where the

world is going, the world that thinks of doing everything without the Father, and which wanders in the darkness of temptation. I am offering to you the light of the Truth and the Holy Spirit. According to God's plan I am with you to help you to have my Son, His Cross and Resurrection, triumph in your hearts. As a mother, I desire and pray for your unity with my Son and His works. I am with you; you decide. Thank you." June 2, 2011

Vicka Ivankovic was age seventeen when the apparitions began. Her cheerful, outgoing, radiant smile awarded her the position of ambassador for the group. Her intention is to pray for people who are sick and for people with disabilities. She currently lives close to Medjugorje, is married, and has two children. She has felt crushing pain and sickness within the time of these apparitions. She gained much wisdom about illness through her own suffering. She is still receiving daily visits from Gospa and is filled with gratitude for every moment she has spent with Our Lady. Also, Our Lady dictated her life story to Vicka, over a two-year period. This is to be revealed to the world when it is time.

Ivan Dragicevic was sixteen years old and very shy when he first saw the vision. He ran away; he was frightened and taken aback. He had wanted to become a priest after the apparitions began. However, this was not what happened. He is married, has three children and lives in Massachusetts. He travels, telling his story and sharing what the Blessed Mother desires for all of us. He also spends time in Medjugorje each summer. His intention is to pray for the youth and for priests. He still has daily visits with Our Lady.

Marija Pavlovic was sixteen at the time that her sister, Milka, saw the lights and vision on the first day. Milka could not return on the second day, so she was not with the other visionaries and did not see Our Lady again. Marija wanted to devote her life to God after the apparitions began. She is devoted to God, though it is not her vocation. She resides in Italy, is married, and has four children. It is through her that the message is spread throughout the world on the twenty-fifth of each month. She continues to have daily visitations from Gospa. Her prayer intention is for the souls in purgatory.

Jakov Colo, the youngest visionary, was only ten when it began. He was a soccer player and not much into church and prayer, but the Blessed Mother changed that. He was a strong-headed boy with an age-appropriate attention span. His young spirit and dedication to the messages were very influential among the people of Medjugorje and all the pilgrims who heard and saw him. He belongs to the parish of Medjugorje, where he lives with his wife and three children. He no longer has daily visits but has a yearly apparition on Christmas Day. Jakov's mission is to pray for all sick people and people with disabilities.

In the apparitions of the Blessed Mother Mary in Fatima, visionaries received secrets. These had to do with future world events. In Fatima in 1917, during World War I, Mary told the three visionaries:

> "This war is going to end; but if people do not cease offending God, a worse one will break out during the pontificate of Pius XI. When you see a night illumined by an unknown light, know that this is the great sign given you by God that He is about to punish the world for its crimes, by means of war, famine, and persecutions of the Church and of the Holy Father ... To prevent this, I shall come to ask for the consecration of Russia to my Immaculate Heart, and the Communion of Reparation on the First Saturdays. If my requests are heeded, Russia will be converted, and there will be peace; if not, she will spread her errors throughout the world, causing wars and persecutions of the Church. The good will be martyred, the Holy Father will have much to suffer, various nations will be annihilated. In the end, my Immaculate Heart will triumph. The Holy Father will consecrate Russia to me and she will be converted, and a period of peace will be granted to the world."

Twenty years after the Our Lady of Fatima apparitions, the skies over Europe glowed inexplicably. World War II occurred, and we know through history of the spread of Communism and the atrocity that followed. In 1984, Pope John

Paul II did consecrate Russia to the Immaculate Heart of Mary.

The three children of Fatima were uninformed of the world and unassuming in nature. Similar to the visionaries in Medjugorje, they carried so much in their young hearts. Ivan has shared, and it is believed by many that Medjugorje is a continuation of Fatima. Ivan was quoted as saying, "Our Lady told one of the other visionaries that what she began in Fatima, she is going to complete in Medjugorje."

As in Fatima, there are secrets. The ten secrets of Medjugorje include both personal information for the visionaries and details which affect the Church and the world. These secrets will not be disseminated until a time that is directed by God. Our Lady has guided the children with these confidences; three of the seers have been entrusted with the ten secrets. Gospa does not appear to them on a daily basis. In 1982, Mirjana received all ten. In 1985, Ivanka was told. In 1998, Jakov was told.

Gospa has allowed the third secret to be shared with us and it involves a permanent visible sign which will be left on Apparition Hill in the village of Medjugorje, for the world to see. Here is the message she gave regarding the sign.

"This sign will be given for the atheists. You faithful already have signs and you have become the sign for the atheists. You faithful must not wait for the sign before you convert; convert soon. This time is a time of

grace for you. When the sign comes, it will be too late. As a mother I caution you because I love you. The secrets exist. My children! Nothing is known of these now, but when they are known, it will be too late. Return to prayer, nothing is more important than this. I would like it if the Lord allowed me to reveal some of the secrets to you, but that which He is doing for you is already a Grace which is almost too much."

Throughout the messages of Medjugorje, there is a repeated thread of motherly wisdom and love. Our Lady wants us to experience peace in our families and in the world. Mothers tend to repeat rules and behaviors to instill values for their children. Mothers do this subconsciously. Our Lady has given us a map to guide us so we can follow what she desires for us, her children, with these five tools given to us through her messages.

First, she wants us to **PRAY** with our hearts to her Son Jesus. She does not want us remotely saying the words. She wants us to open our hearts when we begin, "Our Father ...." She calls us to recite the Rosary each day, thinking about the life, death, and glory of her Son, with sincerity and devotion. She asks us to pray all the way through our day, for guidance in the decisions we have to make and in thanksgiving for all we have received. To pray with the heart is to pray with love, trust, and abandonment. Prayer is needed to experience God.

"Dear children! These days I am calling you to family prayer. In God's name, many times I have been giving you messages, but you have not listened to me. This Christmas will be unforgettable for you only if you accept the messages which I am giving you. Dear children, don't allow that day of joy to become my most sorrowful day. Thank you for having responded to my call." December 6, 1984

The second message is to **FAST**. In Medjugorje, the people fast on bread and water every Wednesday and Friday. Fasting teaches self-control and humbles us to rely on faith. In both the Old Testament and the New Testament, there are many examples of fasting. We know that Jesus fasted frequently. This sacrifice also teaches us how little we need. Children can fast from media or electronic devices, something that is of value to them. September 26, 1985: *"Dear children: Thank you for all the prayers. Thank you for all the sacrifices. I wish to tell you, dear children, to renew the messages which I am giving you. Especially live the fasting because, with fasting, you will bring happiness that the whole plan which God plans here in Medjugorje will be realized. Thank you for your response to my call."*

The third consistent message is to **READ THE BIBLE** daily. God inspires the Bible; He is the author, so we must read. Stick with it; the more we read, the more we can see the relevance of the Scriptures in our personal journey. As

Christians, we are called to read the Holy Scriptures and learn from them. October 18, 1984: *"Dear children, today I call you to read the Bible every day in your homes and let it be in a visible place so as always to encourage you to read it and pray."*

The fourth is monthly **CONFESSION**. We must make ourselves pure and clean inside, getting rid of the sin that has plagued our being. Once we begin to practice this sacrament, the clearer we begin to see what is needed in our lives and how God wants to work with us. June 26, 1981: *"Make your peace with God and among yourselves. For that, it is necessary to believe, to pray, to fast, and to go to confession."* February 10, 1982: *"Pray, pray! It is necessary to believe firmly, to go to confession regularly and, likewise, to receive Holy Communion. It is the only salvation."* July 24, 1982: *"Whoever has done very much evil during his life can go straight to Heaven if he confesses, is sorry for what he has done, and receives Communion at the end of his life."*

The last tool is to receive the **EUCHARIST** as often as possible. The more we receive, the more we want to listen to the words of the Gospel and feel the presence of Jesus in Mass. Keeping holy the Sabbath is one of the commandments, and if daily Mass is available, we should attend. April 3, 1986: *"There are many of you who have sensed the beauty of the Holy Mass ... Jesus gives you His graces in the Mass."* April 25, 1988: *"Let the Holy Mass be your life."* May 23, 1985: *"Open your hearts to the Holy Spirit. Especially during these* *days the Holy Spirit is working through you. Open your hearts and surrender your life to Jesus so that He works through your hearts."*

This time with Mary, here on our planet, is a time of grace. She is our mother, Theotokos, the bearer of Christ. She loves us profoundly. Her apparitions and messages are a gift to show us the way. The apparitions began in Yugoslavia and continue in the country now named Bosnia and Herzegovina. The name is different, but her words and presence are still intended to move us closer to her Son Jesus. Our world is challenged in so many ways, and Mary wants us to follow the way of the light. Faith is part of our personal journey. Faith is what made my mom announce to my brother, "I am taking you to my heavenly Mother for a miracle." The faith of my mother powered our journey and propelled us into action, and faith is what continues to guide me now.

Map Images

In 1991, we traveled NY to Rome for a layover
and rest before flight to Dubrovnik.

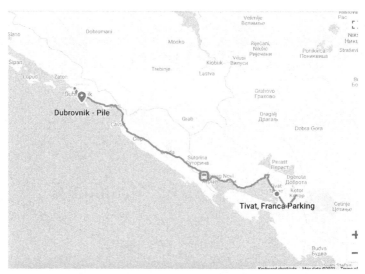

We were rerouted midair from original destination of
Dubrovnik to Tivat, so we traveled to Dubrovnik by bus (1991).

In 1991, we connected with Marion Tours in Dubrovnik
and traveled to Medjugorje via van.

References

Albom, Mitch. *The First Phone Call From Heaven*. Harper
Collins, 2013.

Barbaric, Slavko. *Pray with the Heart*. Franciscan University Press, 1988.

Cavins, Jeff, et al. *The Great Adventure: A Journey Through the Bible*: *Bible Timeline Seminar Workbook*. 2005.

Emmerich, Ven. Anne Catherine. *The Life of the Blessed Virgin Mary*. Tan Books, 1970.

Gaitley, Fr. Michael E. *33 Days to Morning Glory*. Marian Press - Association of Marian Helpers , 2011.

Gillespie, Hugh. *Preparation for Total Consecration to Jesus Christ Through Mary*. Montfort Publications, 2011.

Hahn, Scott. *Hail, Holy Queen*. Doubleday, 2005.

Ilibagiza, Immaculee, and Steve Erwin. *Left to Tell*. Hay House Inc, 2014.

Kidd, Sue Monk. *The Invention of Wings*. Penguin, 2014.

Merton, Thomas. *The Seven Storey Mountain*. Houghton Mifflin Harcourt, 1999.

Montfort, Saint Louis. *True Devotion to Mary*. Tan Books and Publishers , 1941.

Ruffin, Bernard. *Padre Pio, The True Story*. Our Sunday Visitor Publishing, 1991.

Soldo, Mirjana, et al. *My Heart Will Triumph*. Catholic Shop Publishing, 2016.

Weible, Wayne. *Final Harvest*. CMJ Publishers and Distrib.,
    2002.

---. *Medjugorje The Message*. Paraclete Press, 1989.

---. *The Joy of the Medjugorje*: *My Greatest Medjugorje Sto-
    ries, Moments, Memories and More*. New Hope Press,
    2017.

Medjugorje Magazine, Catholic Shoppe USA, Westmont, IL

United States Conference of Catholic Bishops. *The New
    American Bible*: Washington, DC: 1991.

About the Author

Barbara Lorenzo is a wife, mother, sister, teacher, story-teller, and a seeker of faith. A recent graduate of The Cenacle of Our Lady of Divine Providence School of Spiritual Direction, she loves to share her story of transformation and conversion through her witness of extraordinary faith. She has served as a Catholic elementary media specialist, a pastoral council member and contributed to ministries in her former parish in New Jersey. She was a contributor for the Metuchen Catholic Spirit newspaper, Evangelization Here and Now newspaper and prior to her conversion, she had a career in the fashion industry. Former participant of the NJCWG for children's books. She currently lives in Ponte Vedra Beach Florida with her husband and is a practicing Spiritual Director with Saint John Paul II Parish. She holds a Masters in Elementary Education and a Bachelor's in Fine Art in Fashion Design. This is her first book.

Made in the USA
Columbia, SC
27 March 2022